Jon Hutchison
'991

Burnsiana

BURNSIANA

James A. Mackay

Alloway Publishing

Alloway Publishing Limited, Ayrshire

Alloway Publishing
First published, October 1988
for
Jamieson & Munro

© James A. Mackay, 1988

ISBN 0-907526-35-7
Alloway Publishing, AYR

Printed and bound in Scotland

Design and Printing
Sunprint, Perth

Binding
Hunter & Foulis Ltd.
Paper
Wiggins Teape Paper Limited.

Contents

The front cover depicts a medley of cigarette cards, the chair made from the Wilson printing press, the Mausoleum, Staffordshire flatback figures of Tam o Shanter and Souter Johnny, the Nasmyth bust-portrait, a Burns medallion, a luggage label from the Monument Hotel, Alloway, a polychrome pottery whisky jug, the painting 'Burns in Edinburgh' by C. M. Hardie, an early 'undivided back' postcard from Mauchline, a rug by Gray of Kilmarnock, a shortbread tin, a painted wooden roundel after Skirving and a sheet of Burns labels. The back cover illustrates the standing full-length portrait of Burns by Nasmyth.

For
Debra and Maurice Pitman

Preface

It is to Peter Westwood, Publicity Officer of the Burns Federation, that credit must be given for suggesting a book on Burns memorabilia. Peter originally envisaged a fairly comprehensive catalogue of stamps, labels, philatelic souvenirs and postcards, but the more we looked into the subject, the more we realised that, so far as postcards were concerned, we were merely scratching the surface. It was at this juncture that I gave serious thoughts to resuscitating an earlier project, utilising my research into such disparate media as Stevengraphs and treen, crested china and horse-brasses in order to produce a book which would encompass all the many and varied fields in which Burns has been immortalised.

Not only has Peter Westwood been a tower of strength in supporting my endeavours, but he has been invaluable at a practical level. It was through his good offices that the project was brought to the attention of Ian McCracken, the Trustee of The John Jamieson Munro Trust of Stirling, to whom thanks are due for making the publication of this book possible. Peter, in his capacity as Technical and Development Manager with Scottish and Universal Newspapers, acted as the go-between for me and the production team at Perth where the book was designed and printed. My thanks are due to Alex Cargill, Director of Scottish and Universal Newspapers and Bill Lockhart, the Manager of Sunprint's Book Printing Division. Arthur Ingham, the Studio Manager, designed the book and marshalled what must have seemed at times a chaotic mass of illustrations into the pleasing order and balance shown within. Those pictures which do not bear a specific credit were taken specially for this project by Robert McAusland of Robert Stewart Photography, Ayr. I must say that Robert has a genius for transferring some of the least promising material into really eye-catching pictures.

Considering how few portraits were painted of Burns in his lifetime (and the controversy regarding just how true a likeness any of them were), the range of iconography is nothing short of astonishing. It is remarkable to think that about sixty sculptors and more than a hundred painters have applied their skills, in varying degrees, to producing likenesses of Burns — even more remarkable that the vast majority have been dependent, to a greater or lesser extent, on the painting by Alexander Nasmyth, although augmented in some cases by an examination of the casts made from the poet's skull in 1857. From the paintings and sculpture, in turn, have been derived the countless manifestations of Burns on postage stamps, banknotes, tea towels, shortbread tins and chocolate boxes, rack-plates and caddy-spoons, horse-brasses, leather bookmarkers, Mauchline-ware snuff boxes and trinkets of all kinds. Second only to the features of the Poet himself have been the myriad reproductions of his birthplace, the Mausoleum, the Alloway and Edinburgh monuments, Alloway's auld haunted kirk and other landmarks associated with his life and times. In the chapters of this book I have attempted not only to enumerate the different classes of Burnsiana but to analyse the trends and fashions over the past two hundred years since the Burns souvenir industry began with the Miers silhouettes and proofs of the Beugo engraving in 1787. The tastefully printed silk handkerchief of yesteryear has become the gaudy T-shirt of the present day. One thing is certain: I cannot in all honesty say that any other person, living or dead, has had the same diversity of commemoration, spread over so many parts of the world — which surely tells us a great deal about the timelessness and universality of Burns and the appeal of his songs and poetry. Even Shakespeare, arguably the greatest writer in the English language, has not enjoyed the popularity and inspired the devotion accorded to Burns.

I do not regard this book as the last word on the subject, by any means. A few examples will suffice to illustrate how research into Burnsiana is an on-going process. As a result of my wife's article in *The Burnsian* regarding her search for Burns monuments in North America, we received details of the Burns 'shaft' (a 15-foot column surmounted by a bust) which was erected in Jacksonville, Florida on 27th August 1930. Contemporary press accounts make copious mention of the principal subscribers and the organising committee but omit the name of the sculptor who may have been a Mr Pedroni. The Burns Club of Atlanta kindly sent us details of the replica of the Cottage which had been a feature of the St Louis World's Fair in 1904 and was subsequently copied by Atlanta and is used for Burns Suppers and other convivial gatherings to this day. The Cottage contains a bust of Burns, sculpted about 1920 by James Watt (a member of the club), and there is a 'full-length statuette' of Burns nearby, but tantalisingly no fuller details were given.

I ran into my old friend Stanley Hunter at the Scottish Philatelic Congress in Falkirk in April 1988 and he remarked casually that there was a statue of Burns in Quincy, Massachusetts but could give no precise details — so that will be on my itinerary during my next trip to America. Incidentally, Falkirk's High Street boasts a plaque on the building where Burns slept during his tour of Stirlingshire in 1787 but I have yet to discover who sculpted the stone bust of the Bard surmounting this plaque, and showing him anachronistically in a bow tie!

In May 1988 my wife visited Timaru in the South Island of New Zealand, to photograph the marble statue there. In attempting (without success, alas) to discover the identity of the Italian sculptor, she spent some time delving into contemporary newspaper reports. These reported the speeches at great length, from the 1913 unveiling ceremony, but omitted details of where and by whom the statue was carved. Passing mention was made, however of a statue of Burns which it was expected would shortly be erected in

Halifax, Nova Scotia — a fact hitherto unknown to us. The very day that I received a postcard with this exciting bit of news, I had a telephone call from John Inglis, Secretary of the Burns Federation, to say that he had just had an enquiry from Canada regarding the whereabouts of Burns statues. The enquirer mentioned casually that he only knew of the statues in Halifax and Toronto, but was sure there must be others elsewhere! By an amazing coincidence, I had already booked an air ticket to fly from Prestwick to Halifax, prior to attending the Burns Conference in Hamilton, Ontario — utterly oblivious to the fact that a Burns statue existed in Halifax. There are times when I genuinely perceive Divine intervention in my Burns quest! What started out as a survey of Burns memorabilia has become a project that has taken both my wife and me right round the world. In particular, the memorials, monuments, statues, busts, cairns and plaques which, directly or indirectly, commemorate Burns have proved to be a much vaster subject than we could ever have dreamed of. The third chapter of this book must perforce be regarded only as a preliminary survey which I earnestly hope will merit much fuller treatment in a separate book eventually.

This book has, truly, been a labour of love, combining a lifelong interest in Burns with an obsession for stamps, coins and other collectables; *Burnsiana* has provided the opportunity to bring these consuming passions together. It would not have been possible, however, without a great deal of help from a great many people. I should like to take this opportunity, therefore of expressing my gratitude to the following who furnished information or assisted with the illustrations: the Curators of the Museums in the Burns Country, notably David Lockwood of the Burgh Museum, William Sinclair of Burns House, Robert Hutton and Donald MacLachlan of the Robert Burns Centre in Dumfries, Mrs Jan Kelso of Burns House in Mauchline, Mr and Mrs James Irving of Ellisland Farm, Mr and Mrs John Manson and the staff of the Cottage and Birthplace Museum in Alloway, Glenn Croft-Smith of the Alloway Monument, the staff of the Tam o' Shanter Inn Museum in Ayr and Robert Brown at Wellwood in Irvine.

I am also greatly indebted to the libraries of the Burns Country, many of which have extensive collections of ephemera, manuscripts and other Burns memorabilia. Thanks are to William Anderson of the Dick Institute, until recently also Secretary of the Burns Federation, and to Mrs Rita Turner, Assistant Secretary of the Burns Federation at Kilmarnock, to Jospeh Fisher and the staff of the Burns Room at the Mitchell Library in Glasgow, to Marion Stewart, Regional Archivist for Dumfries and Galloway who has in her care the collection of books by and about Burns formed by Lord Craig of Glendyne and to Alistair Cowper and Mrs Sheila Wise of the Ewart Library in Dumfries. Thanks are due also to members of the staff at the Scottish National Portrait Gallery, the Royal Museum of Scotland and the National Library of Scotland, all in Edinburgh, and to Lawrence R. Burness of the William Coull Anderson Library of Genealogy in Arbroath.

Many private individuals have given unstintingly of their time and trouble to help me with the compilation of this book. I am indebted to Ian McLellan, late of the Clydesdale Bank in Glasgow, to John Inglis, Sam Gaw and the other Directors of the Irvine Burns Club, to Peter Westwood, Publicity Officer of the Burns Federation and a fellow-philatelist, to my friends and neighbours in Dumfries, Mrs Sarah Paling, Mrs Mary Grierson, Noel Dinwiddie, David Smith and Bill Sutherland of the Burns Howff Club and Donald Urquhart of the Southern Scottish Counties Association of Burns Clubs. Colin Morton of Dumfries also supplied much useful information concerning Burns and the Theatre Royal. H. George McKerrow and his daughter-in-law, Mrs Maureen McKerrow, were most helpful regarding the Globe Inn. David Hope kindly supplied the illustration of the Octocentenary collage in the Robert Burns Centre.

Farther afield, the following people have given me a great deal of help in many ways: James Anderson (Edinburgh), Alistair Campsie (Montrose), William Dawson (Clackmannan), James Davie (Huddersfield), R. Y. Corbett (Paisley), Stanley K. Hunter (Glasgow), James McCaw (Coventry), Mrs R. Meldrum (Guardbridge), William Park (Kincardine), and Dr George Philp (Glasgow), Bob Carnie, Andy Hay, Tommy Miller and Graham Underwood (Calgary), Douglas Muir (Edmonton) and John D. Ross (Fredericton), James M. Montgomery (Atlanta), David Skipper (Tallahassee), Mary Lucile and Chase Sheridan (Jacksonville), Professor G. Ross Roy (Columbia, SC), Marcia Pindara (Cheyenne), Frankie Nevins (New Jersey) and Liz Holland (Philadelphia); Mrs Stella Brown (Melbourne), Mattie and Grev Ferris, and Raoul and Airdree Neil (Brisbane), Leslie Carlisle and Pat Boland (Sydney), Lynda Wallace (Hokitika, New Zealand) and George Kelly (Booysens, South Africa).

I am also greatly indebted to all the secretaries and officials of Burns clubs, Caledonian and St Andrew's societies around the world who have so ably assisted me by sending me their syllabuses, Burns Supper menus, tickets and programmes to add to my rapidly burgeoning collection of Burns ephemera. I cannot thank them individually, but I take this opportunity to accord them my sincere thanks for all their help.

A very special debt of gratitude is due to Allan Stoddart, Honorary President of the Burns Federation, former Curator of the Tam o' Shanter Inn Museum and one of the great private collectors of Burnsiana, whose generosity is matched only by his hospitality. Last, but by no means least, I must thank my wife Joyce for her support and encouragement in the preparation of this book. In search of statues, busts and plaques commemorating Burns she has travelled all over Canada, the United States and New Zealand in the past twelve months, endured numerous overnight bus journeys, walked more weary miles and cursed the sun for being in the wrong place more times than she would care to remember.

James A. Mackay
Dumfries, June 1988

Portraits of Burns

Bust portrait of Burns by Alexander Nasmyth.

Standing full-length portrait of Burns by Alexander Nasmyth.

The portraits of Robert Burns, Scotland's national bard and the Poet of all Humanity, are legion — but only half a dozen can be regarded as authentic, in the strict sense of having been produced from the life, backed up by such documentary evidence as the poet's own correspondence. Burns spent a considerable time, from the latter part of 1786 till early 1788, in and around Edinburgh. During the winter of 1787 in particular he had plenty of time on his hands, and it is at that time that one would have expected him to have been the frequent subject of the many portrait painters in the capital. That he did not take advantage of this situation is explained by none other than James Nasmyth, son of Alexander Nasmyth, who states in his own autobiography: 'The Poet had a strange aversion to sit for his portrait, though often urgently requested to do so. But when at my father's studio, Burns at last consented, the portrait was rapidly painted. It was done in a few hours, and my father made a present of it to Mrs Burns.'

Burns himself (in a letter of May 1795 to George Thomson) mentioned the fact that he had sat to Nasmyth half a dozen times, which gives the lie to James Nasmyth's claim. James Nasmyth's autobiography is unreliable on many other matters, and his statements that his father and Burns were introduced by the poet's future landlord, Patrick Miller of Dalswinton, and that the idea of the portrait originated with Alexander Nasmyth, have to be treated with caution. It is now generally accepted that the idea came from William Creech, publisher of the Edinburgh edition of the Poems, who wanted a portrait of Burns which could subsequently be engraved for reproduction on the frontispiece. Tantalisingly, Burns makes no reference to this portrait at the time it was being painted. It was probably commissioned late in December 1786 and completed by 24th February 1787, on which date Burns wrote to John Ballantine 'I am getting my Phiz done by an eminent Engraver', which implies that the painting was in Beugo's hands by that date.

As a result of this one portrait, Alexander Nasmyth is best remembered as a portrait-painter but this was not his *forte* at all. He was primarily a landscape artist and, in a city which boasted numerous portraitists of the first rank, the choice of Nasmyth seems an odd one. There is some grain of truth in what James Nasmyth said. Nasmyth was the one painter whom Burns knew socially. Furthermore, Nasmyth shared the poet's radical politics, a stance which was to alienate him from many wealthy clients. Burns and Nasmyth became firm friends and spent a lot of time together and, as noted later, one of their country excursions together was to produce one of the other early portraits of Burns.

Later in life Nasmyth reminisced about the painting of Burns's portrait with his biographer, William Hall and confessed that the painting was never actually finished. Having captured the likeness of Burns, Nasmyth was afraid to continue lest he might spoil the portrait. This is borne out by the fact that Burns had to give several additional sittings to John Beugo when he engraved the portrait for Creech. In 1830 William Walker produced a new engraving of Burns based on the Nasmyth original and the old man congratulated Walker saying 'It conveys to me a more true and lively remembrance of Burns than my own picture of him does, it so perfectly renders the spirit of his expression.' Even if we make allowances for the fact that Nasmyth was recalling the image of Burns forty years after the event, we must respect his candid admission. The sculptor D.W. Stevenson, who modelled the head of Burns on two occasions in the 1880s and had made a close study of all the authentic portraits of the poet, was generally satisfied with the Nasmyth portrait — 'but the eyebrows I have always felt defective in form, the curve is common in its sweep, and is carried too far.' He added that this had not escaped the observation of several of the earlier engravers, noting that Walker had been the first to introduce more variety into the detail of this feature.

Stevenson was also mildly critical of Nasmyth's rendering of the upper lip — 'it has too much of the Cupid's bow line'. This, too, was a feature toned down in subsequent likenesses, notably the chalk drawing by Archibald Skirving, discussed in greater detail later. The original bust-portrait by Nasmyth passed into the hands of Alexander Cunningham in 1796 and was in his possession till 1808 when it was presented to the poet's widow. In due course it passed to Colonel William Nicol Burns who bequeathed it to the National Galleries of Scotland in 1872.

Nasmyth painted two other versions of this bust-portrait. The first of these was produced some time after he made the acquaintance of George Thomson in September 1792. The chief difference between this replica and the original lies in the eyes, which are more fully orbed and have an upward gaze. The eyebrows are more elevated and the hair more extended at the back of the head. On the back of the canvas appears the inscription 'A.N. pinxt' but at some subsequent date this was altered in pen and ink to read 'Sir Hy. Raeburn and A. Nasmyth pinxt'. The circumstances surrounding this alteration have never been satisfactorily established and art historians nowadays lend little credence to the story that Sir Henry Raeburn had a hand in this work.

It has long been a matter of speculation why Raeburn, the greatest portrait painter of his day, never painted Scotland's greatest poet from the life. Raeburn spent much of 1787 in Italy, but had returned to Edinburgh while Burns was still in the capital. There is no authentic record of their ever having met socially, far less that Burns gave sittings. The legend that Raeburn retouched the Thomson version (at Thomson's request) rests solely on George Thomson's own statement to this effect (quoted in his biography by Cuthbert Hadden, 1898) and that Raeburn revised and retouched the painting in Thomson's presence. Thomson's 'manipulation' of his dealings with Burns and his doctoring of the poet's correspondence, however, show Thomson in his true light. One cannot rule out, therefore, that Thomson

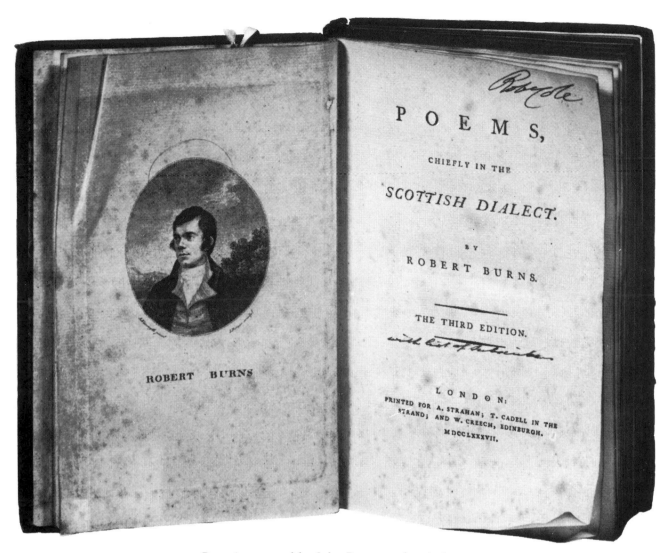

*Portrait engraved by John Beugo, as frontispiece
of the 1787 edition.*

doctored the inscription at some later date to enhance the value of the painting by associating it with Raeburn. The Thomson copy was eventually purchased from the London dealer, Colnaghi, by John Dillon who presented it to the National Portrait Gallery, London in 1858.

Nasmyth painted a third version of the bust-portrait many years later. Its exact date of composition is unknown, but in 1824 it was acquired by Elias Cathcart of Auchendrane, whose estate Nasmyth was then landscaping and whose wife had been one of his art pupils. This version differs in minor details from the 1787 original, but such differences are likely to have been accidental rather than representing a deliberate attempt by Nasmyth to produce a more accurate picture than the original. The 'Auchendrane' portrait eventually passed into the hands of the Earl of Rosebery who bequeathed it to Glasgow Art Gallery.

Nasmyth accompanied Burns on a number of jaunts into the countryside surrounding Edinburgh. On a visit to Roslin Nasmyth did a lightning sketch of the poet standing, wrapt in thought. The pencil drawing shows Burns full-length and hatted. Be that as it may, however, the background to the drawing is not that of Roslin, but Alloway, as the Auld Brig o' Doon and the Kirk appear to left and right. This pencil sketch formed part of an album of drawings by Nasmyth which was sold to the National Galleries of Scotland in 1928. Intriguingly, a *second* drawing exists, purchased by the late James McPhail and now in the possession of Irvine Burns Club. This drawing is very similar to the National Galleries drawing, but for the fact that Burns has his left arm folded over the right, and not the other way round. The McPhail version is that which Nasmyth used in producing his small oil painting of the subject in 1828. Commissioned by Robert Chambers in November 1827, it was later engraved for the frontispiece of Lockhart's *Life of Burns*, published by Constable in 1828. It is not

12

impossible, however, that the drawing in the possession of Irvine Burns Club was produced *after* the painting, as the working model for the engraving.

John Beugo

Although the engraving by Beugo was derived from the first Nasmyth bust-portrait it deserves recognition in its own right because Burns himself sat to Beugo, thus enabling the engraver to make such improvements as he felt necessary. Beugo, born in Edinburgh in 1759, was the same age as Burns and established a *rapport* with him. They became good friends and studied French together, under Louis Cauvin. Beugo's intimacy with Burns is reflected in his sensitive engraving. Burns himself was exceedingly well pleased with it. On 9th September 1788 he wrote to Beugo 'I might tell you a long story about your fine genius but as what every body knows cannot have escaped you, I shall not say one syllable about it.' He asked Beugo 'Whenever you finish any head, I should like to have a proof Copy of it.' This implies that Burns had the notion of forming a collection of Beugo's engravings but Beugo responded by sending the poet 36 India paper proofs of his own portrait. Burns distributed them to close friends, and there are several references to these proofs in his letters. These proofs, in fact, may be regarded as the earliest collectables associated with Burns and, as such, they are much-prized rarities nowadays. The plate was subsequently retouched by Beugo as it became worn, and later states are known from 1793, 1794, 1797, 1798 and 1800: the later the impression, the lesser the value from the collector's viewpoint.

Peter Taylor

If legend is true, then strictly speaking the portrait painted by Peter Taylor should be given pride of place as the earliest portrait of Burns. The existence of this painting, however, was never mentioned by Burns himself. Nasmyth claimed in 1787 that he was unaware of any other portraits of Burns at that time, although it cannot be ruled out that Burns sat to Peter Taylor soon after his arrival in Edinburgh. The painting itself bears the inscription 'T.1786' on the back, but this may have been added later. D.W. Stevenson, commenting on the fact that the same view of the head was given by both Nasmyth and Taylor, ingenuously adds 'being friends, they would probably see each other's work' — a flat contradiction of Nasmyth's own avowed ignorance of any other portrait .

The earliest record of this painting belongs to 1812 when James Hogg and two friends paid a visit to Taylor's widow. Mrs Taylor appears to have been the only person who saw this portrait in progress and on the death of her husband in 1788 she is said to have locked up the picture and it was only as a special favour that a sight of it could be obtained. According to her testimony, her husband became very intimate with Burns and offered to paint his portrait. To this Burns agreed and gave the artist three sittings, taking breakfast with him before each session. Mrs Taylor was present at the last, and by far the longest, session which she claimed took place shortly before Burns left Edinburgh on 5th May 1787. It seems, therefore, that even if the work were commenced in December 1786, several months elapsed between sittings. Moreover, the story that Burns had met Taylor at a dinner party which extended into the wee sma' hours and agreed on the spur of the moment to sit for his portrait the very next morning bears an uncanny resemblance to the story which James Nasmyth put about concerning his father's portrait of the bard. The Nasmyth story has been disproved, but in a curious way it lends credence to the rumour that Burns had, in fact, met an artist in such circumstances and had given a sitting the following morning and thus this gives some weight to Mrs Taylor's story.

Taylor was some three years Burns's senior and actually was employed as a coach-painter and interior decorator. Clearly he had artistic aspirations, but his untimely death in 1788 brought these ambitions to an end. No other portrait that can definitely be assigned to him is known. The painting is a seated half-length portrait, showing Burns in beaver hat and with his right hand self-consciously tucked *à Napoleon* inside his waistcoat. The painting is a small oval, in oil on a wood panel (a medium with which Taylor, as a coach-painter, would have been most familiar). Hogg mentions Mrs Taylor opening a clothes press and removing the picture from a little box, so this points conclusively to the small panel, now in the Scottish National Portrait Gallery, as having been the picture he actually saw. The position is complicated, however, by the existence of a larger version, executed in oils on canvas. It is now considered that the canvas was a later version painted by Taylor, and that the panel version was that painted from life.

Painted wooden lid, after Peter Taylor.

Silhouette by John Miers, 1787.

The panel version was used as the basis for an engraving, executed by J. Horsburgh in December 1829. At first glance, the Taylor portrait is not recognisable as being of Burns, but that probably arises from our familiarity with the Nasmyth bust-portrait. A careful comparison with the other contemporary portraits, however, leaves less room for doubt. Several of the poet's contemporaries, when they were shown the Taylor portrait, failed to recognise Burns either. Jean Armour, when shown the painting, expressed her belief in its being an original, adding that 'the likeness to the upper part of the face is very striking' — not exactly an enthusiastic endorsement! Clarinda was much more positive. She was shown the portrait in October 1828 and wrote 'In my opinion it is the most striking likeness of the Poet I have ever seen and I say this with more confidence having a most pcrfcct recollection of his appearance.' Sir Walter Scott, who, as a boy of fifteen, met Burns only once, confessed that he was 'a bad marker of likenesses and recollector of faces' and wrote (14th November 1829) 'I should, in an ordinary case, have hesitated to offer an opinion upon the resemblance, especially as I make no pretention to judge of the Fine Arts. But Burns was so remarkable a man, that his features remain impressed on my mind as if I had seen him only yesterday and I could not hesitate to recognise this portrait as a striking resemblance of the Poet, though it had been presented to me amid a whole Exhibition.'

The panel painting was shown at the Crystal Palace centenary celebrations in 1859 and was taken to Australia when the Taylor family emigrated. It subsequently served as the model for the statue of Burns by John Greenshields, erected at Camperdown, Victoria. It was eventually bequeathed by William Andrew Taylor to the Scottish National Portrait Gallery in 1927. The existence of the canvas painting was not known until July 1893 when it was mentioned in a letter to the *Kilmarnock Standard*. This painting — or another and hitherto untraced version — was exhibited at the Ayr Academy Bazaar in 1895. This may be the painting which was acquired by the Portrait Gallery in 1938, formerly in the collection of Captain Wardlaw Ramsay of Whitehill.

John Miers

John Miers, a year older than the poet, worked as a silhouettist in Leeds before spending the years 1787-8 in Edinburgh. He subsequently moved to London where he was established as a profilist and jeweller at 111, and later 162, Strand. Little is known of his later career, but in the closing decade of the eighteenth century he was one of the most prolific artists in this exacting medium, preferring to work in pen and ink, rather than in cut paper. Otherwise known as profiles or shades, these portraits date from the seventeenth century, although they attained their greatest popularity in the late eighteenth century. Their popular name was derived from Etienne de Silhouette, who was not only an enthusiastic amateur

which surrounded this portrait. Who was the intended recipient of this miniature? We shall probably never know. Nothing was, in fact, known of this miniature until 1885 when it turned up in the collection of William F. Watson. D.W. Stevenson (1892) mentions having seen this miniature, executed on ivory, on many occasions in the house of Mr Watson, and of Watson's firm belief that it was, indeed, the Reid miniature. Watson's collection was acquired in 1886 by the Portrait Gallery, but as it was Watson's inclination to suppress as confidential the sources of his various acquisitions the antecedents of the miniature were never communicated to the Gallery. Doubtless Watson himself knew the provenance of the painting and it is now generally accepted that it is the Reid miniature. The heraldic bookplate of John Mitchell, Collector at Dumfries, was affixed to the back, and this lends further weight to its origins, although, of course, this is not conclusive. The left-facing profile shows the poet as he was in the last year of his life and presents a more bucolic impression of Burns than the Nasmyth or Beugo portraits. Reid, a native of Kirkennan, had a studio in Dumfries and it is averred that Jean Armour also sat for her portrait in this medium but no miniature of Mrs Burns, painted on ivory, is now known to exist.

The only other portrait which has some remote claim to being authentic is the so-called Swinton portrait, executed in oils. Its close affinity to the Nasmyth bust is very obvious and it has been suggested with some plausibility that it came from Nasmyth's brush and was designed as a cartoon or sketch for the original painting, or may even have been a preliminary attempt, abandoned in favour of the larger bust. Its provenance, however, has not been fully established and until such time as clearer documentary evidence is forthcoming, judgment will have to be reserved.

Derivative Works

The paintings by Nasmyth, Taylor and Reid, the Beugo engraving and the Miers silhouette are the only portraits which can be regarded as both contemporary and authentic. One other picture was produced in the poet's lifetime, but must be regarded as deriving — like so many later works — from the Nasmyth bust-portrait. This was the painting of 'The Cotter's Saturday Night' by David Allan (1744-96), popularly known as 'the Scottish Hogarth'. Allan never met Burns, but in 1786 he was appointed Director of the Trustees Academy and this brought him in close contact with the Principal Clerk, George Thomson, who recruited Burns to provide lyrics for his *Select Scottish Airs*.

Thomson commissioned the painting which shows the cotter's family, modelled on the family of William Burnes, with the figure of the eldest son bearing a striking resemblance to Burns himself. Allan produced a copy of this painting, which Thomson presented to Burns. Acknowledging this gift, in the long letter of May 1795 already quoted, Burns said: 'I have shewn it to two or three judges of the first abilities here, they all agree with me in classing it as a first-rate production. — My phiz is *sae kenspeckle*, that the very joiner's apprentice whom Mrs Burns employed to break up the parcel (I was out of town that day) knew it at once... Several people think that Allan's likeness of me is more striking than Nasemith's *[sic]*...' Burns was particularly taken with the small boy about to cut the cat's tail — 'the most striking likeness of an ill-deedie, damn'd, wee, rumble-gairie hurchin of mine, whom, from that propensity to witty wickedness & manfu' mischief, which, even at twa days auld I foresaw would form the striking features of his disposition, I named Willie Nicol after a certain friend of mine...'

Allan also engraved the convivial scene from 'Tam o Shanter', with the shadowy figure of the poet hovering in the background. This work may also be regarded as contemporary, as Allan died on 6th August 1796, a fortnight after Burns himself.

Archibald Skirving's celebrated drawing of Burns in red crayon on grey paper was for many years regarded as authentic. Certainly it was regarded by many of the poet's contemporaries as the finest representation of him and it continues to occupy a special place in the affections of Burns enthusiasts to this day. But that it is not authentic was proved by the discovery of Skirving's manuscripts in relatively recent times. In a letter to his brother Skirving refers to the drawing of Burns 'taken from a picture, for him I never saw'. Skirving spent some time on the Continent, but returned to Edinburgh towards the end of 1796. The drawing must have been executed between that time and October 1798 for engravings based on the portrait were then advertised in the *Morning Chronicle*. The original engraving was made by Paton Thomson, but three years later John Beugo produced a sensitive version for the *Scots Magazine* and the Belfast edition of Burns's poems, published in 1805. Sir Walter Scott wrote in 1816 of Skirving going to London 'with the only good portrait of Burns'.

Painted wooden roundel, based on Archibald Skirving.

Clearly derived from Nasmyth, it nevertheless possesses a very special quality and is aesthetically most pleasing.

Mention has already been made of the supposed involvement of Sir Henry Raeburn in retouching the Thomson copy of the Nasmyth bust-portrait. It was even supposed that Raeburn had touched up the Nasmyth original while it was in Alexander Cunningham's possession. In 1802 Mesrs Cadell and Davies, who held the copyright of Burns's writings and published Dr Currie's editions, wished to obtain a copy or drawing of the Nasmyth bust-portrait which could then be engraved for use as a frontispiece. Cunningham very generously arranged for such a copy to be made, by 'our finest artist here, Raeburn, who will do it every Justice'. Subsequent correspondence revealed that Raeburn was willing to make the copy for 20 guineas. Cadell and Davies agreed to this, for on 14th November 1803 Raeburn himself informed the publishers that the portrait was now completed and he suggested that it could be transported to London by sea. 'I have frequently sent pictures by that mode of conveyance, and they always went safe.' Subsequently Raeburn had the painting consigned to London in a case, and sent the receipt for it by separate letter on 1st December. The picture was conveyed by the smack *Sprightly* and in due course it was safely delivered. Cadell and Davies appear to have been very well satisfied with the portrait, if we may judge from Raeburn's letter of acknowledgment, dated 22nd February 1804: 'Gentlemen — nothing could be more gratifying to me than the approbation you expressed of the copy I made for you of Robert Burns.' In the same letter he mentions a portrait he had executed of Henry Mackenzie which was about to be shipped to London. The 20 guineas were paid by Cadell and Davies to James Lyon in London, enabling Raeburn to draw on the latter for that sum in settling some London accounts. Incidentally, it is worth noting that Nasmyth executed the original bust-portrait for nothing — and Beugo likewise took no fee for engraving it.

The Raeburn portrait vanished from sight for sixteen years and it is not known where it hung in the interim, although we may conjecture that it adorned the premises of Cadell and Davies. On 1st April 1820, this company advertised a new edition of Currie, revised by Gilbert Burns, the poet's brother. The work was issued 'with a new portrait' and this appears as a frontispeice in the first of the four volumes, engraved by W.T. Fry after A. Nasmyth, from which it may be inferred that Raeburn, having but copied the Nasmyth, did not displace the painter's name on the engraved plate. The portrait shows a strong intellectual expression and was a welcome departure from the Beugo engraving. In an advertisement of March 1823 Thomas Cadell mentions the portrait as 'from an original Picture by Raeburn'. Cadell was in error in describing it as 'original' but after an interval of twenty years he could be forgiven for this mistake. It was not again used by Cadell, but re-emerged, engraved by H. Robinson, in the first and second

Aldine editions of **Burns's** poetry, published in 1830 and 1839 respectively. As to the painting itself, however, its present whereabouts are unknown. Incidentally, a large canvas showing a seated portrait of the poet may be seen in the Burns bedroom at the Globe Inn. It is unsigned, but a brass plate proclaims optimistically 'School of Raeburn, possibly painted from life'.

It has been estimated that upwards of a hundred artists have produced paintings of Burns since his death. About forty of them were represented at the Centenary Exhibition in Glasgow in 1896, but no attempt was made to assess their artistic qualities. Some of these works, notably the bust-portraits by James Gilfillan and James Tannock, were painted in the decades immediately after the poet's death, by men who may have had some clain to know Burns in life, and this has imbued these paintings with a quality of near authenticity. Others, by W. Dobie, James Nasmyth, William Spier, Charles K. Robertson, William Simpson, Alexander S. Mackay, Thomas J. Ford, John Andrew, George Watson, R. Ramsay Russell, Alex McCubbin, Joseph Semple, Sir Theodore Martin, James B. Alexander, and Sir Daniel Macnee were modelled to a greater or lesser degree on Nasmyth's original. Sir William Allan painted a rather lugubrious portrait of Burns seated at his desk, in the throes of composing 'The Cotter', and this was subsequently engraved and published as a popular print. One painting which was *not* exhibited in 1896 was the bust-portrait painted by William McQuhae. Apart from a vague resemblance to Nasmyth's seminal work, this painting cannot be regarded as a good likeness of Burns. The painter was born in Balmaghie in May 1779 'from where he moved to Edinburgh, where he and Burns roomed together. He early exhibited remarkable talent as a painter, and while rooming with Burns he painted from life this portrait, which was then pronounced a good likeness. About 1805 Mr McQuhae came to America, bringing with him the picture, which he presented to an art society in Philadelphia...' This account, written by George M. Diven who subsequently acquired the painting, is utterly ludicrous. McQuhae must have been twenty years younger than Burns, which would have meant him 'rooming' with Burns at the tender age of eight! Remarkable his talent may have been, but such precocity is unheard of. Yet this ridiculous story was readily accepted, and an engraving of the McQuhae portrait made by T. Johnson for publication in an American periodical, *The Century Magazine* (volume LV).

No fewer than nineteen of the portraits shown in the Centenary Exhibition were described in the catalogue as being by unknown artists — and it must be admitted, the less said about them the better. Right down to the present time, the Nasmyth bust has been cloned *ad nauseam*. Just as innumerable rhymesters and poetasters feel impelled to emulate the Master with their doggerel verse, so countless artists, many without training of any sort, feel inspired to turn out their own versions of the bust, and usually with indifferent results. Poor Nasmyth's bust has been stylised and stereotyped almost to the point of parody and caricature, and this process, as we shall see, has extended from the fine arts into every conceivable branch of the applied arts.

The 1896 Exhibition represented the acme of Victorian adulation of Burns, coinciding with the highwater mark of the Romantic movement. The result was an astonishing array of genre paintings. It would require a large book to do justice to all of these works individually so I can only summarise them here. Undoubtedly the most important of these works were

Burns as Depute-Master Mason, engraved by Charles Ewart, after Stewart Watson.

Burns and the Vision, by James Christie (by courtesy of Irvine Burns Club).

those which illustrated scenes from the poet's life. First and foremost in this group is Charles Martin Hardie's painting of the meeting of Burns and Scott at Sciennes House in the winter of 1786-7. The same artist painted two versions of 'Burns in Edinburgh, 1787' showing the poet reciting one of his works before a gathering of the *literati* at the Duchess of Gordon's home. In both of these works Hardie has gone to great lengths to obtain good likenesses of the various personages. Stewart Watson painted a similarly panoramic canvas showing the inauguration of Burns as Laureate of Lodge Canongate Kilwinning, while James Edgar used the same treatment in his rendition of 'Burns and his Correspondents' and William Borthwick Johnstone in his splendid canvas 'Circulating Library of John Sibbald'. In the heroic mould are paintings of the procession of St James's Lodge, Tarbolton, by David O. Hill and W.E. Lockhart's sombre 'Funeral of Burns'. Sir Noel Paton executed a watercolour of 'Burns and the Vision', and James Christie later produced the same subject in oils. Sir William Allan painted 'Burns composing the Cotter', while Gourlay Steell painted 'Burns at the Plough'. One of the earliest of the posthumous paintings was 'Young Burns at the grave of his father' painted by Buck and engraved by Bate for publication by William Holland in 1808. The 1896 exhibition also had paintings of 'Burns and friend in village ale-house' and 'Burns and the Souter', both by unknown artists. One of the most interesting of these genre paintings, in point of detail, is 'The meeting of Burns and Captain Francis Grose' by R.S. Lauder, now in the Birthplace Museum. The same museum has Alexander Carse's painting of the Jolly Beggars gathered in Poosie Nansie's Inn at Mauchline. It

Burns in Edinburgh, by C. M. Hardie (by courtesy of Irvine Burns Club).

Above and opposite (top): two of the series of five oil paintings by Angus Scott illustrating 'Tam o Shanter', (by courtesy of Irvine Burns Club).

ROBERT BURNS.

Reversed portrait, after Beugo, by Halpen, in the Dublin pirated edition.

merits a mention in this chapter because it incorporates a seated figure of the poet observing the 'gangrel bodies', but it has to be admitted that portraiture was not Carse's strong point. The same may be said of Carse's great masterpiece 'Mauchline Holy Fair', where Burns is shown as a minor character on the extreme right of a very crowded canvas. James Edgar also executed a picture showing Burns at a party at Lord Monboddo's, with eighteen of the leading figures of the Enlightenment looking on in rapt attention. Then there are all the paintings of Burns and his heroines. J.E. Christie alone seems to have dealt with the subject of 'Burns and Bonie Nell', but Highland Mary inspired many an artist, famous and not so well known. C.M. Hardie, R.B. Nisbet, James Archer, Thomas Faed, R. Macaulay Stevenson and G.W. Brownlow have essayed paintings in this theme, while G. Fidler has given us 'The Brook' where Burns and Mary Campbell vowed eternal fidelity and W.H. Midwood has painted the touching scene in which Burns and Mary exchanged Bibles as a token of their betrothal. This was a subject to which Sir Daniel Macnee also applied his considerable talents. By contrast, Jean Armour, the wife who was remarkably loyal to Burns and survived him by 38 years, was only painted in relative old age, by James Gilfillan (at least two versions being known), and

"Burns and Highland Mary" by W. H. Midwood. Birthplace Museum.

"The meeting of Burns and Captain Grose," by R. S. Lauder, Birthplace Museum.

Murals in Irvine Burns Club: Burns in Irvine, by Ted and Elizabeth Odling.

there is also a frankly derivative portrait by an unknown hand. S. McKenzie painted the well-known portrait of 'Bonie Jean' with her favourite grand-child, Sarah Burns Hutchinson, but it may be significant that no artist has been inspired to paint a picture of Burns and Jean together.

Probably the most imaginative, and certainly the most ambitious work of more recent years to portray the bard, is the series of murals which were commissioned by the Irvine Burns Club to decorate the walls of the Burns Room in Wellwood House, Irvine. This room, which preserves the atmosphere of two centuries ago in its dark beams and polished stone floor, its ingle-nook and contemporary furnishings, is dominated by the frescoes executed by Ted and Elizabeth Odling to illustrate the episode in the early life of Burns when he lived in Irvine (1781) and learned the trade of flax-dressing. The murals present a medley of scenes: the arrival of Burns, a visit to Templeton's bookshop, the budding poet in the throes of composition or suffering black despair, at the flax dressing or practising his violin, conversing with his brother poet, David Sillar, or the sea-captain, Richard Brown. These murals are remarkable not only for their superb draughtsmanship but for the meticulous attention to detail and the accuracy of the eighteenth century costumes, furniture and rural scenery.

I have discussed the portraits of Burns, especially those executed in his lifetime, in some detail for directly or indirectly they affect the depiction of the poet in every other medium. Paintings of scenes from the life and works of Burns will be found treated separately in the next chapter.

Funeral of Burns at Dumfries, July, 1796.

Pictures from the life and works of Burns

The earliest pictures associated with Burns, available to the public, were the various reproductions of his bust-portrait that appeared in editions of his Poems from 1787 onwards. The engraving by Beugo has already been discussed at some length, because it ranks among the handful of authentic portraits. In the same year as the first Edinburgh edition (1787) there appeared at Dublin a pirated edition of the Poems, and this was illustrated, with superb effrontery, by a bust-portrait as frontispiece. The Irish engraver, Patrick Halpen, must have held one of the Beugo prints to a mirror and engraved a portrait which showed Burns facing right instead of left. Inevitably the 'speaking likeness' of the poet, rendered so sensitively by Beugo, suffered considerably by this treatment. Nevertheless, the Halpen engraving deserves pride of place as the first in a seemingly endless line of portraits which become less and less like the Bard the farther they get away from the original, and yet continue to bear some resemblance to the Nasmyth bust, however slight.

There were, of course, many later engravings based on the Nasmyth bust which were more accurate and these appeared initially in some of the innumerable editions of the Poems and accompanying biographies that proliferated in the course of the nineteenth century. One may cite in this group the engravings by John Zeitter, Edward Mitchell, George Aikman, R.B. Parkes and, above all, the excellent portrait executed by William Walker and Samuel Cousins in 1830 and reprinted in 1842. H. Bell Scott made a fine engraving from the Auchendrane bust, as well as an engraving of the Nasmyth full-length portrait. Some of these engravings are known, like the Beugo of 1787, as India paper proofs, and by the 1830s it was also customary to issue editions of the engravings separate from the printed volumes, mounted and framed. By means of the pantograph, enlarged engravings based on Beugo, or taken direct from the Nasmyth bust, were published either plain or delicately aquatinted. There was a rash of such pictures in 1859, the year of the worldwide celebrations of the poet's birth, and this fashion continued to gather momentum over the ensuing forty years, culminating in the great Centenary celebrations of 1896. The earliest prints were taken from copperplate engravings, but by the 1830s steel engraving — or siderography as it was sometimes called — was more popular, as the plates did not wear out so readily. Although lithography had been invented in the year of the poet's death, it does not appear to have been widely applied to Burns portraits until the second half of the nineteenth century, when some remarkable multicoloured reproductions of the Nasmyth bust were produced. A fairly early exception to this, however, was the lithograph by W. Grattan entitled 'Burns's Departure from Scotland' which was published by the London print-seller Ackermann in 1825. There were experiments with other forms of reproduction. At the Centenary Exhibition of 1896

there was a platinotype by Alexander McCubbin of his oil painting and an 'autotype sepiagraph' of the Tannock bust of Burns. I have not been able to ascertain what sort of reproduction this was, but suspect that it was some kind of photographic process. By the 1890s collotypes were extensively used — the Exhibition catalogue, published in 1898, was replete with such plates produced by P. Gardner from original photographs by the well-known Glasgow firm of Annan and Sons. Other photographic processes, known as rotogravure, heliogravure or photogravure, were being developed at the turn of the century, and were employed to produce monochrome prints, often rendered in rather peculiar shades of brown, blue or green. In recent years multicolour photogravure has been widely used, but surprisingly little use of this process has been made in the context of Burns pictures. An exact facsimile of the Skirving chalk drawing, in red on grey, was produced by one of these early photographic processes in 1891. The famous Glasgow collector of Burnsiana, W. Craibe Angus, commissioned an edition of twelve of these prints from Dixon & Son, and one of them may be seen at the Birthplace Museum in Alloway. In the 1890s, however, chromolithography reached its peak of perfection as the preferred medium for colour prints. A splendid example of this was the lithograph of 1893 produced by the British and Colonial Fine Art Association of James B. Alexander's watercolour portrait of Burns.

Apart from the portraits that adorned the editions of his Poems, published in Burns's lifetime, the earliest portrait to appear in print was a rather crude line drawing, based on Nasmyth of course, which accompanied an obituary notice of the poet in the *Newcastle Chronicle* in July 1796. This was produced by the letterpress process and a proof of this curious portrait was shown at the Centenary Exhibition in 1896.

Scenes and characters from the works of Burns

None of the editions published in the poet's lifetime contained illustrations of the poems. The only illustration — and that of a topographical nature — was the engraving of Alloway's auld haunted kirk which appeared in the second volume of Grose's *The Antiquities of Scotland* (1791). In this instance a poem — 'Tam o Shanter' — was used as an accompaniment to the picture, and not the other way round. Similarly, David Allan executed some twenty etchings for George Thomson, to illustrate *Select Scottish Airs*, but they were never published in their entirety. Several of Allan's works illustrated poems by Burns, notably 'Tam o Shanter' and 'The Cotter's Saturday Night', but these pictures appeared posthumously.

Apart from Allan's paintings of Tam and the Cotter, which were subsequently engraved for reproduction in books, the only contemporary painting derived from a poem of Burns is the curious little panel done in oils illustrating 'Willie brew'd a Peck o Maut' which hangs in the Burns Centre,

Tam o Shanter, by Joseph Shearer.

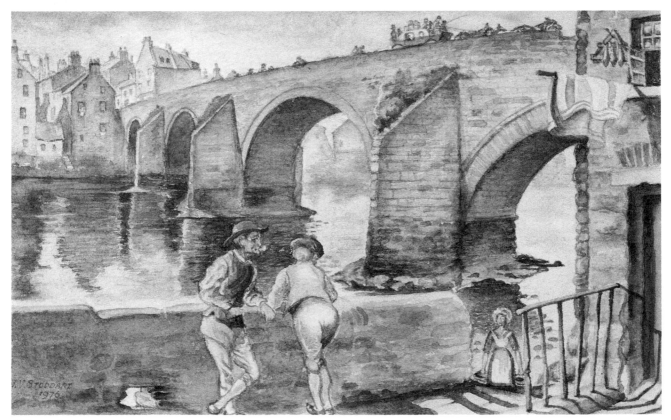

"The Auld Brig o Ayr" by John V. Stoddart (Allan Stoddart Collection).

Dumfries. According to the caption, it was 'painted by a friend of William Nicol, Laggan, Nithsdale in 1793, who presented it to Burns and was in his possession at his death. Afterwards purchased by Captain Ewart at the sale of Burns's effects at Dumfries on 11th April 1834, who afterwards gave it to his daughter who was married to Mr William Kitchen, Solicitor, Newcastle-on-Tyne and was in her possession after her husband's death, 11th May 1879. The above particular was all told me by Captain Ewart's daughter — George Hannah, Albert Square, Edinburgh'. This painting, with its ungrammatical but interesting provenance, was presented to Dumfries by the Earl of Rosebery in 1942.

Pride of place among the characters created by Burns must go to Tam o Shanter who has been reproduced in more media than all the others put together. Among the artists who have helped to immortalise the bibulous Tam in oils are Samuel Bough, John Burnet, Thomas Davidson, Heywood Hardy, W. Thomas Smith, L. Adams and J. Ward. James E. Christie produced at least four different versions of Tam o Shanter, as well as paintings entitled 'Warlocks grim and wither'd hags', 'Tam skelpit on thro dub and mire', 'The Carlin claught her by the rump' and — most famous of all — 'Cutty Sark'. E. Nichol's painting of Tam and Maggie confronted by the 'towzie tyke' hangs in the Birthplace Museum. Tam's approach to Alloway kirk, by an unknown artist, featured in the Centenary Exhibition. The best known series of paintings illustrating this great epic poem, however, was that executed by John Faed in watercolours. Chromolithographs of these wonderfully evocative pictures were subsequently published by W. & A.K. Johnston of Edinburgh, but steel engravings, monochrome lithographs and halftone reproductions of them have appeared in various editions of 'Tam o Shanter' published as a separate work right down to the present day. R.C. Lucas, better known as a sculptor, executed a folio collection of drawings illustrative of 'Tam o Shanter' which was published in 1841 and is now much sought after. In more recent years there is the lively and atmospheric series of five oil paintings by Angus Scott, which was commissioned by Irvine Burns Club and now adorns the entrance to 'Wellwood'. As a rule, sculpture tends to be derived from two-dimensional works such as paintings and drawings, but there are instances in which pictures have been inspired by statuary. The stone figures of Tam and Souter Johnny carved by Thom are discussed elsewhere in this book, but it should be noted here that they inspired an etching by W. Geikie. A painting of Tam by L. Adams was subsequently etched by C. Hamburger, and there is also a well-known chromolithograph of this subject by Harry Harwood. In addition there are numerous prints of Tam o Shanter which were produced by unknown artists. The Centenary Exhibition displayed a rare broadsheet version of the poem, illustrated by a rough woodcut of Cutty Sark and the dance of the witches. Moreover, Tam o Shanter was included in the repertoire of miscellaneous scenes and characters executed by many other artists to illustrate editions of the Poems. The most visually exciting illustrations of Tam are those which were executed by Joseph Shearer of Sydney, Australia in the last few years. Examples of his work may be seen in the Tam o Shanter Inn, Ayr.

'The Cotter's Saturday Night' comes a poor second, although it has been immortalised on canvas by Sam Bough, P. Macgregor Wilson, H.J. Dobson, Charles M. Hardie and C.S. White in addition to David Allan. Engravings were produced by Paton Thomson after Allan and by Francis Sennewick after White and there are also several anonymous prints associated with this great sentimental poem. 'The Jolly Beggars' inspired paintings by William Fulton Brown and Sir William Allan, and Alexander Green returned to this theme on several occasions. Other paintings based on Burns's great comic cantata include 'When lyart leaves bestrow the yird' by David Fulton, and 'Gangrels' by J.C. Wyper. James E. Christie has given us two wonderful paintings of 'Hallowe'en', while the same poem was the subject of a fine painting by Robert Gemmill-Hutchison.

'Duncan Gray' was painted by Alexander Carse and also by Sir David Wilkie (the latter painting being later published as an engraving by F. Engleheart). Both Thomas Hunt and Niels M. Lund have painted scenes from 'A Winter's Night', while 'The Haggis' was immortalised in paintings by Alexander Fraser and G. Ogilvy Reid. Charles M. Hardie produced a veritable gallery of paintings inspired by various poems of Burns, including 'Mary Morison', 'Red, Red Rose', 'Silver Tassie', 'Ca' the Yowes', 'Tam Glen', 'My Heart is Sair' and 'Auld Lang Syne'. The last-named poem also inspired Robert Gemmill-Hutchison to paint his canvas entitled 'We twa hae paidled in the burn'. James Christie and William Whittet have given us their versions of 'Willie brew'd a peck o maut', but paintings of this subject by unknown artists, in addition to the Ewart painting already mentioned, have also been recorded.

Among the other poems which have been honoured by oil paintings may be mentioned 'The Deil's awa wi th 'Exciseman' by J.M. Wright, 'Twa Dogs' by George Pirie, 'Braw Wooer' by G. Ogilvy Reid, 'The Lea Rig' by W.D. McKay and Marshall Brown, 'Sweet fa's the even on Craigie-burn' by Andrew Hyslop, 'Beneath the milk-white thorn that scents the ev'ning gale' by T. Corsan Morton, 'In gowany glens' by John Lawson and 'We'll gently walk and sweetly talk' by Norman M. Macdougall. E. Sherwood Calvert painted 'Crystal Devon' and 'The charming month of May', while J. Lochhead produced 'John Barleycorn' and 'Bonie Day in June'. The Centenary Exhibition included a painting entitled 'A blast of Janwar win' by an unknown hand and several anonymous paintings illustrative of 'Tam Samson'.

Many of these paintings were subsequently engraved in order to illustrate editions of the Poems, but there were also numerous anonymous engravings. In this category come the series, published by James

Thin, which illustrated 'Auld Lang Syne', 'Rantin, Rovin Robin', 'Hallowe'en', 'Tam o Shanter', 'The Braw Wooer', 'The Cotter's Saturday Night' and that disdainful line from 'A Man's a Man' — 'You see yon birkie ca'd a lord'. William Hole produced a series of twelve engravings to illustrate the famous centenary edition compiled by Henley and Henderson. James Bryden produced a number of etchings in 1895,

"The Jolly Beggars", etching by James Bryden, 1895.

"The Cotter's Saturday Night", etching by James Bryden, 1895.

including 'The Cotter' and 'The Jolly Beggars'. A curious feature of these etchings is the manner in which the artist's name and the date are cunningly concealed in the detail of the pictures.

Most of the editions of Burns published in the course of the present century have tended to fall back on the paintings and engravings executed in the nineteenth century, but there have been some notable exceptions. Ted and Elizabeth Odling produced a series of drawings which were later used to illustrate a guide published by Irvine Burns Club. John Mackay, best-known for his work as an illustrator in the *Scots Magazine*, has produced some delightful vignettes which were used to illustrate James Veitch's *Junior Life of Burns* and, more recently, a series of twelve watercolours based on the life and works of Burns which were published in the form of a calendar for 1988.

Scenery and Landmarks associated with Burns

Captain Francis Grose unwittingly initiated the spate of pictures devoted to the Burns country when he published the engraving of Alloway Kirk already mentioned, which was accompanied by the first publication of 'Tam o Shanter' in 1791. Scenery and landmarks associated with the poet lagged a little behind, in terms of reproduction. The earliest editions of the Poems were not illustrated, other than by the portrait of Burns himself, but early in the nineteenth century engravings evoking the Burns country began to appear, both as separate works and as illustrations to the Poems.

Probably the earliest of the separate works was the aquatint of the poet's birthplace by Robert Scott, from an original drawing by William Score, published by Robert Chapman of Glasgow in November 1801. An exceedingly rare trial proof of this engraving is displayed in the Birthplace Museum and shows trees at the back of the cottage; these trees do not show in the published plate. It seems strange that the cottage which had been vacated by the Burnes family in 1766 should have become a place of veneration to Burns devotees within a few years of his death. The first recorded Burns dinner was held at Alloway in the summer of 1801 by a group of the poet's Ayrshire friends and in subsequent years they would foregather for a meal and good fellowship in the cottage itself which, at some time prior to 1800, had become an ale-house. Samuel Bough was an enthusiastic painter of the cottage exterior — at least five different versions of the subject are known from his brush, but other paintings of the poet's birthplace are known by Lockhart and David Small. David Octavius Hill (1838) was the first artist to paint the interior of the cottage, and this has proved to be a very useful documentary painting in assisting the trustees to restore the cottage to the condition in which it would have been at the time the poet lived there.

Among the earliest illustrations of the life and works of Burns were those engraved on wood by the celebrated artist Thomas Bewick. These exquisite woodcuts were used to illustrate the only edition of the Poems ever to be published at Alnwick, in 1808. Reprints from the original wood blocks were made in a limited edition in 1896 to celebrate the centenary of the poet's death and these are now much sought after.

In 1809 Thomas Stothard and Robert H. Cromek (author of the well-known *Reliques*) made a pilgrimage to the Burns country. Incidentally, they travelled from London by sea, intending to call at Newcastle to visit Thomas Bewick. Altogether they spent nine weeks touring Scotland in quest of material with which to illustrate a new edition of Burns. Stothard then returned to London, having completed his drawings, but Cromek tarried four weeks longer. They spent a month in and around Edinburgh, obtaining sketches of Roslin Castle, Roslin Chapel, Hawthornden, Edinburgh in general and views of the High Street, Allan Ramsay's old shop, the Castle, St Anthony's Chapel at Holyroodhouse and Fergusson's tombstone in particular. They toured East Lothian and called on Gilbert Burns at Grants Bracs, sketching his portrait, and also that of old Mrs Burns, the poet's mother. Cromek gave the old lady a ten-pound note 'with which she was well satisfied, and I was also greatly gratified' as he wrote to his sister Ann. Portraits were also sketched of Lord Woodhouselee, Lord Monboddo, James Gray (who taught the children of Burns at Dumfries Academy), John Murdoch, Robert Burns junior and Neil Gow, the celebrated fiddler. As Gow had died two years previously, it must be supposed that the sketch was done from some other portrait, as was a posthumous sketch of Elizabeth Burnet whose death in 1790 had inspired Burns to compose his well-known elegy.

In a letter written on 2nd August 1809 from Edinburgh to his wife, the day before they set out for Dumfries, Cromek wrote: 'I have thought it prudent to alter our route, on account of the precarious state of Mrs Dunlop's health, who is between eighty-ninety, & may suddenly give us the slip. We shall therefore draw *Jean*, get done in Dumfries, and in Nithsdale, and go immediately down to Mauchline to Mrs Dunlop &c... As for Jean, I do not doubt of her and then the family will be secured, which is a grand object.'

Continuing their tour from Dumfries, Cromek and Stothard crossed Nithsdale and went via Tarbolton to Mauchline, Mossgiel, Kilmarnock, Stewarton and Neilston, and thence to Glasgow. Thereafter they toured the west Highlands before returning to Greenock at the beginning of September. Despite almost continuous rain that summer, Cromek and Stothard had succeeded in their object beyond their wildest hopes. In one respect, however, their hopes were dashed. Jean refused their reasonable request. In March 1810 James Gray wrote to Cromek about this unfortunate matter: 'I saw Gilbert Burns a few days ago. He was sorry to learn that Jean had refused to sit to Stothard. He said he thought she owed this to Cadell & Davies and had he suspected it he would have written to her on the subject.' Cadell & Davies apparently financed the tour, hence Gilbert's remarks. Stothard *did* produce a sketch of Jean — a

fact mentioned by his biographer, Mrs Bray, in her articles in *Blackwood's Magazine*(May-June 1836), but it seems likely that Stothard sketched the portrait from memory, and significantly no use was ever made of it to illustrate any edition of the poet's works.

Cromek died in 1812 before the fruits of the tour could be harvested. Two years later, however, Stothard's twelve scenes illustrating the poems of Burns were published. The illustrations in question were actually engraved on copperplate by Cromek and were issued as a set of prints in 1814. Nine years later they were employed to illustrate the edition of the Poems edited by Gilbert Burns. These engravings, however, are said to have borne little relation to Stothard's original drawings which were never published. After Cromek's death these drawings passed into the hands of his sister Ann who disposed of them at Christie's in June 1845. This invaluable record of the tour was thus dispersed and the present whereabouts of these drawings is unknown. A sketch of Burns's cottage by Stothard, dated 1812, was reproduced in Allan Cunningham's edition of Burns in 1834, and an etching entitled 'Brig o' Doon and Alloway's auld haunted Kirk' is preserved in the Mitchell Library, Glasgow. No explanation has ever been forthcoming why the projected edition was abandoned, but as Cadell & Davies were its backers it is reasonable to assume that the withdrawal of their financial support rendered its completion impossible.

Allan Cunningham's sumptuous two-volume *Life and Works* (1834) was beautifully illustrated not only with scenes and landmarks associated with Burns, but also with engraved portraits of many of the poet's associates and correspondents. These engravings were also made available as separate prints and a series of them, mounted and framed, may be seen in the Tower at Mauchline. William Forrest and Robert Anderson made engravings from drawings by Alexander Nasmyth, Sam Bough, William Lockhart and Clark Stanton which appeared in the 'Library Edition' of Burns in 1880. The set of fifteen engravings, however, is also known as proofs without the letterpress captions.

William Simpson produced a series of engravings showing the poet's birthplace, Alloway Kirk, the Brig o Doon and the Monument, subsequntly published by Allan and Ferguson. William Young published engravings of eight views in the Land of Burns, while W. Bell Scott issued a set of sixteen copperplate etchings illustrative of the life and works of Burns.

As the nineteenth century progressed interest in the places associated with Burns gathered momentum. The scenery of the southwest of Scotland began to attract the serious attention of painters from all over the British Isles. Lockhart, David Law, John Wallace and James M. Mackay painted views of the cottage. In addition to David Hill, already noted, W. Bell Scott and Robert Alexander painted interior views of the poet's birthplace, and Andrew Allan painted a scene at the fireplace. Gavin Hamilton's house in Mauchline was painted by J.C. Wyper, while Thomas

Morton and F.W. Scarborough produced paintings of Mauchline Castle. The poet's last home in Dumfries was the subject of oils by Hamilton Maxwell who painted at least two different versions. R. Macaulay Stevenson painted Afton Water while Robert Nisbet painted 'On the Nith'. Both of these subjects were also the subject of paintings by David Law. Landseer was not the only artist to cash in on the Victorian penchant for humanoid animal subjects, as is shown in G. Fidler's painting entitled 'The Guardian of Highland Mary's Monument'. Among the paintings shown at the Centenary Exhibition were 'Mouth of the Doon' by William Dalglish, 'Valley of the Doon' by Helen Thornycroft and 'Brow Well' by T. Marjoribanks Hay. George Thomson painted the Globe tavern, the poet's 'favourite howff' in Dumfries, while an engraving of the Globe Close by J. Rogers was based on a painting by W.H. Bartlett. Mossgiel from the time of Burns was painted by John Kelso Hunter and James Clark, who also produced a fine painting of Nanse Tinnock's ale-house in Mauchline.

Inevitably, certain subjects were more popular than others. Various aspects and views of Ellisland, romantically situated above the bank of the Nith, inspired Sam Bough, David O. Hill, John Wallace, James Paterson, Wilfrid Lawson and G. Fidler, among others. The poet's monument at Doonside, Alloway, usually with the auld brig in the foreground, found expression in paintings by Patrick Downie, David Law and J.D. Scott, while P.C. Auld produced at least two versions of this subject. Susan F. Crawford, R.M.G. Coventry, W.E. Lockhart, R.A. Cruikshank, Patrick Downie, F.W. Scarborough and David Farquharson painted oils of the Auld Brig at Ayr, and various watercolours of this subject were produced by William Young. The Brig o Doon, without the monument, attracted the attention of Robert Alexander and Hugh Allan. Alloway Kirk was painted at one time or another by James Clark, Hugh Allan, W.E. Lockhart, David Law and Marjoribanks Hay. Only one painting of Lochlea appeared in the Centenary Exhibition, and that was by an unknown artist.

Undoubtedly, however, the most ambitious of all the artistic coverage of the Burns country was that produced by David O. Hill who visited the haunts of the poet at various times between 1837 and 1840 and produced a prodigious series of 82 views. These exist in the form of oils, watercolours and pencil drawings, which were subsequently produced on steel by a veritable army of engravers: W. Richardson, W. Howison, W. Miller, J. Horsburgh, W. Forrest, T. Grundy, J. Giles, T. Higham. J.T. Willmore, T.J. Kelly, J. Appleton, T. Jeavons, D. Wilson, R. Sands, P. Lightfoot and E. Goodall. They were published by Blackie in two handsome quarto volumes entitled *The Land of Burns* in 1840-1. The title page of this work indicates that the landscapes were from paintings, but it is now known that Hill was one of the first artists to use the camera as an aid to his work. Rather unfairly, Hill's artistic output tended to be decried on that score. Ironically, his reputation at the present day rests mainly on his skill as a pioneer photographer! The rights to these engravings subsequently passed to Blackie and Son who published later editions of these volumes, as well as the individual prints. Cashing in on the Centenary celebrations in 1896, an oblong folio was produced entitled *In the Land of Burns* — note the similarity of title to the original production. Seven etchings by David Law were published in 1893, with brief descriptions by Edward R. Dibdin. Oddly enough, the Mausoleum in Dumfries has received scant attention from artists, despite its distinctive appearance. Architectural drawings by Thomas Hunt exist, and steel engravings, either plain or hand-coloured, by S. Rawle after an original drawing by Burney, executed in 1819 but this subject has never received serious attention from painters working in oils other than W.H. Bartlett.

Various engravings of Burns scenes and landmarks may also be found in many of the early guidebooks and tourist literature of the nineteenth century. John MacWhirter contributed illustrations of this sort to *Caledonia*, published in small folio format in 1878. By the last decade of the nineteenth century, however, photography was rapidly ousting engraving, and the artistic contribution to Burnsian illustration was drastically reduced. Nevertheless, as late as 1920 George Houston was producing watercolours of the Burns country which were subsequently reproduced in a full-colour pamphlet.

The vast majority of the pictures, both paintings and engravings, allude to scenes contemporary with the life and works of Burns, but there are several important pictures which are concerned with later events. I have already mentioned, in the previous chapter, William Lockhart's panoramic canvas of the poet's funeral at Dumfries in 1796. This painting of epic proportions was not actually painted till almost a century later, but has been much reproduced since then, usually without any comment so that the viewer is left with the implication that it was an eye-witness scene. In 1844 a great festival was held on the banks of Doon in honour of the re-union of the three surviving sons of the poet, and this scene was captured on canvas by an unknown artist. The painting itself is now preserved in the Birthplace Museum at Alloway.

The celebrations marking the centenary of the poet's birth, in 1859, occasioned a number of works, of which the anonymous painting of the procession of the incorporated trades with banners flying, through the High Street of Dumfries is perhaps the most noteworthy. In connexion with this event, however, Sir Daniel Macnee painted his portrait of Burns based on Skirving. This was subsequently steel-engraved and married to a series of charming vignettes illustrative of the life and writings of Burns by A. Maclure. This montage was lithographed as a folio sheet and published by Maclure and MacDonald of Glasgow. Significantly no artistic interpretation appears to exist concerning the 1896 celebrations; by that date the camera was supreme.

Burns Sculpture

Burns Mausoleum, Dumfries. Photo: James Mackay.

Statues of Robert Burns are to be found in Scotland, England, Ireland, the United States, Canada, Australia and New Zealand, not to mention plaques and roundels, panels in low and high relief, and busts in bronze, wood, plaster or marble. Apart from the public monuments and memorials, sculpture exists in the form of the clay models and maquettes fashioned by sculptors as a preliminary to producing their full-scale works, or as reductions which were subsequently sold to the general public. Allied subjects, which are a form of sculpture in the strict sense, will be found elsewhere in this book under the headings of numismatics, ceramics, pewter, brass and furniture.

Monumental Statuary

The monuments erected in many parts of the world to Robert Burns are the most tangible and enduring medium in which the poet's memory has been kept alive. Oddly enough, the first attempt to have a memorial erected to Burns was made as far back as 1812, by John Forbes Mitchell of Bombay, and it is ironic that the first expression of a national, as opposed to a local, nature, should have come from overseas. Although Mitchell eventually collected a large sum of money for this purpose, it was not until he returned to Britain in 1819 that he could take practical steps to implement his proposals. In the meantime, plans for monuments to Burns had been maturing elsewhere.

Late in 1813 William Grierson and John Syme, close friends of the late poet, took the first steps towards doing something to perpetuate the memory of Burns in a practical form. A fund for the erection of a mausoleum in St Michael's churchyard was launched on 24th November 1814 and designs were solicited from architects. More than fifty designs from

The Muse of Poetry discovering Burns at the Plough: marble statuary, Herman Cawthra after Peter Turnerelli, in the Mausoleum, Dumfries. Photo: James Mackay.

every part of Britain were submitted, an indication of the widespread interest in Burns at that time. The design submitted by Thomas Frederick Hunt of London was finally chosen, but Hunt very generously waived the fee due to him, regarding it as a great honour to be chosen for so prestigious a project. The building was entrusted to a local contractor, John Milligan and the work was completed by September 1815.

As befitted the sepulchre of Burns and those of his children deceased, some form of sculpture was thought desirable. The honour of producing the first image of Burns in stone was given to Peter Turnerelli (1774-1839), an Irishman of Italian descent working in London. Turnerelli produced a marble group alluding to Burns's dedication of his first volume — 'The Poetic Genius of my country found me, as the prophetic bard Elijah did Elisha, at the plough and threw her inspiring mantle over me'. To be sure, the phraseology of the dedication was rather high-flown, so it was inevitable that in translating this sentiment into marble Turnerelli produced an allegorical composition which has endured a measure of criticism over the years and which nowadays strikes us as mannered. But it must be remembered that Turnerelli was working at a time when classicism was at the height of fashion, and in the context of the early

nineteenth century it was no worse than other marble groups of the period. It was well received at the time; the criticisms on aesthetic and factual grounds came much later. Turnerelli took two years to complete the statuary, but its conveyance (by sea) to Dumfries was delayed till 1819 while the sculptor haggled with the Mausoleum committee over his fee. In this respect he had gone back on his word; while not as public-spirited as the architect, Turnerelli promised to let the committee have the sculpture whether their fund reached its target or not. Later, however, he held out for the full amount, impelling the committee to mount a last-ditch campaign in the national press to secure the necessary sum.

Turnerelli's statuary endured for over a century, but by the 1920s it was in a poor state. Not only was the marble showing signs of decay but the Mausoleum itself was scandalously neglected. A fund for the restoration was launched in 1928 but it failed to reach its target. Initially it was considered that the statuary should be remodelled in bronze, as likely to last much longer, but the cost of doing this was prohibitive. Even the cost of restoring the statuary was estimated in excess of £3,000. The task of restoring the sculpture was given to Hermon Cawthra who completed the job in 1936, taking the opportunity to rectify the glaring inaccuracies perpetrated by Turnerelli, notably in the footwear and leggings of the ploughman-poet. Turnerelli's original was transferred to Burns House and was for some years displayed on the upper floor alongside the famous punch-bowl. Subsequently it was withdrawn from the House and ended up in a builder's yard. It was at one time offered to the Theatre Royal but no space was available. When Burns's first home was refurbished a few years ago consideration was given to housing the statue there but by that time it was too late. The builder had died and his yard had been sold, and the statue has long since disappeared.

While the citizens of Dumfries were getting their Mausoleum campaign under way, the devotees of the bard in his natal district were not letting the grass grow under their feet. Alexander Boswell of Auchinleck issued an invitation to a preliminary meeting at Ayr on 24th March 1814 to discuss a memorial project. Only one person answered this invitation, and that was the Rev. Hamilton Paul who had played a leading role in the Alloway anniversary dinners from 1801 onwards. These two gentlemen, however, soon overcame the apathy of their fellow-citizens and eventually raised £3,300 — a relatively large sum for those days. The money was used for the erection of a national monument on the bank of the River Doon at Alloway, near the poet's birthplace. The monument was designed by the noted Edinburgh architect, Thomas Hamilton, who later designed the Burns monument on Calton Hill in his native city. Hamilton was steeped in the classical tradition, as these two monuments testify.

The Alloway monument consists of a three-sided rustic basement supporting a circular Corinthian peristyle, surmounted by a cupola. The massive substructure was carefully sited so that each side faced one of the three divisions of Ayrshire — Carrick, Cunninghame and Kyle. The interior of the basement formed a circular chamber, intended as a repository of relics of the poet. The superstructure consists of nine columns, representing the nine muses, and the frieze of their entablature is richly decorated with chaplets of laurel. The design of the central column was copied from the temple of Jupiter Stater in the Campo Vaccini in Rome.

No plans were made for some form of sculpture to occupy this monument, and it was not until 1845 that anything was done to remedy this defect. In the summer of 1844 the great Festival in honour of the sons of Burns was held at Alloway. One of the participants was the sculptor Patric Park, who remarked to several of his friends at the time that it was a great pity there was no figure of the poet in the monument. From this discussion Park formed a plan to sculpt a bust of Burns in white marble. The work was completed by September 1845 and then offered as a gift to the monument committee. Two years elapsed before the committee got around to having the bust installed, on a pedestal of Aberdeen granite. The bust is clearly based on the Nasmyth painting, but it was subject to a great deal of criticism at the time, on the grounds that it was not a very good likeness and devoid of those natural features which were characteristic of the popular conception of the poet. It has to be admitted that such views, like the sculptor's interpretation, are entirely subjective.

Whereas Ayr got a monument without a statue, Edinburgh got a statue, and then decided to have a monument, almost as an afterthought because the money raised for the statue exceeded actual requirements. Mitchell's original idea was to have a colossal statue of Burns in some conspicuous site in the Scottish capital, but like some other of Edinburgh's colossal schemes, it shrank considerably before it came to fruition. Inevitably the initial enthusiasm soon waned, and subscriptions came in very slowly, forcing the committee to revise their ambitions very drastically. Five years after the fund was launched, the commission to sculpt the statue was given to John Flaxman in July 1824. Flaxman (1755-1826) was the foremost British sculptor of his day and he worked on a life-size marble statue of the poet. The head was clearly modelled on Nasmyth, but the rest was the London sculptor's own concept of what Burns would have looked like. He is shown clad in a plaid and knee breeches. A broad bonnet with a thistle in it lies at his feet, beside a ploughshare. His arms are folded and, rather self-consciously, he holds a bunch of daisies in one hand and a scroll of paper in the other. The square pedestal has a panel in bas-relief showing a seated figure of the bard being crowned by his muse.

Edward Pinnington, the celebrated art critic, discussed the Flaxman statue in the *Art Journal* (August 1897) as 'a fair example of the sculptor's mastery of technique. The chiselling is superb. In certain passages a desire may arise for finer

Marble statue by John Flaxman, Scottish National Portrait Gallery. Photo: James Mackay.

Left: Burns National Monument, Edinburgh.
Photo: James Anderson.

Detail of the bust of Burns by Flaxman.

Bronze statuette of Burns,
after Flaxman.

Glasgow statue, by George Ewing. Photo: William Doig.

discrimination, a more sensitive appreciation of the subtleties of texture, but as a whole the statue is the product of a highly accomplished sculptor who found a keen delight in the practice of his art.' In point of fact, Flaxman died before he could finish the statue, so this task fell to his pupil and brother-in-law, Joseph Denman. Flaxman, following in the selfless traditions of Nasmyth and Beugo, Hunt and Hamilton, generously agreed to carry out the work regardless of remuneration. In the end, however, the fund raised twice as much as the £1,400 required and the unexpended portion was then put to erecting the monument. The foundation stone was laid in 1831 and the temple was completed within the year. The monument was transferred to the City of Edinburgh by the committee in September 1839. A few years later Henry Scott Riddell, the all but forgotten author of 'Scotland Yet', donated the proceeds from his song to defray the cost of an ornamental railing round the monument. An East Linton worthy is credited with a cynical couplet:

Puir Burns amang the Calton Rocks
Sits lanely in his pepper-box.

The edifice was soon found to be too cramped to show the statue to advantage, and fifteen years later it was removed and re-erected in Edinburgh University Library. Dr John Lee, Principal of the University, objected to this on the specious grounds that Burns did not have a college education. Following a protracted correspondence between the University and the Town Council of Edinburgh, the statue was removed in 1861 to the National Gallery of Scotland in Princes Street. There it remained until the Scottish National Portrait Gallery was opened in 1889. It has stood in the entrance hall of the Gallery ever since, where it can be seen and admired in an ideal setting. From 1846 onwards the monument itself, like its Alloway counterpart, was used as a museum for Burns relics, but in 1901 the relics themselves had to be moved to the Corporation Museum on account of damage from damp. The Edinburgh monument is, in very truth, a cenotaph — literally 'an empty tomb'. Extensive renovation was carried out in 1961 and the monument re-opened to the public, but there has never been any suggestion that the Flaxman statue should be returned to its original location.

Flaxman's preliminary model of the statue was subsequently acquired by George Thomson who presented it to Colonel William Nicol Burns in 1847. John Irvine made a drawing of it in 1844 which was later engraved by H. Cook. One of these prints may be seen in the Birthplace Museum. Bronze reductions are also known, one being displayed in the Globe Inn, Dumfries. A half-sized replica in painted bronze occupies a niche above the Robert Burns Lounge in Perth.

James Crawford Thom (1802-50), whose career is discussed at greater length towards the end of this chapter, went to the United States in 1836 in pursuit of a bad debt and never returned to Scotland. He settled in Newark, New Jersey where he 'executed and had erected an imposing statue of Robert Burns'.

There is no mention of this in Edward Goodwillie's book on Burns memorials, published at Detroit in 1911, so it may be assumed that Thom's statue had disappeared long before that date. It seems likely that this stone figure was erected about 1840, before Thom gave up sculpture and became a gentleman farmer. He died of the 'white plague' in April 1850, but it is interesting to note that his grandson became Governor of New Jersey in 1932 — at that time the youngest man ever to have held gubernatorial rank.

Glasgow lagged far behind Edinburgh in erecting a statue to Burns, although it must be conceded that Glasgow has, in the long run, accorded greater and more public honour to the bard, whose statue is such a prominent feature of George Square to this day. Agitation for a statue of Burns began in 1872 as the result of an article in the *Evening Citizen* of 6th June, following the unveiling of a statue to Thomas Graham, the Glasgow-born scientist. The writer hinted that so long as Burns, Thomas Campbell and Adam Smith were without suitable commemoration in Glasgow, it could not be said that subjects were wanting, worthy of illustration in bronze of marble. John Browne, a commercial traveller and Burns enthusiast, responded immediately by starting a shilling subscription sheet which he took to the editor of the *Citizen*. The paper then gave the fund full publicity and in the space of a year some £1,680 was raised. The cost of a bronze statue and granite pedestal was estimated at £2,000 so George Edwin Ewing (1828-84) was commissioned to model a full-length figure of the poet. Ewing, a native of Birmingham who later settled in New York, spent the middle part of his career in Glasgow and was eminently qualified to execute the commission. Ewing's figure was cast in bronze at a Thames Ditton foundry in October 1876 and stood nine feet tall. No fewer than 30,000 people crowded into George Square on 25th January 1877 to watch the unveiling ceremony. Ewing's concept of Burns was quite original, and on that score alone it was subjected to a great deal of adverse criticism at the time. The poet is shown in pensive mood, with a daisy in his left hand and a Kilmarnock bonnet in his right. He was dressed in the costume of a Scottish farmer, in loose coat, knee breeches, stockings and buckled shoes. The figure, if somewhat heavy, is graceful in outline and the drapery has been treated in an effective and free manner.

George Ewing also designed the massive pedestal of Aberdeen granite, and about the turn of the century this was embellished with a series of three bas-relief panels in bronze, sculpted by Ewing's younger brother James (1843-1900). These depicted scenes from the 'Cotter', 'Tam o Shanter' and 'The Vision'. Plaster maquettes for these panels may also be seen in the Birthplace Museum.

The campaign for a statue of Burns in Kilmarnock likewise began in 1872, but dragged on rather longer, and it was not until 9th August 1879 that the monument was actually unveiled. The chief protagonist in this scheme was James McKie who personally raised most of the £2,893 necessary for the erection of the impressive monument which stands in the Kay Park to this day. Undoubtedly the most pretentious of all Burns monuments, this curious structure was designed by the Kilmarnock architect, Robert Ingram, and can best be summed up as an eclectic fusion of Scots Baronial, neo-Gothic and Italianate, with a dash of Baroque and a hint of Romanesque. The 80-foot tower of red sandstone dwarfs the statue of the poet, of Sicilian marble eight feet tall. The statue itself was chiselled by William Grant Stevenson (1849-1919) who also sculpted the colossal statue of William Wallace at Aberdeen and was noted for his statuary of historic personalities. He made a study of the various authentic portraits of the poet and also used a cast of his skull when modelling the head. The result is very pleasing, and also the closest to the original Nasmyth bust. Burns is shown in the act of composition, with a pencil poised in his right hand while the left grasps a notebook resting against a tree-stump. Like the Alloway and Calton Hill monuments, the Kay Park extravaganza was intended as the repository of Burnsiana, in this case the fine collection of books, manuscripts and relics which had been assembled by Mr McKie. Sad to relate, however, the tower has been in a poor state of

Painted half-sized statue by W. Grant Stevenson, Tam o Shanter Inn Museum, Ayr.

repair for some years now, and the McKie collection has been removed to the greater safety of Dean Castle and the Dick Institute.

Stevenson had been the winner of a competition to find the most suitable design for a statue. His brother David was awarded a prize of £50, while William McBryde got £25. The models for the statues by the Stevenson brothers and McBryde were thus acquired by the monument committee and were displayed at the Centenary Exhibition in 1896. So far as can be ascertained, the McBryde model was never subsequently realised in any form, but W.G. Stevenson also carved at least one copy of his statue, and this was exhibited in the place of honour at the Centenary celebration. D.W. Stevenson's model was subsequently executed full-scale and casts were erected in Leith, Newcastle upon Tyne and Toronto, discussed later in this chapter. The three models from the competition were until recently on display inside the Kilmarnock monument but have now been removed temporarily to Dean Castle. Probably the most distinguished sculptor to turn his hand to the subject of Burns was Sir John Robert Steell (1804-91). The son of an Aberdeen wood carver of the same name, he himself was apprenticed to a wood-carver but also studied at the Trustees Academy, where he came to the attention of George Thomson. Later he won a scholarship which enabled him to spend several years studying in Rome. Following his return to Scotland he received many public commissions. His marble figure of Sir Walter Scott for the memorial in Princes Street, Edinburgh was the first marble statue to be commissioned from a native Scot. He was appointed Sculptor to the Queen in Scotland and at the unveiling of his memorial to the Prince Consort in 1876 he was knighted by Queen Victoria. Although pre-eminent as a carver of marble statuary he also introduced the technique of bronze-casting to Scotland and established his own foundry, which was subsequently used by most Scottish sculptors of the period.

In 1872 a statue of Sir Walter Scott was unveiled in New York's Central Park and, not to be outdone, the Burnsians of that city immediately formed a committee to get a companion figure erected. Sir John Steell was given the commission and in due course his statue of Burns was unveiled on 2nd October 1880 — the first statue of Burns to be erected outside Scotland. Like Stevenson, Steell closely followed the Nasmyth portrait, helped by a cast of the poet's skull. Unusually, the statue shows Burns seated — or rather sprawled - on the fork of an old elm tree, his head thrown back to gaze at the evening star. His features are supposed to wear an air of intense abstraction, although critics have said that it is a pained expression. The right hand holds a quill-pen as if ready to note down the poetic thoughts suggested by his gaze, while his left arm dangles listlessly. The position of the legs gives the appearance of muscular power in repose. A plough sock lies near the right foot, partly concealed by a scroll bearing lines from 'To Mary in Heaven'.

Statue by Sir John Steell, Dundee. Photo: James Mackay.

*Statue by Sir John Steell, Thames Embankment.
Photo: James Mackay.*

Nowadays the Steell statue is not as highly regarded as it was when it first saw the light of day. Such was Sir John's pre-eminence that he was very soon commissioned to provide casts of his statue for Dundee, London and Dunedin. Only a fortnight after the unveiling in Central Park, another of these seated statues was unveiled in Albert Square, Dundee in the presence of some 25,000 people. This was the culmination of a campaign dating back several years in which the leading role was played by the Rev. George Gilfillan, compiler of several editions of Burns's works, but a highly controversial figure on account of his interpretation of the poet's life.

The Minute Book of the Dundee Burns Club (1880), discusses the Steell statue in considerable detail and, reading between the lines, we may sense something of the controversy that surrounded this sculpture. 'The pose of the limbs has been censured as awkward, but the critics who so write fail to perceive that when a human being's consciousness is entirely absorbed by some high inspiration, the airs and graces of posture are undreamt of... Sir John Steell's insight into poetic idiosyncrasy has prompted the thought that true art consisted in the negligent disposition of the statuesque limbs. Yet how wonderfully subtle is the manner in which the lines of the limbs are blended with the lines of the drapery, in order to produce the necessary amount of light and shade. The highest poetic grace of the statue is found in the rapt expression of the upturned face, which appears instinct with thoughts that burn...'

The third cast of Steell's seated figure was presented to London by John Gordon Crawford and unveiled by Lord Rosebery on 26th July 1884. Incidentally, it was while looking for a suitable site in the Thames Embankment Gardens that Colin Rae Brown, Provost Mackay and Captain Sneddon of Kilmarnock chanced upon the idea of forming a Federation of Burns Clubs, an idea which became a reality in August the following year. Significantly, the London version differs in some respects from those in New York and Dundee, most notably in the pose of the head. The Dunedin statue was unveiled on the Queen's birthday, 24th May 1887 and is an exact replica of the New York figure, standing on a pedestal of Peterhead granite at the top end of the Octagon, the little square at the very centre of the 'Edinburgh of the South Pacific'. That Dunedin should be the first city in New Zealand to honour the bard was hardly surprising, as Dunedin owed its very foundation to the Rev. Dr Thomas Burns, son of Gilbert, and thus a nephew of the poet. The unveiling ceremony was actually performed by Miss Burns, a great-grand-niece of Robert.

Sir John Steell demonstrated his versatility by producing several busts carved in marble and based on his bronze statue. One of these was placed in Poets' Corner, Westminster Abbey, and unveiled by Lord Rosebery on 7th March 1885. Sir John received this commission in 1883 and the money was raised by a shilling subscription, the Prince of Wales heading the subscribers' list. Another marble bust based on

Marble bust of Burns by Sir John Steell, Birthplace Museum, Alloway.

the statue can be seen in the Birthplace Museum on a plinth indicating that it was presented to the Cottage by John Keppie A.R.S.A. A plaster cast of the Steell bust of Burns is to be found adorning the facade of a building at 38 Queen Street, Edinburgh. A bronze reduction of the statue, cast from Sir John's original model, was shown at the Centenary Exhibition in 1896.

In the previous chapter the prodigious output of David O. Hill, landscape painter and pioneer photographer, was discussed. His wife Amelia, the sister of the celebrated Edinburgh painter, Sir Noel Paton, was a sculptress of no mean repute who exhibited bust-portraits, animal figures and genre statuettes at the Royal Academy from 1870 onwards. Elements of all three specialisations are to be found in her best-known work, the statue of Burns which stands in Church Place at the top of the High Street in Dumfries. Although Dumfries could take pride in being the first town to erect a memorial to the poet, there was a feeling that the Mausoleum, tucked away in a quiet corner of St Michael's churchyard on the edge of town was hardly sufficient. A committee was formed by members of the Tam o Shanter and Queen of the South Burns Clubs, now both long defunct, and the necessary funds raised. Mrs Hill was commissioned to produce a suitable statue and she modelled the seated figure of the poet, with a collie at his feet, in clay. The clay model was then shipped to Italy to be cut in Carrara marble on an enlarged scale. In the process much of the fine detail was lost. This was not the fault of the sculptress, although it is doubtful whether she was capable of direct-carving such a large work herself. Edward Pinnington, in the

Art Journal, wrote: 'The statue suggests sprightly activity and vivacity, something of bubbling vitality and buoyant energy, rather than thought. It is, however, the nearest existing approach to a woman's sculptured thought of Burns, and it is interesting, even if it never was a lofty embodiment of the poet.' One may detect some male condescension in this criticism. Philip Sulley, Secretary of the Dumfries Centenary Celebration of 1896, may have been no art critic, but he surely echoed the feelings of his townsmen when he wrote: '... the expression is stolid, vacant, meaningless, certainly not the inspired, commanding look of Burns. The base is crowded with inartistic, paltry details — a bonnet, shepherd's pipe of an Italian type, mice, daisies and thistle, while the alleged collie defies description.'

Dunedin's ambition of having the first statue of Burns in the Southern Hemisphere was dashed by the Australian gold-rush town of Ballarat whose Scottish citizens formed the customary committee in November 1884 and published a circular announcing their intentions. Where Ballarat scored over Dunedin was in turning to local talent, for the design was produced by a Mr Thomson who fashioned a clay model of the poet in conventional garb, complete with plaid, a pen in one hand and a book in the other. The facial expression bespeaks deep thought as if he were about to compose a poem. At his side sits his faithful dog, gazing up affectionately at his master. The likeness is not particularly close to Nasmyth, but this may be due to the fact that Thomson's model suffered enlargement, for it was sent to Italy to be carved in Carrara marble by John Udney. The statue was erected on a tall pedestal of Bluestone and Harcourt granite decorated copiously with quotations from some of the best-loved poems. The statue was unveiled on Labour Day, 21st April 1887, in the town centre opposite the Post Office.

Even Ballarat, however, was pipped at the post by another town, barely 60 miles away. Perhaps news of the Ballarat project came to the attention of W. A. Taylor, a farmer at Rennyhill, who was in possession of a statue of the poet. In 1885 he presented it to the town of Camperdown, and it stands in the tiny Botanic Gardens on a hilltop overlooking the lakes — surely the most scenic location of any Burns statue. The statue was carved by John Greenshields in 1830 and reproduces the hatted portrait of Burns by Peter Taylor painted in 1786. The poet is shown seated with his dog alongside. The statue remained in the hands of the Taylor family which migrated to Victoria in the 1850s. The sandstone group suffered considerable damage over the years; but was beautifully restored by the Camperdown Lions Club in December 1987.

The generosity of Miss Mary McPherson resulted in the very fine seated bronze which was unveiled in Washington Park, Albany on 30th August 1888. As executor for Miss McPherson, Peter Kinnear secured the services of Charles Calverley, a New York sculptor, who spent two years working painstakingly on a plaster model, which was then cast larger than life-size. The poet is shown seated in the traditional

Statue by George Lawson, Ayr.

Marble statue by Amelia Hill, Dumfries. Photo: James Mackay.

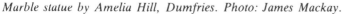

garb of the ploughman, in breeches, boots and leggings, with a plaid slung nonchalantly over his shoulder. Interestingly, the poet's features, while clearly derived from Nasmyth, are not unlike those in the Macnee portrait of 1859. The pedestal of red Scottish granite was embellished with four bronze bas-reliefs showing 'The Cotter's Saturday Night' (front), 'Auld Lang Syne' (rear), with the ploughman Burns leaning against his horse compsoing 'To a Daisy' (right) and Tam o Shanter on the auld brig closely pursued by Nanie (left).

Alloway may have had its Grecian temple, but the people of Ayr felt that a statue of Burns in some central position would be more appropriate. Through the exertions of the local Burns club the necessary funds were raised and the London sculptor George

Statue by Charles Calverley, Albany, New York. Photo: Joyce Mackay

Statue by George Lawson, Vancouver. Photo: Joyce Mackay.

Statue by Frederick Pomeroy, The Domain, Auckland. Photo: James Mackay.

Statue by Henry Bain Smith, Aberdeen.

Statue by Pittendrigh MacGillivray, Irvine.

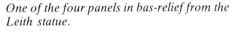
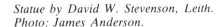

One of the four panels in bas-relief from the Leith statue.

Statue by Frederick Pomeroy, The Domain, Sydney.

Statue by David W. Stevenson, Leith. Photo: James Anderson.

Anderson Lawson (1832-1904) was commissioned to sculpt the standing figure which was unveiled on 8th July 1891. For once art-critics and laymen were united in their praise of this statue. Pinnington echoed popular feeling when he wrote: 'At Ayr, Mr Lawson has quickened intellectual force with poetic fire and passion. The arms are crossed, the hands clenched, and the gaze earnest and concentrated to the simple grace of the figure elements are added of both thought and repressed feeling. Burns might have stood thus reading his poems to Edinburgh society; thus he might have written his impassioned farewell to Clarinda, conned his ode to Mary, or finished the ringing Scots wha hae. The work can neither be located by incident, nor specialized in respect of sentiment. It is Burns broadly generalized the inseeing, rapt, intense poet... The freedom, grasp and breadth of the basic idea of the work indicate a sculptor whose knowledge of Burns was not exhausted upon his coat and breeches.'

Lawson's statue was widely regarded as the most successful statue of Burns sculpted up to that time, and it is hardly surprising that soon it began to rival the Steell figure in global esteem. Replicas were erected at Melbourne (Princes Bridge, St Kilda Road) on 23rd January 1904, Detroit on 23rd July 1921, Vancouver (Stanley Park) on 25th August 1928, Montreal (Dominion Square) on 18th October 1930 and Winnipeg (Manitoba Legislative Assembly Grounds) in 1936. In the case of the last-named a bronze plaque was added and unveiled on 25th October 1952. Bronze reductions of the statue were unveiled in Belfast's Free Library and Art Gallery in September 1893 and later installed in Ayr Old Church. Another was presented in 1938 by James B. McLennan of Coylton to the British Institute at the Sorbonne in Paris. During the Nazi occupation the statue was hidden in a box in a cellar underneath a pile of empty coal sacks. When Paris was liberated in

Statue by Grant Stevenson, Denver, Colorado. Photo: Joyce Mackay.

Granite statue by J. Massey Rhind, Barre, Vermont. Photo: Joyce Mackay.

Alto-relievo panel from the Barre statue. Photo: Joyce Mackay.

Statue by Earl Cummings, San Francisco. Photo: Joyce Mackay.

Statue by Albert Hodge, Stirling. Photo: James Mackay.

1944 the statue was removed from its hiding place, cleaned and restored to its original position. In recognition of the care taken by the Institute in preventing the statue falling into German hands, the Burns Federation in 1946 presented a set of the Scottish National Dictionary to the Sorbonne. The Lawson statue is also known to have been cast as a reduction, standing a metre high, in solid silver. One of these statuettes was sold in 1940 to A.E. Pickard, the Glasgow eccentric and self-styled 'Independent Millionaire'.

The Ayr statue has a set of four bronze bas-reliefs set into the pedestal. Lawson himself sculpted the panels showing Tam o Shanter and 'Cutty Sark' at the keystane of the auld brig, and a scene from 'The Cotter's Saturday Night'. A young Ayrshire sculptor, David McGill, sculpted the third panel, presented by the Freemasons of Scotland and showing a racy scene from 'The Jolly Beggars'. The fourth, or American,

panel was the gift of 25 citizens of the United States and was sculpted by George E. Bissell of Poughkeepsie, New York, showing the tender parting scene of Burns and Highland Mary. The Melbourne statue (now in the Treasury Gardens) likewise has decorative panels which show scenes from 'The Cotter' and 'Tam o Shanter' as well as Burns at the plough.

Dr William Alexander, an Aberdeen author and journalist, was the prime mover behind the campaign to erect a statue of Burns in the Granite City. In time-honoured fashion a public subscription was launched and the commission to execute a bronze figure of the poet was given to Henry Bain Smith (1859-95), a local sculptor. The statue stands about ten feet high, on a pedestal of white Kemnay granite bearing the solitary word BURNS cut in the front. Pinnington, as usual, had something to say about this statue, which was unveiled on Union Terrace on 15th

September 1892. 'The Aberdeen statue is mildly expressive of dignity and thought. It shows the graver and sterner side of Burns, and standing close by the busiest thoroughfare of Aberdeen, although robbed of a fuller eloquence by its stiffness and frigidity, its message to humanity is at least salutary and bracing. The peasant deserved respect and homage, and he won them.'

Australia's third statue of the bard was unveiled in the Reserve, Adelaide on 5th May 1894. William J. Maxwell, a native Scot domiciled in South Australia, was commissioned to carve the life-size figure of the poet in Angaston marble, mounted on a pedestal of Monarto granite. Maxwell broke with the tradition which had been fixated on Burns's ploughman image, and portrayed the poet in Fox livery, top coat, buckskin and top boots, as he would have appeared during his sojourn in Edinburgh. Maxwell's figure was clearly derived from Charles M. Hardie's painting showing the bard reciting one of his poems at a salon held by the Duchess of Gordon. Incidentally, tradition asserts that the poem he recited was 'A Winter's Night', but in view of that poem's radical sentiments it seems highly unlikely that he would have chosen that particular work for such a patrician assembly. Maxwell was one of the runners-up in the competition for the statue erected at Kilmarnock, and it is thought that the Adelaide figure was based on the model he produced on the previous occasion.

Like London and Albany, Irvine was fortunate enough to receive its statue of Burns as the result of the generosity of one individual, John Spiers, a native of the town who had made a fortune in mercantile business in Glasgow. The task of producing this splendid bronze was entrusted to James Pittendreigh Macgillivray (1856-1938), who has the unique distinction of being the only sculptor of Burns who was himself a poet. Macgillivray hailed from Inverurie and received his artistic training in the studio of William Brodie. He moved to Edinburgh in 1894 and became one of the most fashionable sculptors of his time, and Sculptor Royal for Scotland.

His statue is one of the few which does not follow the Nasmyth portrait. Pinnington commented 'Equally self-contained and original is Mr Macgillivray's Burns at Irvine. The face and head are not slavishly copied from any misleading portrait, and the features are of a finer mould than the pen pictures ascribe to Burns. The figure is strong, in no sense fine, and there is no straining after grace, although the more prominent lines are all gracefully rhythmic in movement.'

Four bronze panels adorn the red granite pedestal: a wreathed shield simply inscribed (front), the toil-worn cotter welcomed home by his wife (north), Burns and Highland Mary (west) and the muse of poetry crowning Burns with laurel (east). A bronze reduction of this statue was presented to Newcastle-upon-Tyne in January 1935 and may be seen in the Laing Art Gallery. The figure, less than a metre high, was Macgillivray's original model for the

Irvine statue and was originally displayed at the 1896 Exhibition.

The London sculptor Frederick William Pomeroy (1856-1924) sculpted the most original of all the Burns statues ever produced. Proceeds from the concerts given by the Tannahill Choir were used to defray the costs of erecting statues in Paisley to Robert Tannahill and Robert Burns. The latter statue was unveiled by Lord Rosebery on 26th September 1896. The bronze figure, ten feet high, is mounted on a twelve foot pedestal of grey granite and stands in Fountain Gardens. Burns is shown in tail coat, knee breeches and a broad Kilmarnock bonnet, leaning languidly against a plough and holding a pencil and notebook in contemplative mood.

Pinnington commended Pomeroy for abandoning precedent and convention without roughly defying prevailing views of physical likeness. 'Burns looks every inch a man; somewhat ponderous, perhaps, across the loins for agility, but muscular, broad and strong. An ample plaid lends the burly peasant all the grace he needs, and, falling over the plough at the back, partly hides a thistle. The emblem is not obtruded, because the sculptor wishes the poet to be seen as the Poet of Humanity first, and as that of Scotland afterwards. Mr Pomeroy tried for something original and he succeeded. In his Burns he has portrayed the thinker and poet of boundless potentiality, without neglecting the toil-bent worker or the athlete. Capable as a work of art, the statue is endowed with a life-like vigour and picturesque grace which ensure its acceptance.' A bronze bas-relief of Tam being pursued by witches adorns the pedestal.

Copies of the Pomeroy statue were unveiled in the Domains of Sydney, Australia and Auckland, New Zealand in January 1905 and November 1921 respectively, on colossal pedestals without the bronze bas-relief.

David Watson Stevenson (1842-1904), elder brother of Grant Stevenson previously noted, was responsible for the lively bronze figure which was unveiled at Leith on 15th October 1898. Standing three metres high on an elaborately carved pedestal, it shows Burns in tail coat and breeches striding forward. Bronze roundels and panels were subsequently added to the pedestal by various private individuals. At the front there is a bas-relief of 'The Cotter's Saturday Night', while, at the rear, there is a panel showing 'Death and Dr Hornbook'. On the right is a scene from 'Hallowe'en' while the left side shows a scene representing:

When Vulcan gi'es his bellows breath
An ploughmen gather wi their graith

A replica of this statue was subsequently erected in the Walker Park, Newcastle-upon-Tyne on 13th January 1901 and another was unveiled in Toronto's Allan Gardens on 21st July 1902. The latter has a grey granite pedestal decorated with four bronze panels sculpted by the local artist, Emmanuel Hahn, best-known for designing Canada's 'canoe' dollars. These panels show scenes from 'The Cotter', 'Tam o Shanter', 'To a Mouse' and 'John Anderson my Jo'.

Barre, Vermont, is not, at first glance, the likeliest place to find a statue of Burns, but in fact this part of the Green Mountain State was settled by Aberdonians, and had a very flourishing Burns club at the turn of the century. A monument, consisting of life-size statue, pedestal and base, was carved in local granite by John Massey Rhind (1860-1936), a native of Edinburgh who migrated to the United States. It certainly deserves credit for originality, as Burns is shown bare-headed, shirt-sleeves rolled up, his coat over his arm, his eyes looking down, the whole attitude and expression suggestive of thought and inspiring meditation at the end of a hard day's toil in the fields. One of the most noteworthy features of this monument, however, are the panels on the pedestal, carved in high relief by James B. King, a native of Aberdeenshire who settled in Barre. On the front is a scene from 'The Cotter', while the back shows the poet's birthplace. Tam o Shanter on the Brig o Doon and Burns at the plough are featured on the respective sides. The monument was unveiled on the Spaulding Campus on 21st July 1899. Massey Rhind also sculpted the bronze statue which was unveiled on 27th October 1914 at Schenley Park in Pittsburgh, Pennsylvania.

William Grant Stevenson later sculpted a bronze figure of Burns, based to a large extent on the marble figure used for the Kay Park monument in Kilmarnock. This statue was erected on a pedestal of Colorado granite and Wisconsin sienite in the City Park of Denver and unveiled on 4th July 1904. A replica was subsequently erected in Garfield Park, Chicago on 26th August 1906. The pedestal of Vermont granite is decorated with bronze panels representing 'The Cotter', 'Tam o Shanter', 'The Twa Dogs' and 'To a Daisy' (Burns at the plough). Stevenson's interpretation of Burns was widely acclaimed, and later replicas were erected at Fredericton, New Brunswick (18th October 1906) and Milwaukee, Wisconsin (26th June 1909). The Fredericton version has bronze panels showing 'The Cotter', 'John Anderson' and Burns at the plough, turning up the daisy, while the Milwaukee statue has the panels of 'The Cotter' and 'The Daisy' alone. The Fredericton statue was erected on Fenety Avenue (now Queen Street) opposite the entrance to the New Brunswick Parliament Building, on The Green, overlooking the St John River. Bronze reductions of this statue were also produced. Thomas Smith & Sons of Edinburgh published statuettes in bronze or silver to commemorate the centenary of 1896 and these were sold in very limited editions.

A campaign to have a Burns statue in San Francisco was started by John McGilvray in 1905. The necessary cash was soon raised and Melvin Earl Cummings of Salt Lake City whose grandparents were born in Scotland was commissioned to produce the figure. Cummings modelled a standing figure of the poet which was sent to the De Rome Foundry in San Francisco for casting but on 18th April 1906 the foundry and its entire contents were destroyed in the San Francisco earthquake and the fire that swept the

city in the aftermath. The rebuilding of the city took all the time and energy of the Scottish community as well as all other citizens alike, and it was not until the middle of 1907 that the project was resurrected. Cummings started all over again, but by the end of that year the model was successfully cast, and the statue itself was unveiled in Golden Gate Park on Washington's birthday, 22nd February 1908. The statue itself is eleven feet high and stands on a pedestal of Californian granite nine feet high. Burns stands to attention, right hand by his side, his left holding a small book. The head is closely modelled on Nasmyth's bust.

William Birnie Rhind (1853-1933), elder brother of Massey Rhind, enjoyed a high reputation at the turn of the century for his portrait busts and statuettes of historic personalities, but carved directly in marble and cast in bronze from plaster models. At the Centenary Exhibition he displayed a marble bust of Burns, and he returned to this theme fifteen years later when he was commissioned to sculpt the stone statue which was unveiled at Montrose on 7th August 1912.

James Craigie, M.P. presented a full-size statue of Burns to Timaru in the South Island of New Zealand and this was unveiled on 22nd May 1913. The Prime Minister, Sir Robert Stout gave the eulogy which was reported at great length, but few details were given about the statue itself. It was apparently modelled locally, but the model was then sent to Italy where the statue was carved in Carrara marble. The eight-foot statue was erected on a base of bluestone surmounted by a pedestal of grey Coromandel granite, on which were carved the words of Thomas Carlyle — 'The largest soul of all the British lands' — and a couplet from 'A man's a man':

> The rank is but the guinea's stamp
> The man's the gowd for a' that.

A bronze statue of Burns was erected in a commanding position between the old and new town of Stirling, formed by the triangular plot between the Corn Exchange Road and Dumbarton Road, and unveiled on 23rd September 1914. The statue was the gift of Provost Bayne to his adoptive town and it was unveiled by his daughter. Burns is shown 'poised in an easy but graceful attitude'. Albert Hemstock Hodge (1875-1918), born in Glasgow but latterly working in London, gave a fine conception of the poet in his Edinburgh period. The Aberdeen granite pedestal, standing twelve feet high, has a frieze on top of the die in raised lettering: 'Then gently scan your brother man, still gentler sister woman'. The pedestal bears four bronze panels in bas relief, showing Burns at the plough, 'The Cotter's Saturday Night' (the expectant wee things), Tam o Shanter at Alloway Kirk and 'The Guiding Star'. The pedestal was executed by Kirkpatrick Brothers of Manchester while the statue and panels were cast by A. B. Burton of Thames Ditton, Surrey.

Boston, Massachusetts holds the unenviable record of taking the longest time to bring its plans to fruition. A Burns Memorial Association was formed in 1899,

Statue by Henry Kitson, Boston. Photo: Joyce Mackay.

Silvered statue by James Watt, Portpatrick. Photo: James Mackay.

but it took twelve years to raise the $15,000 considered necessary for the erection of a suitable memorial to the poet. Designs were solicited and in the autumn of 1911 the commission was awarded to Henry Hudson Kitson, a native of Yorkshire who had emigrated to America at the turn of the century. Kitson planned an elaborate memorial consisting of a broad, decorative pylon flanked by low walls surmounted by balustrades and other architectural embellishments. A bronze statue of Burns was to be erected on a pedestal projecting from the base of the pylon. The figure was unusual in that it showed Burns leaning on a walking stick, with a book and spray of laurel tucked under his left arm. Characteristically, the work was subject to seemingly innumerable delays, compounded by the entry of the United States into the First World War in 1917. It was not, in fact, until New Year's Day 1920 that the statue was unveiled in the Caledonian Grove, along the Charles River Embankment. Some years ago, however, the statue was relocated in a small park opposite One Winthrop Square Building, at the junction of Franklin and Devonshire Streets.

Kellock Brown (1856-1934) was born in Glasgow and spent most of his working life in that city. From the end of the nineteenth century onwards he enjoyed considerable popularity and sculpted many of the large monuments and memorials to be found all over the west of Scotland. Yet today he is best remembered for one of his smaller works, the bronze statuette of Burns which was unveiled in the Glasgow Art Gallery in 1919. This arose from a plaster model executed a quarter of a century earlier, but sad to relate Brown never received a commission to execute the full-scale work. A bronze cast was shown at the Centenary Exhibition in 1896, and it seems probable that this was the very figure unveiled at Kelvingrove 25 years later. Kellock Brown also produced a bust of Jean Armour, intended as the basis of a full-scale statue, but regrettably there was never any serious proposal to transform this into reality.

It is a sad fact that the costs of erecting statuary escalated during and after the First World War, and as a result this method of perpetuating the memory of famous personalities has been comparatively little used since then. It is, in fact, all the more remarkable that several other statues of Burns were erected in various parts of the world in the inter-war period. A local sculptor, James Watt of Stranraer, produced the statue of the poet which was erected at Portpatrick on 1st May 1929. Henry Snell Gamley (1865-1928), a pupil of D.W. Stevenson, was one of Scotland's leading sculptors in bronze in this period and at one point was consulted as to the feasibility of reworking the Turnerelli group in this medium, but it had to be abandoned on grounds of expense. Gamley gave some indication of his capabilities in the memorial erected over the grave of Mrs McLehose in the Canongate churchyard, unveiled on 10th June 1922; the modelling of Clarinda's features in low relief is particularly expressive. Gamley never had the satisfaction of seeing his project for a full-scale statue

Left: Statue by Robert Aitken, St. Louis, Missouri.
Photo: Joyce Mackay.

Statue by Scott Sutherland, Arbroath. Photo: James Mackay.

Burns Memorial, Canberra.
Right: Bas-relief of "Clarinda" (Mrs McLehose) by Henry S. Gamley.

Bronze maquette of the statue in Cheyenne, Wyoming, by Henry Snell Gamley, Ellisland.

Bust by Giusti, Dick Institute, Kilmarnock.

Figure of Burns, Ellisland.

of the poet come to fruition, for he died a year before his bronze was unveiled in Gilchrist Park at the corner of Randall and Pioneer Avenues, Cheyenne, Wyoming on 11th November 1929. The statue stands on an elegant pedestal of local granite and was the gift of Mary Gemmell Gilchrist, widow of one of Wyoming's most colourful cattle-barons and a native of Ayrshire. A bronze reduction of this figure may be seen at Ellisland, while another was displayed at the two exhibitions held at Lady Stair's House, Edinburgh in 1953 and 1959.

A statue by Robert Aitken was unveiled in St Louis Missouri in 1931, as a result of the exertions of the local Burns club. It may be seen at the campus of Washington University, on Skinker Parkway and Lindell Boulevard. Ward Willis (1870-1948) executed the fine bronze statue of Burns which was eventually erected in Centenary Place, Brisbane in 1932. It was the culmination of a long campaign by the local Scottish community which had hoped to erect the statue in 1929. Shortage of funds almost aborted the project, but it was then that the City of Brisbane and the Queensland Government came to the rescue and provided the balance required. A magnificent bronze statue of Burns was sculpted by Samuel Davie and unveiled in the Australian Commonwealth capital of Canberra on 26th January 1935. A bronze statue by James McLeod was to have been erected in Perth, Western Australia in 1937, but the necessary £1200 was never raised. A full-size statue of Burns in Sicilian marble was imported from Scotland and erected at Hokitika, New Zealand in June 1933. Like Timaru, the identity of the sculptor is unknown.

The cost of sculpture has escalated in the last four decades. The only full-scale statue of Burns to be erected since the Second World War was unveiled at Arbroath on the poet's bicentenary. The seven foot bronze was the work of Dundee sculptor Scott Sutherland, best-known for the Commando monument at Spean Bridge. This realised an ambition which had been cherished by the Arbroath Burns Club for almost seventy years. A life-size figure of Burns, sculptured in fibre glass and papier mache by Alastair Smart of Jordanstone College of Art, was unveiled at the gallery of Scottish farming, in the granary of Ellisland, on 25th October 1979. The figure is clothed in replica costume by Ellice Miller of Glasgow, with shoes, buckles and wooden buttons supplied by the Country Life department of the National Museum of Antiquities, and socks knitted by Mrs Harkness of Closeburn. A seated figure of Burns in his familiar town garb was created by Gems Models of Kensington and may be seen in the upper gallery at the Burns Centre, Dumfries, inaugurated in 1986.

Apart from the full-scale works used for public memorials, plaster models and bronze casts from them are known of figures of Burns, executed by John Tweed, James Fillans, H. Daniel Webster and Paul R. Montford. The statue by Tweed was later executed, and purchased by Sir Francis Vernon Thomson who bequeathed it to the National Library of Scotland in Edinburgh. In addition to these models, most of the statues previously noted were also edited in bronze reductions in limited editions for sale to collectors and Burns enthusiasts. Montford's figure of Burns was also published as a statuette in bronze or terracotta, sold in limited editions to the public at ten guineas or twenty-five shillings respectively by J. M.L. Tregaskis of London to commemorate the centenary of the poet's death. One of these statuettes was given to the painter, Thomas Faed in exchange for his endorsement: 'I was very pleased with the Statuette of our beloved Burns, and think it a great success. I hope the world may pronounce the same verdict.' Hugh Cairns, a sculptor of busts and statues of famous personalities at the turn of the century, also sculpted a statue of Burns which was commissioned by the Caledonian Club of Boston, Massachusetts, and installed there about 1890.

Busts of Burns

James Crawford Thom, born at Skeoch near Tarbolton in 1802, is best remembered for his droll figures of Tam o Shanter and Souter Johnny. He was apprenticed to a firm of stonemasons in Kilmarnock and while working on the renovation of a tombstone in Crosbie kirkyard, Troon in 1828 he came to the notice of David Auld, the custodian of the Monument at Alloway. Auld was impressed with the young man's stone-carving and procured a block of sandstone, asking Thom to try his hand at a bust of Burns based on one of the Nasmyth portraits. Auld was so pleased with the results — Thom's very first essay in sculpture — that he commissioned him to carve the life-size figure of Tam. What became of the bust of Burns, however, is a complete mystery. Had it survived, it would undoubtedly rank as the earliest bust of the poet. Conversely, there *is* a bust of Burns hewn in stone and as I have not been able to trace its origins I am tempted to suppose that this may, indeed, have been James Thom's handiwork. This bust may be seen in a niche below the gable of the house in Maybole High Street where William Burnes and Agnes Broun are reputed to have first met.

Several other busts of Burns have been erected in public places; without exception, these pieces of sculpture have closely followed the Nasmyth bust-portrait. The marble bust by Patric Park has already been mentioned in connexion with the Alloway monument, but forty years elapsed before another bust of the poet was installed in Scotland for the public view. It was singularly appropriate that the first bust to be installed in the Hall of Heroes in the Scottish National Wallace Monument on Abbey Craig, Stirling, was the marble of Burns, sculpted by D.W. Stevenson. This fine bust was presented by Andrew Carnegie and unveiled on 4th September 1886. The same sculptor also produced the marble bust of Burns which was installed in the Main Hall of Tullie House, now the civic museum, in Carlisle, on 21st July 1898. Stevenson was engaged on modelling the head for his statue at Leith about that time, and the Carlisle bust, in white Sicilian marble, was closely modelled on that statue.

Burns appears to have been a popular subject for busts carved in marble by the Italian portrait sculptors of the nineteenth century. Fidardo Landi, Professor in the Academy of Fine Arts at Carrara, produced several versions of the poet's bust and one of these may be seen in the Public Library of Fall River, Massachusetts, where it was installed in 1899. J.W.

Dods, the Dumfries stone-mason and sculptor, inevitably paid his own tribute to the bard. There are in the Burgh Museum, the Globe Inn and the Theatre Royal painted plaster busts of Burns modelled by Dods in 1886 and there was also, at one time, a similar bust in the County Hotel before it was demolished. These plaster busts were probably taken from a preliminary model for his large bust carved direct in local red sandstone, which was presented by William Ewart to the town and which was placed originally in a niche on the front of the Ragged School in Burns Street, next door to the house in which the poet died. When the Ragged School was demolished the bust was removed and is now preserved in the basement of the Robert Burns Centre.

A bronze bust of Burns by F. Doyle Jones was placed on a granite pedestal and erected at Galashiels on 31st May 1913. William Lamb, the well-known Montrose sculptor, produced the fine bronze of Burns which was presented to the Sunderland civic museum on 7th April 1936. A bronze bust of the poet was sculpted by Guido Giusti who flourished in Venice at the turn of the century and is best remembered for his papal busts. A cast of this work is preserved in the Dick Institute, Kilmarnock, headquarters of the Burns Federation. A larger than life-size bust, cast in epoxy resin by John Letts, may be seen in the entrance to the club-house of the Coventry Tam o Shanter Burns Club and a replica was presented to Ellisland in the summer of 1987. There are even some interesting busts of the poet which were cast in iron at the Carron Foundry, Stirlingshire, at the end of the last century for sale to the general public. The modelling, by an unknown artist, is quite competent. Marble busts carved by T. Nelson MacLean and William Brodie were on show at the Centenary Exhibition in 1896. The latter is now in the possession of the Edinburgh museums and libraries department and was displayed at the exhibitions of 1953 and 1959. Another bust by Brodie, with pedestal panels by Robert Pringle, is in the Mercantile Library at St. Louis, Missouri. It was installed in 1866 and is thus the earliest extant Burns memorial in America. A

Bust by John Letts, Coventry Tam o' Shanter Club and Ellisland.

Cast iron bust of Burns (mould found at Glenfield Pub).

Bas-relief panel from the Stirling statue.
Photo: James Mackay.

Bas-relief panel from the Albany statue.
Photo: Joyce Mackay.

Bas-relief panel from the Winnipeg statue. Photo: Joyce Mackay.

Bas-reliefs by Emmanuel Hahn, from the
Toronto statue. Photo: Joyce Mackay.

Burns Memorial Shelter, Prestonpans.
Photo: James Anderson.

Bronze plaque, Theatre Royal,
Dumfries. Photo: James Mackay.

Below left: Bronze plaque, Lodge
St. Ebbe, Eyemouth.

Below: Cast iron roundel, in gold
and black.

head of Burns was sculpted by the Glasgow artist Benno Schotz in the 1960s, using the celebrated actor John Cairney as his model. Cairney, whose features and facial expression bear an uncanny resemblance to Burns, virtually built his career on the life of the bard.

Panels, plaques and roundels

Many of the statue groups mentioned above were mounted on pedestals decorated with bas-relief panels, the vast majority of them being cast in bronze. It will be noted that several of these panels, notably those sculpted by D.W. Stevenson, were mounted on more than one statue, and other casts of these panels were also produced for sale to private collectors. Replicas of these bronze panels were also published in white plaster or terracotta, or are known to exist as the original maquettes, in clay. Grant Stevenson showed his bas-relief of 'The Cotter's Saturday Night', later installed on the Chicago monument, at the Centenary Exhibition. James Ewing's bronze panel of Alloway Kirk was also on display — a replica of the bas-relief mounted on the pedestal of the Glasgow statue. James Fillans (1808-52) is known to have modelled an *alto-relievo* group devoted to the birth of Burns, but it is not known whether this was ever published in a commercial edition. John Flaxman produced a demi-relief bronze cast taken from a side view of the bust sculpted for Poets' Corner, Westminster Abbey. William Mossman (1843-77), noted for his many memorials, monuments and historic busts executed in the Glasgow area, sculpted a bas-relief portrait of Burns which was subsequently cast in bronze. John Steell, father of Sir John and

Gourlay Steell, who flourished in the early years of the nineteenth century, produced a medallion profile of the poet carved in oak. The most recent works in this genre include the bronze plaque with a bas-relief portrait based on the Nasmyth bust, by a local artist Ian Douglas, and mounted on the outer wall of the Theatre Royal, Dumfries and the carved stone roundel with profile of the bard which features prominently in the Burns memorial shelter erected at Prestonpans. As the cost of erecting full-scale statuary has become prohibitive in recent years, there has developed a vogue for freestone cairns which can be constructed relatively cheaply, and provide an admirable medium for the display of bas-relief plaques in bronze. Examples of these monuments have been erected in very recent times at Leglen Wood, Wauchope and Covington Mains but their commemorative plaques are non-figural.

The most recent memorials which actually feature Burns on plaques, however, have both been erected in Canada. On 19th July 1981 a memorial of rough-hewn local granite was unveiled by Dr Jim Connor in the Elmo Curtis Rose Gardens, Springbank Park, London, Ontario. The granite slab bears a thirteen-line inscription surmounted by a bas relief roundel of the poet, cast in bronze. On 21st July 1984 a cairn was unveiled in Gage Park, Hamilton, Ontario and this incorporated a plaque embellished with a bas-relief portrait of Burns after the Nasmyth bust, sculpted by Nicholas Jon Neu. A large roundel with a bas relief profile of Burns in glazed pottery was at one time mounted above the doorway of Burns

*Stone statues of Tam o Shanter and Souter Johnny by
James Thom.*

House in Mauchline, but when the house was refurbished some years ago the roundel was removed and may now be seen in the Tower museum nearby. Other plaques and roundels in stucco, terracotta and other ceramic materials are discussed in Chapter 8.

Sculpture of related subjects

John G. Mossman (1817-90), father of William Mossman, already noted, was born in London but spent his working life in and around Glasgow, where he sculpted a large number of statues, fountains, and bas-reliefs. Probably his best-known works are his statue of David Livingstone and the bronze figure of the Lady of the Lake for the Loch Katrine commemorative fountain in Kelvingrove Park. To Burnsians, however, he is remembered chiefly for designing the tomb of Mary Campbell in the Old West Kirkyard of Greenock. The monument was erected by public subscription on 25th January 1842. Two marble panels were inserted into the stone and depicted the allegory of Grief weeping over an urn, with the Lingering Star above, and the historic parting of Burns and Highland Mary at Failford in 1786, shortly before the latter's tragic death.

Of all the poet's heroines, Mary Campbell has excited the popular imagination to a remarkable extent. Statues of Highland Mary are to be found in Dunoon, Liverpool, New York and Victoria, British Columbia. D.W. Stevenson executed the large bronze which was unveiled at Dunoon, overlooking the Firth of Clyde, on 1st August 1896, and reductions in bronze and terracotta were subsequently edited. Benjamin Evans Spence sculpted the beautiful white marble statue of Mary, wearing a shawl and with eyes demurely cast down, which was unveiled in Sefton Park, Liverpool on 5th October 1896. A copy of this statue was subsequently erected in New York's Public Library on 5th Avenue. A small statuette of Burns and Highland Mary by Hamilton P. McCarthy may be seen in the Birthplace Museum. Apart from the portrait sculpted by Kellock Brown, already mentioned, Jean Armour was the subject of a marble bust by an unknown hand, which is now preserved in the Burns Museum at Mauchline.

Hamilton Patrick MacCarthy, the son and grandson of portrait sculptors, flourished in the second half of the nineteenth century and produced busts and statues of historic personalities. He sculpted a group of Burns and Highland Mary which was cast in bronze. This unusual little group may be seen on top of the drinking fountain in Beacon Hill Park, Victoria, British Columbia.

Undoubtedly the most popular sculpture associated with Burns consists of the life-size figures of Tam o Shanter and Souter Johnny which were carved in freestone by James Thom (1802-50), the Tarbolton stone-mason. Edward Goodwillie (1911) describes them as 'crude statues', which scarcely does justice to Thom who trained as a mason but later turned to the modelling and sculpting of busts and statues of historical and contemporary Scottish personalities. Admittedly he was catapulted to fame with his effigies of Tam and the Souter which were installed in the gardens of the Monument at Alloway. The story of how Thom was discovered has already been told. The young stonemason became the protege of David Auld who commissioned the statues of Tam and the Souter which were publicly exhibited at Ayr in July 1828. Afterwards Auld organised a tour of Edinburgh, Glasgow and London for the statues and a great deal of money was raised in this manner, the proceeds being divided equally between the Trustees of the Monument, Auld and the sculptor himself. With their share of the money the Trustees were able to enlarge the gardens at Doonside.

In light of Goodwillie's comments, it is interesting to note that the statues, when exhibited in London in the summer of 1829, took the metropolis by storm, and were even hailed by one art critic as ushering in a new era in realistic sculpture. Many replicas were ordered and in the ensuing years Thom was kept very busy indeed. It is estimated that sixteen pairs of these statues were carved in 1828-35, each figure differing in some respects. William Brown, the tenant of Trabboch Mill near Stair, sat as the model for Tam, and some of his personal relics can be seen in the Tam o Shanter Inn at Ayr to this day. Controversy exists, however, over the original for the Souter. A certain resident of Kilmarnock was reputed to have a face and form very much resembling Johnny. This individual was approached to sit for the portrait, for a consideration. His answer was characteristic of the independent Scot: 'Weel, I'm fond o a gless o whisky, and whyles tak mair than I can haud, but I'm blist if I'll be the example o that drucken body, Johnny Davidson!' Other accounts say that Thom modelled the Souter on a couple of Ayr children, but they must have been gey precocious weans to furnish the features of the leering shoemaker.

In 1829 Thom sculpted a pair of these figures and, for good measure, the landlord and landlady of the Tam o Shanter Inn. The four figures are now to be seen in the garden of Johnny Davidson's house at Kirkoswald, a National Trust for Scotland property which celebrated its own bicentenary in 1986. Sometime in the early 1830s Thom also sculpted the figure of Nanse Tinnock — not Poosie Nansie (Agnes Gibson) as is sometimes stated — and this was purchased by David Auld who displayed it for several years in the garden of the adjoining inn, now the Monument Hotel, Doonside. An oak tree was blown down across this seated figure, knocking the head off. It was skilfully restored and some time after Auld's death in 1872 the statue was purchased for £70 by the Monument Trustees who installed it beside Tam and Johnny in the Monument gardens.

Thom sculpted another full set of four figures from Ayrshire sandstone in 1834 and this was shipped to Philadelphia where the statues were exhibited in the Masonic Hall in Chestnut Street. Thom's agent, responsible for exhibiting the statues, reneged on the deal and in a bid to recoup his losses Thom went to America in 1836. He managed to recover some of the money, but then settled in America. The Philadelphia statues were removed to the old Franklin Institute in 1837 and a group of local businessmen then purchased them from Thom and presented them to the Institute. In 1845 they were transferred to the Academy of Fine Arts where they remained for thirty years. In 1876 the United States celebrated its Centennial and the statues were moved to the Fairmount Park where they were installed on East River drive, under a rustic shelter. The statues were refurbished in 1935 but are no longer in existence.

Between 1836 and about 1840 Thom produced a further twenty-one sets of Tam and Souter Johnny for various locations in North America, though what has become of them is impossible to say. They were carved from the red sandstone obtained at Little Falls, New Jersey. One pair graced the main entrance of the Colt mansion (of revolver fame) and later appeared in the Free Public Library in the nearby town of Paterson, until destroyed in the great fire of 1902. Another pair was sent on tour round America, but was lost when the boat carrying them across Chesapeake Bay foundered in a storm. Tam and Johnny got a watery grave, an element that was rather foreign to their tastes, by all accounts! Thom also executed monumental statuary for parks and buildings in New Jersey and New York and he is recorded as having sculpted a group for Central Park, entitled Auld Lang Syne.

Numerous replicas of Tam and the Souter have been cast in bronze or iron as well as terracotta or plaster. Small figures of Tam and Johnny with solid backs, but based on the Thom statues, are known in cast iron, either unpainted, black all over, or painted in lifelike colours. They were popular in the nineteenth century as ornaments and door-stops.

Full-size masks cast in bronze, iron or aluminium from the heads of the statues, sometimes plain but more usually decorated with paint in natural colours, were mass-produced long after Thom emigrated to the United States of America. The grinning features of the droll couple may be seen embedded on the walls of many buildings around the southwest of Scotland to this day. Full-size figures by Thom were on show at the Centenary Exhibition and others were erected outside the Palm House in the Liverpool Botanic Gardens, where they may still be seen.

John Greenshields, an Edinburgh sculptor active in the 1830s, carved a group entitled 'The Jolly Beggars' in sandstone. This group of eight life-size figures was taken on exhibition to London and was eventually purchased for £200 by Lord Rothschild who installed them in the grounds of his mansion at Gunnersbury, now a public park in west London. The preliminary models are preserved in the art collection of the Hunterian Museum at Glasgow University and were shown at the Centenary Exhibition.

One must not overlook the large carved and painted wooden figure-head which graces the bow of the famous clipper-ship Cutty Sark. This beautiful vessel was constructed by Scott's of Dumbarton and is now a popular tourist attraction at Greenwich, and visitors can see the young witch Nanie in the short chemise that earned her the nickname bestowed by Tam o Shanter. To celebrate the centenary of this great sailing ship a memorial was erected in 1969 at Market Square, Inverbervie, birthplace of the ship's designer, Hercules Linton (1836-1900). Appropriately the monument shows the eponymous young witch.

Gerrard Robinson carved a large wood panel in high relief of the dramatic incident on the Auld Brig entitled 'Maggie the Meare Losing her Tail to Cutty Sark' and this may be seen in the John George Joicey Museum, Newcastle upon Tyne. Tam, his horse and Nanie are carved in the round, while the 'hellish legion', in lower relief, recede into the panel creating an illusion of wraith-like movement.

Cutty Sark memorial, Inverbervie. Photo: James Mackay.

Burns Relics

As part of their fund-raising activities, the committee for the erection of the statue of Burns at Dumfries staged a bazaar in 1880, at which upwards of a hundred relics of the poet were displayed and excited a great deal of interest. In the following year James McKie of Kilmarnock published his *Bibliography of Robert Burns* and devoted almost forty pages to a survey of the relics preserved at that date in Edinburgh, Tarbolton, Arbroath, Irvine, Alloway, Ayr, Abbotsford, the British Museum, the South Kensington Museum (now the Victoria and Albert Museum), the Bodleian Library, the Liverpool Athenaeum, St Paul's School, London, Burns House, the Ewart Library, the Crichton Institution and the Observatory Museum in Dumfries, the Kay Park Monument and the Ayrshire Burns Library in Kilmarnock, the Hawick Museum and Harvard University as well as sundry Burns clubs and private individuals. The chief value of this survey lay in the details given of the then locations of Burns manuscripts, but nothing associated with the bard was too trivial to be listed. McKie went to enormous lengths in describing these relics and also their extensive pedigrees. The McKie survey, however, was as nothing compared with the 400-odd relics mustered fifteen years later as part of the Centenary Exhibition in Glasgow.

Duncan McNaught contributed the section on relics to the Exhibition catalogue, published in 1898. He commented that while the collection of the editions of Burns which were displayed in the large gallery were an inexhaustible source of interest to the Burns student, he had to admit that 'to the average visitor, unlearned in the bibliography of Burns, they appealed in much the same way as a like number of unknown books on the shelves of a circulating library. After a glance at the rarer, earlier editions, his curiosity was satisfied, and he turned to the relics as more in accordance with his tastes and feelings.' Then he added, rather obliquely, 'This is why such exhibitions need never hope to be great financial successes.'

McNaught contrasted the keen interest of scholars in the manuscripts and printed editions of Burns's works, with 'the hero-worship of the masses' which found expression in the many relics which had been handed down from generation to generation. He spoke of 'popular sentiment', but veneration would scarcely have been too strong a word to apply to the positive mania for everything and anything, no matter how trivial or mundane, which claimed the slightest connexion with Burns.

Speaking of the relics themselves, he wrote: 'They are all personal to the Poet or the individuals upon whom shone the reflected light of his genius. All are redolent of his humanity — scarce one of his spirituality. Burns is no abstraction to his countrymen. His poetry is embalmed in their hearts, and his overshadowing personality pervades and is ever associated with it. Hence it is that everything connected, in the remotest degree, with his earthly pilgrimage is guarded by all sorts and conditions of men with a solicitude that is apt to evoke a smile from those outwith the pale of the national feeling.'

Glancing through the pages of the catalogue, one cannot help smiling at the zeal which went into assembling such a mass of material, and the range and quality of the relics themselves. Man is, indeed, an acquisitive animal but nowadays the desire to collect Burnsiana is fulfilled by the souvenir industry which, a century ago, was still in its infancy. We live in a more sophisticted — not to say sceptical — age but we should not laugh at the naivety of our forebears and their blind unquestioning faith in accepting the authenticity of so many 'sticks and stones' which were imbued with a quality approaching mysticism merely on account of their association with the bard.

McNaught was at pains to point out that 'For the authenticity of the exhibits their possessors are responsible, the Committee rightly deeming that it did not fall within their province to exercise any censorship in the matter. Though no hall-mark of genuineness can therefore be claimed on the ground of admission to the Exhibition, it is not to be supposed that any large proportion of the articles shown were of the nature of counterfeits. On the contrary, in nearly every instance the name of the exhibitor will be found sufficient guarantee, irrespective of the vouchers attached and in a large majority of the entries the most exacting will fail to discover a flaw in the historical record.'

These relics were displayed, and consequently catalogued, in no particular order. As the Catalogue itself is a rarity (only 400 copies were printed), and as such an assemblage of relics could never be brought together again, I have considered it worthwhile to give below a brief summary of them, re-classified into categories of objects which actually belonged to Burns or his immediate family, articles which belonged to people associated in some way with Burns, material only indirectly linked to the poet, and lastly objects manufactured from materials which came from places that were themselves associated with Burns in some way. In passing, it is interesting to note that, such was the intense hold on the general imagination of 'Tam o Shanter', that objects associated with John Davidson and Douglas Graham, the alleged prototypes of Souter Johnny and Tam himself, were displayed in the same spirit of veneration as the personal belongings of those who were near and dear to Burns, and were received by the public with the same unquestioning faith.

'We verily believe', wrote McNaught, 'such is the wondrous hold the immortal Tale has upon the imagination of the Scottish people, that the veritable pipes which made the roof and rafters dirl might have been on view without exciting more than the mildest measure of surprise. When such a trifle as the tobacco pouch of the bleth'rin nonentity of Tarbolton James Humphrey is so carefully treasured as a memorial of the Poet, we need marvel less at the omnivorous stomach of the typical Burns relic-hunter than at the glowing enthusiasm which creates his appetite.'

The numbers in brackets after each entry refer to the order in the Exhibition Catalogue. Those relics which may be seen at the present time in the Cottage (C), Burns House in Dumfries (H), the Mauchline Museum (M), the Tower at Mauchline (T), the Bachelors' Club, Tarbolton (B), Ellisland (E) and the Tam o Shanter Inn at Ayr (S) are indicated by these abbreviations. Similarly the relics which were formerly displayed in the Kay Park Monument, Kilmarnock or the Burns Memorial on Calton Hill, Edinburgh and are now preserved by Kilmarnock and Loudoun District Council and Edinburgh District Council in Dean Castle or the Dick Institute, Kilmarnock (K) or Edinburgh's museums and libraries department and have been displayed in recent years at Lady Stair's House in the Lawnmarket (L) are also indicated. Some of the poet's relics are now in the Royal Museum of Scotland, Edinburgh (Λ). Special exhibitions of Burnsiana were staged at Lady Stair's House in 1953 and 1959 and these are denoted by L53 and L59 respectively. In addition to these museums, open to the public, many of the older Burns clubs are the proud possessors of many items of memorabilia. The vast majority of these objects were on loan to the Centenary Exhibition and it is therefore hoped that the lists which follow account for virtually all of the relics now known to exist.

Personal belongings of Robert Burns
Peerie with which Burns played as a boy (S)
Table belonging to Burns at Dumfries (C)
Top of small table from Dumfries (C)
Two chairs, formerly in Ellisland (C, H)
Two chairs 'which were in Burns Cottage' (907)
Four elm chairs formerly in Burns House, Dumfries (L53, 59)
Rush-bottomed chair, ex 1834 sale (957)
Milking-stool used at Mossgiel (C)
Kitchen chair from Ellisland (961) (T)
Chair on which Burns was nursed (918) (C) a replica of the chair (H)
Burns's nursing-chair and cradle (S)
Bed in which Burns was born (C)
Shelved press and cupboard used by Burns as a bookcase (C)
Cutty stool (917)
Stool from Ellisland (919)
Mahogany writing-desk given to Burns by Mrs Dunlop (1009) (C)
China bread plates, cream pot, teacups and saucers, slop bowl, teapot, sugar bowl, coffee cups and saucers (938-46)
China cream jug inscribed 'To Robert Burns, Dumfries 1st December 1791' (936)
Painted china punch-bowl (877)
Knife and fork (L53, 59)

Large tumbler engraved with details of the Burns provenance, Burns House, Dumfries.

Two silver teaspoons (723)
Wooden mazer (C)
Punch-bowl of Inveraray marble, made by James Armour, the poet's father-in-law (now in the Hastie Collection, British Museum)
Replica of the marble punch-bowl (863) (C)
Wine-glass (867), dram-glass (876), masonic whisky decanter (873) and whisky bottles (869, 871-2)
English cordial glass, c. 1750 (L53, 59)
Glass tumbler (926) (H) and tumbler in a wooden case, with 13-line inscription (927) (H)
Brass candlestick from Mossgiel inscribed 'Robert Burns, Mossgiel, 1784' (925)
Pair of brass candlesticks (929)
Whip (717) and silver-mounted horn-handled whip used on Highland Tour (739)
Walking stick with twisted handle (632) (H)
Pair of spurs (740)
The poet's 'favourite caup', presented by James Armour to Paisley Burns Club (654)
Sword (677), swordstick (710) and blunderbuss (709) (H)
Small pistol, lent by J.W. Devlin (830): see separate note regarding Burns's pistols
Lord Balmerino's dirk (T)
Looking-glass and glass-cutter (S)
Dressing-glass (829) (E), two razors (834), razor and shaving mirror (C)
Silver watch (836), six waistcoat buttons (C) and cravat pin set with cairngorm (H)
Brooch given to Burns by Mrs Dunlop (L59)
Masonic jewel worn by Burns as Depute-Master, St James's Lodge, Tarbolton (728)(B)
Masonic apron (729)(B) masonic mallet and chair (B)
Masonic pottery tankard (H)
Masonic apron, Lodge St Andrew, Dumfries (L53, 59)
Draught-board used by Robert and Gilbert at Lochlea (727) (K)
Clock 'believed to have been owned by Robert Burns' (T)
Brass-handled pocket knife or jocteleg (794) (T — but since stolen)

Burns's shaving mirror, Ellisland.

Excise scales and claw hammer used by Burns, Ellisland.

The poet's copper kettle, Burns House, Dumfries.

Family Bible, purchased from Peter Hill for £2 (C)

Bible 'read by Burns at the Brow, and left behind by him' (721)

Bible from the poet's Lochlea period (B)

Cutty spoon (718), tongs from 1834 sale (747a), kitchen poker and fire tongs (847-8)

Excise ink bottle used by Burns (712), with two quills and penknife (C)

Triple compartment inkstand (A)

Excise chest with silver plate giving its provenance (953)

Pocket scales used on Excise duties (E)

Musket carried on Excise duties (H)

Gauging rod inscribed 'R.B. 1792' (711)

'Wangee' rod, referred to in a letter to Mrs Dunlop, November 1790 (C)

Link of measuring chain used by Burns (719)

Four links of the surveying chain (L53, 59)

Two wooden toddy ladles (742) (H), wooden toddy ladle ex Miller Goudie sale (745)

Silver toddy ladle (691)

Guitar [cittern] (678)

Bone snuff box 'Robert Burns — Ellisland 1787' (796) and snuff horn (C)

Iron pot, from the displenishing sale at Ellisland (910)

Soup ladle, from Ellisland (963)

Copper toddy kettle, with engraved inscription giving its provenance (H)

Brass door-knocker from Burns House, Dumfries (T)

Fire-grate, from Ellisland (C)

Mantelpiece from Ellisland (635)

Cooking range, oven and 'swee' made at Carron and installed by Burns at Ellisland (E)

Travelling trunk made from a tree-trunk and initialled 'RB' (E)

Sword, hammer, musical stock-horn and clothes-brush (E)

Fishing-rod with silver plate bearing a six-line inscription (E)

Small seal mounted on a silver pen and pencil holder but not contemporary (C)

Heraldic seal (700) (C) — see notes

Lock of hair given by Burns to Annie Rankine (722), and another lock (724)

Lock of Burns's hair given by Jean Armour to Jean Wilson at his death (C)

Locket containing the hair of Burns and Jean Armour (699)

Musket used by Burns on Excise duty, Burns House, Dumfries.

Gifts from Robert Burns

Pony-hoof inkwell given to John Lapraik (H)

Soapstone salt-cellar given to Robert Wilson, 'the gallant weaver' (T)

Silver watch given to his cousin John Allan (703)

Horn snuff mull given to John Cunningham (782)

Spectacles given to Hew Ainslie (803)

Scrap of dress given to his cousin, Fanny Burns when she married Adam Armour (640) (T)

Stew-pot given to David Hutchieson — 'Wee Davock' (908)

Parlour chair from Ellisland, given to his servant as a wedding present (952)

Punch-bowl of Lowestoft china, given to Willie Nicol (1007a)

Chair which fell off the back of the cart at the flitting from Mossgiel to Ellisland. Burns gave it to William Smith, his gaudsboy, telling him to give it to his mother (T)

Blue and white china tea service, a wedding gift to Mary ('Mailie') Corsby (E)

Enamelled marble apple, a wedding gift to his sister-in-law, Jean Breckenridge (L53, 59)

Burns's pistols

Duncan McNaught's *caveat* regarding the authenticity of the relics at the Centenary Exhibition could doubtless be applied to quite a few of the items on display but never more so than in the case of the small flintlock pistol (830) which was lent by J.W. Devlin of Carlisle. Fortunately this hand-gun was one of the items actually illustrated, so that we know that it was a small pocket pistol with stepped barrel, of a type fashionable in the 1780s. As if to confirm this, the stock was marked 'R. Burns, 1790'. On the face of it we have a positive identification, giving both the owner's name and the date when it was presumably acquired. The fact that the pistol is thus inscribed, however, should immediately make us suspicious. Ross Roy tells an amusing anecdote about a horn spoon in his possession which purports to be the very one with which the bard supped his porridge, and as if to verify this fact, it actually has his name engraved round the rim. Professor Roy points out how ludicrous this is — as if the poet would have had his own spoon at home and had to have it clearly marked, lest any other member of the household should use it by mistake! Of course, something as valuable and important as a pistol might indeed be engraved with the owner's name yet I must confess that such a practice was not at all common.

It could be argued, of course, that a subsequent owner might have had the poet's name engraved, but if this were the case, the addition of a date of alleged ownership strikes one as very dubious. Fortunately, there are other inscriptions on the stock which cast some light on the mystery. Below the poet's name is 'Miller, Dalswinton', whom we must suppose was none other than Patrick Miller, Burns's landlord during the Ellisland period (1788-91). From these inscriptions it might be inferred that Burns purchased the pistol in 1790 and gave it to Miller as a parting gift the following year. Relations between Burns and Miller cooled latterly, as a result of the 'bad bargain' of Ellisland, so it is extremely unlikely that Burns would have made such a present. In any case, a pocket pistol is hardly the sort of thing one would give to a landed proprietor such as Miller, nor was it likely that Burns could have afforded such a gesture.

All is revealed, however, by the third inscription on the stock: 'Brodie, 1804'. John Brodie described himself as a 'dealer' of Academy Street, Dumfries. Around the town, he was known as 'Poacher' Brodie or 'Jock the Poacher' which give a better indication of his business, and from his part in the fabrication of the provenance for two other *brace* of pistols, it is virtually certain that the Devlin pistol was likewise a fake manufactured with the intention of deceiving Burns collectors.

The antecedents of the Devlin pistol cannot, at this remove in time, be explored, but the other pistols are well documented. First of all, there is the *genuine* pair of pistols which were manufactured by David Blair, the well-known Birmingham gunsmith, who presented them to the poet on 29th October 1788. This much is incontrovertible, as Burns wrote to Blair from Ellisland on 23rd January 1789 thanking him rather belatedly: 'The defensive tools do more than half mankind do, they do honor to their maker; but I trust that with me they shall have the fate of a miser's gold — to be often admired, but never used.' If Burns received such a magnificent gift in 1788, not long after the commencement of his Excise duties, it is extremely unlikely that he would have purchased a pocket pistol of indifferent quality a year later.

In August 1795 Burns wrote to Blair and made him a present of a Jacobite relic which he prized very highly. This was the dirk which had belonged to Lord Balmerino, executed for his part in the Rebellion of 1745. The letter, incidentally, is a fascinating example of how provenance was established in a relic. Burns

Burns's fishing rod, Ellisland.

Left: Burns's travelling trunk, Ellisland.

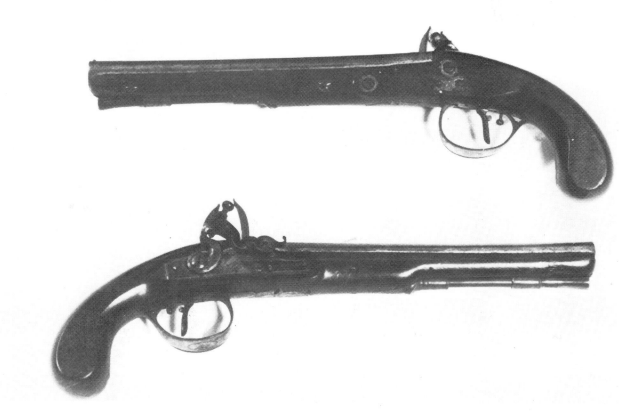

*Cased pair of duelling pistols, erroneously alleged to have belonged
to Burns. Photo: Sotheby, Parke Bernet.*

himself had acquired the dirk from Dr William Maxwell, scion of an old Catholic Jacobite family in the neighbourhood, who shared the poet's radicalism and was both medical adviser and close confidante. Maxwell and Blair were also intimate. Maxwell was in France when the Revolution broke out and in 1792 returned to England to procure weapons for the revolutionaries. Blair played a major role in the affair.

Having given a present from Maxwell to Blair, it was logical that Burns should give Blair's present to Maxwell. Shortly before his death, Burns gave the doctor his one material possession of any value, the brace of pistols. According to the notoriously unreliable Allan Cunningham, Burns said to Maxwell: 'Alas! What has brought you here? I am but a poor crow, and not worth plucking.' And with that he pointed to his pistols and 'desired that Maxwell would accept of them, saying they could not be in worthier keeping, and he should never more have need of them.'

That much was true, and Maxwell did, indeed, fall heir to the pistols. The good doctor treasured the gift for thirty-eight years. On his own deathbed, on 13th October 1834, he gave the pistols to his daughter Elizabeth and she, in turn, left them to her heir, Bishop James Gillis. On 19th April 1859 Bishop Gillis read a paper on the subject before the Society of Scottish Antiquaries, to whom he donated the pistols. The publicity which surrounded his impending gift, however, had created a controversy in the national press, due to the fact that claims were then being advanced in respect of a rival brace of pistols. In his paper, however, Bishop Gillis scientifically traced the history of his own pistols and rebutted the evidence supporting the opposition.

One of the rival claims concerned a brace of pistols which was not even made by David Blair! These pistols were claimed as the ones given by Burns to Dr Maxwell but their subsequent history took a rather different turn. James Hastings, writing to the *Illustrated London News* on 5th January 1859, gave what he purported to be the true history of the pistols. 'When Maxwell died, he gave them to an old friend of his, and an aged one of mine. That old friend also died and the pistols (with the poet's last words graven in brass and inserted in the oaken case) were inherited by his grandson. The latter lately went to America and took the heirloom with him... I was sorry to see these relics of poor Burns leave Old England even for Young England but the bard is well loved on the other side of the Atlantic.' It subsequently transpired that the 'aged friend' to whom Dr Maxwell was alleged to have given the pistols was Provost Fraser, of the King's Arms, Dumfries, and his grandson was Alexander Howat.

Bishop Gillis caused further enquiries to be made in Dumfries, and got a statement from Mrs Howat (mother of Alexander, and daughter of the late Provost Fraser). She frankly admitted that she had never heard her father say that the pistols had belonged to Burns. The only evidence for supposing them to have been such was that they were bought at the Maxwell roup held at Dumfries in May 1834, shortly before the aged doctor moved to Edinburgh, where he died a few months later. She averred that her son stated that he had heard his grandfather say that they were Burns's pistols, and on the strength of that Alexander Howat had taken it upon himself to get a plate engraved and affixed to the case containing the pistols.

The brass plate reads: 'This pair of pistols was given by the POET BURNS on his death bed to Dr William Maxwell, Dumfries, July 1796, with the words I wish them to fall into the hands not of a Rascal but an Honest man presented afterwards by Dr Maxwell to John Fraser, Esq., of Dowie Vale.' Alexander Howat, however, did not retain his heirloom for very long. The paper read by Gillis on 19th April 1859 which resoundingly destroyed all rival claims, was widely publicised in the national press, and it seems probable that Alexander got to hear of it. On 8th June of that year he disposed of the pistols to Captain Robert Leitch, master of the SS *City of Baltimore*, which made its maiden voyage from Liverpool to the United States about that time. Captain Leitch, in turn, added a brass plate of his own certifying that the pistols had been 'Presented by John Frazers (*sic*) Grandson...' There is no doubt in my mind that Alexander Howat disposed of the pistols knowing the truth of the matter, but he concealed this from Captain Leitch who, to the end of his days, cherished them in the mistaken belief that they had once belonged to Burns. They were handed down through successive generations of the Leitch family until September 1977 when they were sold by Leitch's great-granddaughter at an auction held by Sotheby Parke Bernet in Johannesburg. The pistols were illustrated in the sale catalogue, and accompanied by a very detailed (21-line) description, which shows them to have been a case of duelling pistols made by Wilson of Edinburgh — nothing to do with Blair of Birmingham at all!

The relentless Bishop Gillis (who would have made an admirable detective) then examined the roup roll of the Maxwell sale. Dr Maxwell's effects included a number of weapons, and against Lot 21 — a case of pistols — there appeared the name of Provost Fraser, who had paid £2. 6s for them.

Shortly after the death of Dr Maxwell there appeared a story about him and Burns's pistols, in the *Inverness Courier*, subsequently reprinted in several other newspapers. The *Courier* ended its report by quoting from a letter received lately from Allan Cunningham, the poet, author and biographer of Burns ranking second only to Dr Currie for unreliability and a flagrant disregard of the truth. 'Honest Allan' was the son of Alexander Cunningham, a close friend of Burns, and he himself became a fanatical relic-hunter who was not above fiddling the facts to suit himself. The letter stated: 'The poet's pistols and Highland broad-sword, which he gave to Dr Maxwell, were lately sold at a public auction for a mere trifle. I am endeavouring to buy them up if possible. I am collecting all the relics of the great Robert that I can, with the intention of placing them in some public sanctuary.'

Inevitably this *canard* came to the attention of Elizabeth Maxwell and the late doctor's friends who prevailed upon William Innes, the family solicitor, to write in the strongest terms to Cunningham seeking a public retraction. There is evidence that Allan Cunningham replied to this letter — indeed, there was quite an exchange of correspondence — but unfortunately none of these letters was preserved. It must be inferred, however, that Allan refused to give way, and the Maxwell family doubtless destroyed the ensuing correspondence in disgust. Cunningham died in 1842, long before the controversy concerning the pistols arose in 1859. Cunningham's widow upheld the myth to such an extent, however, that the *Illustrated London News* condemned the Gillis and Howat pistols as spurious: 'Allan put them into a very handsome box, with a suitable inscription. They are twice referred to in Cunningham's *Life and Works of Burns* (second edition, 1835, pp. 312 and 341) as made by Blair of Birmingham. Will the Scottish Antiquaries continue to exhibit their newly aquired — treasure, shall we call it?'

Bishop Gillis countered this by examining the roup roll of the Maxwell sale. He soon discovered that Peter Cunningham, Allan's son, had gone to Dumfries after the sale and paid £5 for them from the actual purchaser at the sale. The purchaser was none other than 'Poacher' Brodie! The truth of the matter was, in fact, revealed in the *Glasgow Daily Herald* of 8th February 1859. The purchaser of the pistols in question was given as 'Jock Brodie, a kind of broker, game-dealer, sportsman, and perhaps poacher in a small way but though decent, he was not a person of any consideration.' The *Herald* was equally dismissive of the pistols — 'a very common pair they are.' To be sure, the pistols did have the name of Blair of Birmingham on them — 'Still, Blair of Birmingham was a common inscription for a pistol...'

Alone of all the protagonists in this convoluted tale, Jock Brodie was still alive in 1859 and a statement was eventually obtained from him by Gillis's friend, Wellwood Anderson. When asked who it was that told him that these were Burns's pistols, Brodie admitted that no one had ever told him anything of the sort. Brodie took refuge in a faulty memory, excusable in one of such advanced years, so his answers, for the most part were inconclusive. Nevertheless, the roup roll shows that he purchased the pistols for 15s 6d - a mere trifle indeed. He could remember selling them about half an hour after the sale to Peter Cunningham, so he made a very handsome profit of over £4 on the transaction. Brodie also purchased two swords in the sale, paying 7s 8d and 8s respectively. One of these was the 'Highland broadsword' subsequently acquired by Allan Cunningham, and thereafter paraded as Burns's sword. Significantly neither the sword nor the pistols in the possession of the Cunningham family were entered at the Centenary Exhibition. The Howat

pistols were sold by Sotheby's in good faith, and found a ready purchaser who paid R4,200 (£2,763) for them. The purchaser then very generously presented them to the Birthplace Museum. The late W.H. Dunlop was acutely embarrassed at this, knowing full well the truth of the matter, but was powerless to refuse the gift, and the pistols are on display to this day without comment or clarification.

Incredibly, there is yet *another* brace of Burns's pistols in existence — and this pair is also on display in the Birthplace Museum. If the Cunningham Blair pistols were, indeed, ' a very common pair', then this brace must be regarded as beneath contempt. They are typical of the cheap pistols turned out in their thousands in the late eighteenth century and possess no merit, technically or intrinsically. Their sole claim to a worthy place in this Valhalla of relics lies in their butts, which bear the unmistakeable initials 'R.B.' in pokerwork. But as if this were not enough to convince the faithful, they are displayed with a letter from Mrs Brodie, dated 28th May 1875, certifying that the pistols were given to her husband John by Burns at his decease. Brodie himself died in Dumfries on 4th May 1875 at the advanced age of 98, so he would have been a youth of nineteen when Robert died. In his youth, Brodie lived in a house in Friars Vennel and ran errands for Jean and Robert when they lived in the adjacent Wee Vennel (now Bank Street). In later years he would reminisce about the poet: 'Rob was a lang lingle fallah wi a loot an his een gied through ye like gemlits. His broos were gey aften doon, an he looked like ane that cared mair for ither folk then he did for his sel an his ain.' Brodie's verdict on Jean was 'weel-faur'd and kin', only a wee bit thowless. A better-natured woman I never saw. She needed, for Rob was nae saunct!' Whether Jock was as intimate with the Burns family as he liked to make out is a matter for conjecture, but it is unlikely that Robert valued him so highly as to make him a dying present. Be that as it may, the pistols are displayed at the Birthplace Museum for all to see.

In a letter to Bishop Gillis in April 1859, when the dust had settled on the controversy, John Stuart, Secretary of the Society of Antiquaries, wrote: 'I think the moral to be deduced will not be without its use in showing how rigid we must be in sifting controverted points, even of recent history, and how easy the process is of inventing historical relics, when people are resolved to have them.'

Burns's seals

Robert Burns is known to have used four seals in the last ten years of his life. Before the advent of Uniform Penny Postage in 1840 letters were charged according to the number of sheets comprising them, and as envelopes counted as a second sheet (and thus doubled the postage) it is hardly surprising that they were never used postally. Instead it was customary for letter-writers to fold the writing paper in such a way that the name and address of the recipient appeared on the back of the letter. When the sheet was folded again, into three, one end would be tucked inside the other and the letter sealed by means of an isinglass wafer or a blob of sealing-wax. The latter was by far the commoner device and it was invariably impressed with the sender's seal as a security precaution. Seals came in several forms. The commonest was the signet ring, a popular form of personal adornment, with the owner's monogram or heraldic motif cut into it, so that the wax impression showed the device in relief. Fob seals were rather larger than signet rings and were so called because they were intended as a decorative appendage to the chain attached to the watch carried in the fob, or small pocket near the waistband of gentlemen's breeches. Then there were those seals designed to lie on the writing desk. They were generally much larger than fob seals and affixed to handles of wood, bone or ivory. A variant of these handled seals is the type which was fitted into the end of a ferrule, pen-knife or pencil case.

The first seal, whose wax impressions are known on letters by Burns as early as 1789, was oval in format and showed a figure holding a harp. Figural seals of this type were sold at the time in stationers and fancy goods shops. A second seal was adopted by the poet two years later, and it is first recorded on a letter relating to the birth of William Nicol Burns. Scott

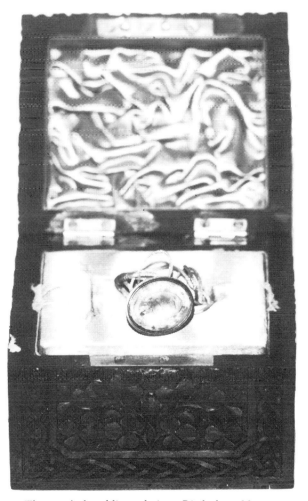

The poet's heraldic seal ring, Birthplace Museum.

Douglas draws attention to this seal, 'with its symbolic impression, as pregnant with meaning. For, nine days before the date of the birth of William Nicol, the Poet's Anna of the gowden locks was delivered of a daughter, who was afterwards brought up by Mrs Burns.' It is possible that the seal was designed by Burns in view of the position he found himself in, but it is hardly likely. It shows a heart transfixed by two arrows, which some Burnsians have interpreted as the bard smitten by love of Jean Armour and Anna Park at the same time. Again, this seal may have been part of the general stock of a stationer, and may therefore have no particular significance, other than that its motif appealed to Burns.

A third seal, however, has a quasi-heraldic device, showing a woodlark perching on a branch, with the motto 'Wood-notes wild'. The seal was cut intaglio into a yellow topaz, set in silver to screw into the top of a pencil case. It is not known how Burns came by this seal but it seems likely that he had it designed for him, or rather it was designed on his behalf. This may, indeed, be the seal to which the poet referred in a letter of 3rd March 1794 to Alexander Cunningham in Edinburgh: 'There is one commission that I must trouble you with. I lately lost a valuable seal, a present from a departed friend, which vexes me much.' This has been interpreted as a gift from the Earl of Glencairn, but there is nothing to substantiate this.

In the letter to Cunningham, Burns goes on: 'I have gotten one of your Highland pebbles, which I fancy would make a very decent one and I want to cut my armorial bearings on it: will you be so obliging as to enquire what will be the expense of such a business? I do not know that my name is matriculated, as the heralds call it, at all, but I have invented arms for myself, so you know I will be chief of the name and by courtesy of Scotland will likewise be entitled to supporters. These, however, I do not intend having on my seal. I am a bit of a herald, and shall give you, *secundum artem*, my arms:- On a field azure a holly-bush seeded, proper in base a shepherd's pipe and crook saltier-wise, also proper, in chief. On a wreath of the colours a woodlark perching on a spring of bay-tree, proper, for crest. Two mottoes — round the top of the crest, Wood-notes wild at the bottom of the shield, in the usual place, Better a wee bush than nae bield.'

Cunningham got a drawing made based on the poet's specifications and this was transmitted to him, via George Thomson. Burns replied to Thomson in May 1794: 'My seal is all well, except that the holly must be a bush, not a tree, as in the present shield. I also enclose it, and will send the pebble at the first opportunity.' There seems to have been some delay in the execution of this commission, for Burns did not receive the seal until shortly before his death. In April 1796 he wrote to Thomson, saying that Mrs Hyslop of the Globe Tavern 'will be a very proper person to bring back the seal you talk of.' In a subsequent letter to Thomson, about 18th May, Burns ends with

Wax impressions from the poet's heraldic seal.

'Many, many thanks for the beautiful seal!' Poor Burns did not live long to enjoy the use of this elaborate seal, for he died only two months later.

The armorial seal passed to the poet's eldest son, Robert Junior, and from him it passed to his daughter, Elizabeth, wife of Assistant Surgeon Bartholomew Everitt of the East India Company. She bequeathed the seal to her daughter, Mrs Martha Burns Thomas of Killinick, Martinstown, Co. Wexford, who lent it to the Centenary Exhibition and about the same time had impressions taken of it in red sealing wax. These impressions were mounted on specially printed cards and a rather faded specimen may be seen in the Birthplace Museum. The descendants of Mrs Thomas emigrated to the United States and recently the present owner of the seal communicated to the Burns Federation that she was willing for it to be returned to Scotland — provided she received $500,000 in payment. Desirable as it would be for the heraldic seal to be displayed in the Birthplace Museum or Burns House in Dumfries, the value placed on the seal is totally unrealistic. In the present circumstances, therefore, it is extremely unlikely that funds would ever become available to make the purchase.

The seal which Burns lost, however, subsequently turned up, and passed to the poet's third surviving son, James Glencairn Burns, who bequeathed it to his daughter Sarah Burns Hutchinson, from whom it passed to her daughter Annie Vincent Burns Scott who emigrated to Adelaide, Australia and took the seal with her. This probably explains its absence from the Centenary Exhibition, but eventually it came, by purchase from her family, into the possession of the Birthplace Museum where it is on display to this day. It is mounted on a silver pen and pencil holder which, however, is not contemporary with it.

Burns House, Dumfries, has on show a small seal with polished bone handle and the face engraved with the monogram 'RB' in cursive script. The provenance of this seal is unknown, but it is extremely doubtful whether it ever belonged to the poet.

Jean Armour Burns

The poet's widow outlived him by thirty-eight years — longer, in fact, than Burns himself lived. The early part of her widowhood must have been in fairly straitened circumstances, but a small government pension, together with the money raised by friends of the poet and latterly the proceeds from the sale of the editions of the *Life and Works* from 1800 onwards must have improved Jean's material position. Her three surviving sons had good, solid middle-class careers and both William Nicol and James Glencairn Burns would have brought their mother presents from India. In view of the foregoing it is surprising how few demonstrably authentic relics of Jean have survived. The following list indicates those items displayed at the Centenary Exhibition, or now displayed in the principal museums of the Burns country:

Hair bracelet (C), gold ring (T), gold wedding ring (H)
Gold brooch with seven stones and lock of Jean's hair (C)
Gold brooch with portraits of Jean (obverse) and two nieces (reverse) (702)
Lock of Jean's hair (775a) (L53, 59)
Piece of lace collar (716)
Two neck napkins, in thread and muslin, worked by Jean (702)
Pocket handkerchief marked 'J. Burns No. 5' (725)
White cotton cap (730) (E) and pillow slip (731) made, spun and worn by Jean
White cotton bedspread made by Jean (S)
Paper fan with coloured print (732)
White kid gloves (736) and silk scarf given by Col. William Burns (737)

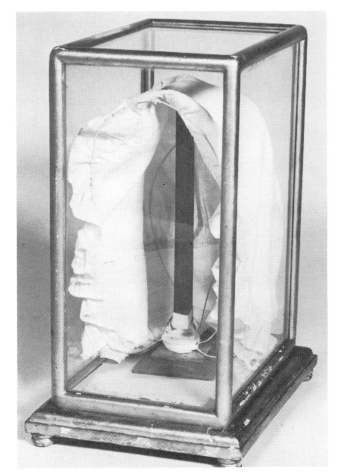

Jean Armour's linen cap, Ellisland.

Piece of a scarf worn by Jean (T)

Silk shawl worn on the occasion of her marriage (S)

Pair of black silk embroidered stockings (747)

Looking glass (902)

Umbrella (L53, 59)

Cup and saucer, and bannock toaster (C)

Rolling pin (738), metal teapots (746) (T) (H)

Fruit knife inscribed 'The widow of Burns to D. Wharton, Dumfries, 1827' (L59)

Tea caddy — a wedding gift from James Armour (741)

Drinking horn and caup — gifts from William Armour (743)

Tea caddy spoon given by Jean to her sister Nelly (846)

Dram-glass from Jean to Peter McPherson, uncle of Highland Mary (878)

Horn drinking-glass given by Jean to a friend (924)

Two table knives from Jean to her niece (H)

China bowl given by Jean to James Adair (H)

Bit of oatmeal cake baked by Jean and given to John Crawford of Alloa, 1823 (L53, 59)

William Burnes (the poet's father)

Spectacles (963.5)

Silver watch, which later belonged to Robert Burns (C)

Chair (C)

Family Bible dated 1762 (C)

See also the discussion of the spurious Cottage collection, later in this chapter.

Agnes Broun Burnes (the poet's mother)

Leather needle-case made by her son William (833)

Looking glass (906) and painted jug with 'Hope' etc (933)

Chest of drawers and stool for wash-tub (C)

Tawse — 'seldom used on Robert' according to John Murdoch (850)

Silk shawl (S)

Armchair (C)

Armchair belonging to the poet's parents, Alloway.

Isabella Begg (the poet's sister)
Butter print given to her by her mother (682)
Stockings knitted of Alpaca wool by her (849) (S)
Quilted petticoat (S)
Gold ring set with turquoise (704)
Scissors (680), chair (960), silver spoon (963) and eight-day clock (C)
Isabella Burns Begg (the poet's niece)
Lock of hair (775b) and Bible
'Dear-bought Bess' (Elizabeth Paton)
Pair of tongs (673a) and chain carved in wood (832)
Elizabeth Burns
Two cups and saucers (L59)
'Highland Mary' (Mary Campbell)
Lock of hair (692), and another given to Manchester Burns Club in 1849 (768)
Gold ring (693)
'Clarinda' (Mrs Agnes McLehose)
Bolt and two hasps of outer door of house in General's Entry where she lived (664)
China cup and saucer — part of a set given to her by Robert Burns (744)

John Rankine
Six toddy ladles and a punch divider (665)
Horn snuff mull given to him by Burns (713)
Armchair with back folding down to form a desk (956)
Tam Samson
China punch-bowl and wooden ladle (860)
Curling stones (911)
Pocket steel shot measures (638)
Dram-glass (K)

Gavin Hamilton
Chair (962) and pair of chairs (T)
Knife and fork (T)
Brass door knocker from his front door, Mauchline (799)
Earl of Glencairn
Silver pocket watch (694)
Snuff box with Oxford crown mounted on lid, given to Robert Burns (H)
'Souter Johnny' (John Davidson)
Pair of child's shoes made by him (648) (K)
Child's chair (955)
Tongs (661), tobacco pipe (764) and pair of brass candlesticks (928)
Cobbler's hand-guard (C), workstool (T) and working tools (T)
Snuff box made from the shank-bone of a racehorse (787) (L53, 59)
Night-dresses (674), apron (676) and back of silk dress (675) worn by Mrs Davidson
Scissors used by Mrs Davidson (679)
'Tam o Shanter' (Douglas Graham)
Two razors (S)
Pair of silver coat-links worn on his wedding day (837)
Snuff box 'made of a hoof of Tam o Shanter's mare' (762)
China cups which belonged to Mrs Smith of Prestwick, Graham's grand-daughter (650)
James Humphrey ('the bleth'rin bitch')
Razor presented by Burns (657)

Razor and matching case (749) (K)
Tobacco 'spleuchan' or pouch (750)
Armchair (905)
'Poosie Nansie' (Agnes Gibson)
Wooden quaich (642), piece of stone from the gable-end (T) and corner cupboard (T)
Other relics may be seen in 'Poosie Nansie's' Inn, Mauchline to this day
Nanse Tinnock
Rafter and pin, four pieces of beams and rafters, and a large beam (T)
Half-gill stoup (644), wooden bicker (646) and pint measure (649)
Wooden platter (760), milk sieve (798)
Bannock plate of Pontypool ware (A)
Horn ladle said to have been used by Burns at Nanse Tinnock's (C)
Quaich said to have been used by Burns at Nanse Tinnock's (L53, 59)
Blue and white china plate given by Burns (858)

Miscellaneous articles
Under this heading I have grouped all those items which can only be regarded as very indirectly connected with Burns — the things associated with people and places which have a passing interest to the life and works of the poet.
Flowered silk skirt worn by Christina Morton (one of the Mauchline Belles) at Burns's kirking (636)
Punch ladle used at Laggan Braes in 1789 by William Nicol, when 'Willie brew'd a peck o maut' (641)
Cup and saucer belonging to Mrs Stewart of Stair 'out of which Burns drank tea' (651)
Ends of Thomas White's dining table, at which Burns often took breakfast (H)
Stools at which Burns sat to correct proofs at William Smellie's (L53, 59)
Wineglasses used by Burns at Craigdarroch (870) and Kirkmichael (874-5)
China cups and saucers used by Burns while visiting Kirkmichael (E)
Dinner bell from Montgomerie Castle, Coilsfield (895)
Tongs (672) and half-mutchkin (C) from the Globe Inn, Dumfries
The poet's favourite chair in Manson's Masonic Inn, Tarbolton (951)
Stirrup-cup from the Tam o Shanter Inn, Ayr (963) (C)
Tuning fork used at Kirkoswald School in Burns's time (C)
Violins belonging to George Thomson (706), Neil Gow (708) and James McLauchlan — the 'thairm-inspiring sage' (1007d)
Two pieces of a spinet belonging to Elizabeth Burgess of Watcarrick, the subject of Burns's song 'Bess and her spinning wheel' (707) (E)
Mallet used by auctioneer John Richardson at the sale of Jean's effects, 1834 (758) (H)
Two silver spoons belonging to Mrs Thom (an aunt of the poet) (696)

Horn snuff mull belonging to Highland Mary's father (792)

Wooden snuff box belonging to John Bishop (Burns's son-in-law) (777)

Dining-chair from Friars' Carse (899)

Pewter baptismal font from the Laigh Kirk, Kilmarnock (843)

Window-frame at 30 St James Square, Edinburgh where Burns lodged in 1787-8 (L53, 59)

Round carved oak table from rafters of Crochallan clubroom, Anchor Close (L53, 59)

Also on display at the Centenary Exhibition were freemason's apron, mallet and punch-bowl from Lodge St Andrew, Dumfries — though it was not claimed that these articles were in any sense personal to Burns. Similarly there was a display of the communion tokens used in Ayrshire churches in the late eighteenth century. There was a cutty stool 'of Burns's time' (909) and the 'Auld Nick' horn — a trumpet fashioned from the horn of a highland bullock which, in the year 1768 (when Burns was a laddie), had strayed from its pasture and got into Alloway Kirk. The horn broke off when the bullock got entangled in the pews. The only relevance of this article was that some poor old lady happened to be walking past the church when this commotion was taking place, and mistook the poor beast for the Devil himself. From this it is easy to suppose that out of this incident came the germ of an idea for the plot of 'Tam o Shanter'. There was also on show a bundle of flax, spun in 1793 — not, it will be noted, claiming to have been dressed by Burns himself during his Irvine period. Perhaps the oddest of the 'association' items on exhibition was a riding whip purchased by Matthew Todd in a shop in Kilmarnock, the same day that Burns happened to be in the same shop and bought his own whip for a guinea!

Caveat Collector

Regrettably, the sorry tale of Burns's pistols is by no means unique. The Centenary Exhibition seems to have stimulated a veritable industry in the production of spurious relics. Fifty years on, and the number of relics associated with the bard seems to have multiplied beyond belief — well, almost beyond belief, for there were no shortage of relic-hunters still eager and willing to be taken in. The relics, promoted solely on the strength of oral tradition transmitted from generation to generation perhaps, had a provenance that was no more reliable than contemporary gossip, only far more enduring. In the run-up period to the bicentenary of Burns's birth, many of these dubious relics attained a status of 'quasi-authenticity', based largely on a provenance which was assuming venerable proportions. These relics followed the bard from the cradle to the grave — quite literally, because the cradle in which he was rocked was claimed by one owner, while others purported to possess fragments taken from his coffin (when the vault was opened in 1834 for the interment of Jean, despite eye-witness accounts that the coffin was remarkably intact). Among the less believable

relics that allegedly came to light between the 1890s and the 1940s was the very trowel used to repair the 'auld clay biggin' at Alloway in 1759 when a portion of the gable fell out at the time of the poet's birth. A silver tray, said to have been given to Burns and Jean as a wedding present, although the circumstances of their marriage make that extremely unlikely, was offered for sale in Glasgow just before the Second World War.

Burns must have had an extensive wardrobe, to judge by the articles of clothing attributed to him. A hat which Burns is said to have worn at Mossgiel turned up in Hamilton, Ontario, and a pair of his shoes, worn as a boy, is to be found in Portland, Maine. For a Tam o Shanter bonnet, which he declared was at one time the property of Burns, the owner was offered 'fabulous prices, but would not part with it either for love or money'. A silk waistcoat said to have belonged to Burns, with purple, brown and cream stripes, was sold in London in 1929. A pair of stockings 'left behind in Richard Brown's house at Port Glasgow, where Burns and Jean and some of their children passed at least one night' was also sold at auction in London — even though the Port Glasgow visit never took place! In 1936 a Warrington gentleman claimed to own Burns's umbrella 'bound round outside with white braid and the name Robert Burns clearly printed on it.'

As pointed out in the story of Ross Roy's porridge spoon, it is safe to say that the presence of an inscription on an article, far from proving ownership, actually casts doubt upon it. It is not the custom now, nor was it ever in Burns's day, for people to give and receive presents elaborately engraved with their names and dates. Yet objects of *vertu* exist with inscriptions implying gifts from the Earl of Glencairn and Dugald Stuart dated '25th January 1787' — a few weeks after they first made the poet's acquaintance. It is unlikely that these gentlemen should have known Burns's date of birth on the basis of such a brief acquaintance, far less gone to the trouble of having gifts specially engraved.

Several watches alleged to have belonged to Burns have also been recorded, invariably inscribed 'R.B.' at least, though one is unbelievably inscribed 'Presented to Robert Burns by his brother-ploughmen of Aire, 1785' — though why they should have made such a presentation when Burns was still an obscure farmer is a mystery. There is, or was, at Cumnock a clock which was claimed as the very one owned by Burns at the time when he planned to emigrate. Another clock, with identical description, was at that time in the proud possession of a lady in Yetholm. Actually, the only clock that the poet ever possessed is in the hands of his descendants in England to this day.

Distance lends enchantment, and this is as true of Burns relics as anything else, to judge by the incredible market for memorabilia in the United States. Describing a sale held in America in 1940, Elizabeth Ewing wrote: 'At this auction there was included a writing-desk which in 1920, when it was

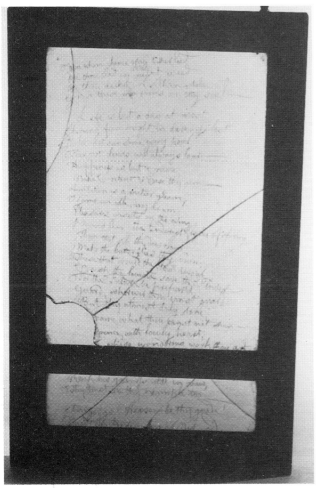

Lines of "O thou whom chance may hither lead", written with a diamond point on a window pane.

first heard of, was reputed to have been the property of Burns and as such brought £100 at auction. But twenty years later it had become a most desirable memento of Burns, a remarkable writing piece indeed and realised £160. There was also offered at this sale Burns's silver inkwell, with a silver pen; on the lid were the initials R.B. Although steel pens were unknown in Scotland in Burns's day and this show-piece had not been heard of before 1916, it was claimed as a birthday gift and sold for £90. A former owner, also an American, declared in the fullest and most unqualified manner I guarantee that this is the ink-well of Burns. He wrote 124 years after the alleged gift had been made, and produced no scrap of writing, no line of print to support his claim.'

The faking of relics by embellishing genuine antiques has known no bounds. A pair of silver tongs which it is alleged had been presented by Burns to the wife of the miller of Tarbolton for sheltering Jean Armour turned up at Kilmarnock: 'Robert Burns, poet' was engraved on them in facsimile of the poet's handwriting. However, this is as nothing compared with the silver coffee pot sold in London in 1902 for 17 guineas. Inscribed 'Robert Burns to Mary', it was claimed to have been presented by the poet to Highland Mary.

Other articles which have at one time or another been invested with a spurious value on account of their supposed attachment to the poet and his family include Jean's frying-pan, the poet's school-satchel from Kirkoswald, an hour-glass allegedly purchased by Burns in Edinburgh, the poet's breakfast table (now in Williamston, Massachusetts) and 'the last razor that Burns ever shaved with — a remarkable memento of his domestic life', which was owned by a Cheshire Scot. This razor was embellished by five small silver plaques, each of which gave the details of a successive owner.

There have been enough gold rings and seals in semi-precious stones to stock a jeweller's shop. Burns took snuff occasionally, as did most of his contemporaries, but the man must have been a positive addict, to judge by the large number of snuff boxes and mulls which are said to have belonged to him. One of these, inscribed 'Presented to Robert Burns, Globe Tavern, Dumfries, January 17, 1796' (when he was actually very ill) passed through the salerooms on several occasions up to the 1940s. Burns's tobacco box came under the hammer in 1930, a nice tortoiseshell confection with a silver plate inscribed 'Bobbie Burns from W. Nicol, Edinburgh, 1787'.

The poet's penchant for graffiti, in the form of lines inscribed with a diamond stylus on window-panes, is well-known, but in addition to the properly documented examples there is a host of spurious claimants. Claims have been made on behalf of a pane of glass from the room in which Burns slept while attending school at Kirkoswald. Burns is supposed to have scrawled the name of Robert Niven on the glass in 1769, when he was ten years old and presumably had his first diamond stylus in his pocket, ready to leave a record for posterity. A similar claim was made shortly before the Second World War on behalf of a window-pane at Finlaystone where the Earl of Glencairn 'once entertained Burns'. As if that were not enough, the seals from the wine-bottles broached on that occasion have also been preserved, despite the fact that the Finlaystone visit was a myth from start to finish.

The spurious Burns Cottage Collection

What was claimed as 'the whole and veritable furniture of the Cottage in which he was born' has, for almost seven decades, been in the possession of a museum in Bath. The Burns Cottage Collection, as it is known, has a curious history that is worth examining, if only to illustrate how spurious relics are made to grow in respectability with the passage of the years. The Bath museum acquired the collection through the agency of Agnew's, the famous Bond Street gallery, about 1920, after it had been on public exhibition there for several months. The catalogue prepared by Agnew's claimed, on the title page, that it was 'The Burns Cottage Collection, comprising the furniture of the Cottage in which the poet, Robert Burns, was born on January 25, 1759.' This may seem a trifle vague, indeed deliberately so, for all that that means is that the furniture on offer had been in the Cottage at some time between 1757, when it was built, and 1918, when it was offered for sale. The foreword, however, was more explicit, for it stated that 'certain outstanding articles in the collection were acquired from the Poet's father, and as such were shown to visitors for many years by John Goudie', tenant of the Cottage, so that the collection claimed to include a considerable portion of the furnishing of the Cottage at the time when Robert Burns was born. Despite the cachet of respectability conferred on this exhibition by the patronage of a certain royal personage, and the fact that it was, in fact, organised by the London Robert Burns Club, the sole interest of this motley collection lay in the fact that it was alleged to have belonged to someone who ran the Cottage as a common ale-house.

The Cottage, as all Burnsians know, was occupied by the Burnes family from 1757 till 1766 when they moved to Mount Oliphant. William Burnes retained the lease of the land as well as proprietorship of the Cottage until 1781, letting the house to a succession of tenants. In 1781 the land and house were put up for sale and were purchased by the Incorporation of Shoemakers in Ayr for £160. The records of the Incorporation reveal that the quondam Burnes house was occupied, at an annual rent of £10, by Matthew Dick, shoemaker in Ayr, from 1782 till 1801. It was Dick who, at some time after 1781, turned the Cottage into an ale-house. John Maitland succeeded to the tenancy in 1801, paying £25 10s a year. He sub-let the Cottage in 1803 to John Goudie. From then until his death in 1842 'Miller' Goudie ran the Cottage as a public-house. John Keats visited the place in 1818 and described Goudie as 'a mahogany-faced old jackass who knew Burns; he drinks glasses, five for the quarter, and twelve for the hour.' After Goudie's death, the business was carried on by his widow until her death in 1843. Thereafter her daughter and son-in-law (Mr and Mrs David Hastings) continued till Martinmas 1845, when the Cottage was let to Davidson Ritchie.

After the death of Mrs Goudie the 'whole household furniture and other effects situated within Burns' Cottage and other premises, lately possessed by Mr and Mrs Goudie' were sold by public roup on 30th September 1843, and two years later the effects of the Hastings were disposed of. Certain of the articles in the Hastings sale were purchased by James Esdaile of Manchester and it is these articles — and they alone — which formed the so-called Burns Cottage Collection.

From the outset, Esdaile seems to have regarded his acquisition as a temporary asset, to be turned to profit as rapidly as possible. In 1866 he attempted to sell the collection to James McKie of Kilmarnock, the noted publisher and Burns-collector, the asking price being £100. McKie turned him down, so four years later he offered the collection to the Trustees of the Burns Monument at Alloway for £50. It is alleged that Esdaile made approaches to other individuals and museums at various times between 1845 and his death, but to no avail.

In due course the collection was inherited by his son, George Esdaile of Rusholme, Manchester. He went even further than his father and came to believe implicitly that he had inherited a large portion of the furniture that had been in the Cottage when Burns was born in 1759, and he devoted a great deal of time and energy in trying to dispose of it at a continually increasing price. He advertised extensively, and as freely offered £300 to the agent who would find him a purchaser for the goods. 'I wish the nation would take up the matter,' he once wailed, 'and restore the Cottage Collection to the Cottage; what is in the Cottage now is not that which was in the possession of the Goudies since 1792. It is all spurious.' He proposed that a company should be formed to acquire his collection. He offered it to any whom he considered a possible purchaser. 'If the promoters like, I will construct a facsimile Burns Cottage and put my collection into it in Glasgow for the sum of six thousand pounds, and the relics will sell for much more after,' he wrote in 1895 to the secretary of the proposed Centenary Exhibition who, very wisely, would have none of it.

Nothing daunted, Esdaile then played on the ancient rivalries of Glasgow and the capital and approached the Corporation of Edinburgh with a similar offer. Unfortunately for Esdaile, however, his offer came while Auld Reekie was still recoiling from the scandal of the 'Antique' Smith forgeries and had no desire to be reminded of the fact that Edinburgh had been condemned before the world as 'a plague-spot of literary forgery'. The *Edinburgh Evening Dispatch*, which had played a major role in unmasking the forged manuscripts, now confronted Esdaile. A series of articles by W. Craibe Angus completely discredited Esdaile and his precious Collection, and the whole business was laughed out of court.

Thereafter little was heard of the Collection until George Esdaile died in 1918. His executors then made a determined effort to dispose of the Collection. The Trustees of Burns Cottage were approached but promptly turned down the offer. Subsequently, according to the Agnew catalogue, 'an acceptable offer was received from a distinguished resident of the United States' (said to have been a Mr Schwabe) and for a time it looked as if the Collection would cross the Atlantic. Then Harry Maconochie, a Scottish Burnsian, made a counter-offer and this was accepted. 'These fascinating relics and mementoes of the Poet' were then exhibited by kind permission of Mr Maconochie who is reputed to have paid £4,000 for the Collection. Subsequently he disposed of the relics to the museum in Bath where they were on show for a number of years — and may well be on display to this day, for aught I know.

In making his offers in 1866 and 1870 James Esdaile stated quite truthfully that he had purchased the furniture at the sale of the effects of David Hastings in 1845. George Esdaile, however, went much further and asserted that the relics comprised 'virtually the entire contents of the Cottage as the Great Poet knew it' and were acquired by his father at the Goudie sale of 1843. It is not unlikely that Hastings acquired some of the Goudie furniture when it was sold in 1843, but most of the bits and pieces were probably new, or recently acquired, when Hastings sold them two years later.

George Esdaile stoutly maintained all his life that he had irrefutable 'guarantees of authenticity' although he never once produced them. 'I assert and can prove,' he wrote, 'that the Cottage collection was in the Cottage when the Souters of Ayr bought it from the father of the Poet, that such furniture became the property of the miller Goudie in 1792, that it was Goudie's till his death in 1842, that my father bought it, and that I have it now.' On another occasion he offered 'a certificate given by the Goudie people, which carries us back to 1792' and which stated that the furniture 'was the furniture of the Cottage in which Robert Burns was born, and where our father resided for 50 years.' The records of the Incorporation of Shoemakers indicate that Goudie lived in the Cottage for only 40 years, so that the certificate only carries us back to 1803, not 1792. This worthless document was manifestly a forgery, and a highly inaccurate one at that.

This leaves a gap of 37 years from 1766, when the Burnes family left Alloway, to 1803. We are supposed to believe that William Burnes left behind 'virtually the entire contents of the Cottage' when he moved house, and that these valuable pieces of furniture were then used by successive tenants and sold to the Incorporation of Shoemakers in 1781 (though the records of the latter show that all they bought were 'houses and land'). We are asked to stretch our credibility still further and believe that Matthew Dick got the Burnes furniture in 1781 and passed it on intact to Maitland who, in turn, passed it on to Goudie in 1803. The supposed provenance of the furniture is absurd from beginning to end.

Goudie, for all his faults, was an honest man who never once claimed that anything in the Cottage belonged to the Burnes period. Furthermore, several books published in the early decades of the nineteenth century — most notably the *New Statistical Account* for the parish of Ayr compiled in 1837 — agree in stating that no part of the furniture of William Burnes was then in the Cottage. In his devastating expose of the Esdaile collection, Craibe Angus pointed out that the furniture on offer was typical, in style and construction, of the furniture commonly found in Scottish country inns in the early nineteenth century, and in no way resembled the rustic pieces typical of the home of a peasant in the 1760s. It is, of course, utterly unimaginable that Burnes, who was struggling to keep above the breadline, should move house, leaving behind his eight-day clock, his corner cupboard, his tables and chairs, which he had allegedly acquired only within the previous nine years, especially as the poor man had to borrow £100 in order to stock Mount Oliphant. Duncan McNaught, writing about the proposed sale by the Esdaile executors in December 1918, to the Editor of *The Glasgow Herald*, spoke of 'the transparent absurdity of William Burnes's furniture having been handed down as heirlooms by the successive tenants of the Cottage, from 1766 to 1843, even on the supposition that he left his furniture behind him, then only some eight years in use, for behoof of a queue of chance strangers, with or without the usual consideration. True, he had a son named Robert, aged seven years in 1766, of whom the world never heard till twenty years afterwards...'

The beginning of the souvenir industry

Those who could not afford to acquire articles purporting to have belonged to Burns or his cronies made do with scraps, fragments and splinters of wood or stone, taken away from landmarks and places associated with the poet. The story is told of a group of itinerant actors who passed through Ayr at the beginning of the nineteenth century. They made an excursion to Alloway and visited the 'auld haunted kirk', then in an advanced state of decay. Someone had the bright idea of hacking off a bit of an oak beam and getting it made into a snuff box by a local craftsman. In this way, it is said that the wooden souvenir industry of mid-Ayrshire (Auchinleck, Cumnock and Mauchline) came into being. The beautiful products of this industry are discussed in a subsequent chapter. These charming trifles were manufactured from sycamore wood prepared specially for the purpose. We are here concerned, however, with the artless mementoes garnered by souvenir-hunters while on pilgrimages to the haunts of Burns.

The following is a list of the souvenirs of this type; most of them were shown at the Centenary Exhibition in 1896, but a few others are, or have been, displayed in various museums:

Piece of old yew tree at Crookston Castle on which Burns carved his initials, 1777 (634)

Mallet from the Crookston yew and a box from the Elderslie Wallace oak (637)

Seven different and assorted fragments from Highland Mary's thorn at Coilsfield

Part of the root of Mary's thorn (629)

Small vase (669) and snuff boxes (767, 781) made from Mary's thorn

Segment of a tree in Ballochmyle Wood (626)

Segment from a tree that grew behind Burns's birthplace (765)

Piece of wood from the Mauchline 'Tent', in the time of Burns (668)

Piece of wood — part of the floor under the bed in which Burns died (621)

Piece of joist under the floor on which the deathbed stood (628)

Study-chair made of flooring from Burns's last bedroom (921)

Paperknives made from skirting board of the bedroom (766, 786)

*Turned-wood vase from part of the
foot of Burns's death-bed.
Globe Inn, Dumfries.*

Piece of turned wood — part of the bed, given to the McIlvean family by Robert Burns Junior in 1843 (633)

Piece of bedstead wood (670)

Two pieces of turned wood from the bedstead, made into small vases (653). One of these — or another like them — is now in the Globe Inn, Dumfries.

Snuff box made from one of the bed posts (779) and a similar one, with Burns's portrait incised on the lid (788)

Dressing case (673), quaich (689), snuff box (772) and necklace made from the rafters of Alloway Kirk

Vase made of wood which grew near Alloway Kirk (S)

Mallet made from the rafters of Alloway Kirk (L59)

Ladles made from the rafters of the Cottage (S)

Pin-cushion whose cover was made from part of the kist made for Burns preparing to emigrate to Jamaica (726) (H)

Egg-cup from rafter of Mossgiel, when the roof was repaired in 1859 (666)

Jewel-box made from Nanse Tinnock's parlour window-shutter (753)

Jewel box from the rafter of Gavin Hamilton's house (790)

Snuff box from Catrine Mill wheel, where Burns first met Lord Daer (T)

Snuff box from part of the roof of the Cottage (756)

Snuff box made from wood of the pulpit of Mauchline Kirk (773) (T)

Snuff boxes made from John Wilson's printing press (S) (L53, 59)

Horn snuff mull with stopper of wood from Alloway Kirk (763)

Fragment of wood from Alloway Kirk (800)

Two oak walking sticks made from a rafter of Gavin Hamilton's house, where Jean and Robert were married

Mallet made from wood grown on the grave of Burns (864)

Mallet from wood of the Auld Brig o Ayr (S)

Oak candlestick made from the wood of the Auld Brig o Ayr (S)

Ring made of shale found on Mossgiel Farm in 1883

Part of the door (622), lock and key (671), fanlight over the entrance (965) and 'lock which replaced the old lock' (660) from St Michael's Church, Dumfries

Dressing-table of wood from the pews of St Michael's where Burns worshipped (964)

Piece of cloth covering the seat in St Michael's where Burns sat (715)

Spence door of Mossgiel from the Burns period (959)

In addition to the above, the Tower at Mauchline boasts two fiddles made of wood from the room in Gavin Hamilton's house where Burns and Jean were wed. Burns House in Dumfries has a paperknife from the ash tree at Linkumdoddie and a gavel from the holly tree at the Mausoleum. I have not been able to confirm, however, that that museum at one time had a phial containing dust from the poet's tomb but on a recent visit I observed a party of American tourists diligently scraping up some of the dust from the red sandstone of which the house is built, and carefully depositing it in a little box. I would dearly like to know what they intend doing with it. Perhaps the grit will end up in an acrylic paperweight or some similar bauble. At least it proves that the age of the souvenir hunter is not yet over.

I will conclude this rather bizarre chapter with reference to two remarkable pieces of furniture whose common factor is that they represent works of applied and decorative art, largely cannibalised from more mundane artifacts. Visitors to Holyroodhouse in Edinburgh will see, in the long Banquetting Hall, an armchair, extravagantly carved with thistle finials and fan-vaulting corner-pieces. The high back is decorated with thistles and has four Gothic arches containing brass panels on which are engraved the lines of 'Tam o Shanter'. The chair itself was made from the rafters of Alloway Kirk by John Underwood, an Ayr cabinetmaker, in 1822. A painting of Tam o Shanter himself appears on the wooden panel behind the back, with a coat of ams at the top. This chair, one of the most elaborate souvenirs imaginable, was eventualy acquired by none other than Queen Victoria.

The Birthplace Museum, however, can cap that with the extraordinary chair made from the printing press on which the first edition of Burns's Poems was printed at Kilmarnock in 1786. One cannot help deprecating the vandalism that destroyed a piece of machinery which would have been of unparalleled interest to Burns bibliophiles and scholars, but this 'conversion' reflects mid-Victorian attitudes. Just as the Victorians loved to embellish everything, no matter how mundane and functional, with florid ornament, so also they took a positive delight in creating something 'artistic' out of ordinary workaday objects. The transformation of an eighteenth century printing press into a mid-Victorian armchair belongs firmly in this tradition. The arm-rests terminate in carvings representing the Twa Dogs, while the finials on either side of the high back feature figures of Tam and the Souter, while a bust of Burns himself (after Nasmyth, of course) towers above the central arch. A roundel carved in bas-relief, set in the top of the back, shows the Monument and the Auld brig o Doon. This oaken extravaganza is one of the chief exhibits in the Birthplace Museum. A silver plaque around the bas-relief has a six-line inscription signifying that the chair was presented by T.M. Gemmell (the lineal descendant in the business of John Wilson) in October 1891. The chair itself was constructed about 1858 in preparation for the Burns Centenary Festival in the County Buildings, Ayr, and the plaque indicates that it was first occupied by Sir James Fergusson, Bart. As a piece of furniture and as a commemorative of the poet's centenary, it is truly unique.

Chair made from the Wilson printing press,
Birthplace Museum.

Printed Ephemera

The printed matter pertaining to Robert Burns is truly prodigious. There have been over 2,000 editions of his Poems alone — an average of ten a year since the publication of that first slim volume at Kilmarnock in 1786 — and translations have been made in over forty languages, from Hebrew to Urdu. The volumes dealing with Burns's prose writings — his letters and the commonplace books — are far fewer in number but the volumes of biography and criticism are legion. On the eve of the bicentenary of the poet's birth the Mitchell Library in Glasgow could boast of over 3,500 volumes by or devoted to Burns, and that figure must have been handsomely augmented in the thirty years which have elapsed since then. Regarding the manuscripts of Burns, there are, or were, in the poet's holograph the text of over 700 poems and songs, and a similar number of letters have been recorded, although the present whereabouts of some manuscripts are not known. The books and manuscripts are outside the scope of this book, but this still leaves a formidable amount of material for the collector of Burnsiana. This chapter deals, therefore, with the various categories of collectable material that exist in two-dimensional printed form, excluding prints and engravings of portraits and illustrations of the life and works of Burns, previously discussed in Chapter 2, and philatelic material which will be found in Chapter 6.

Early printed matter

Without doubt, the earliest piece of printed material pertaining to Burns was the prospectus for the Kilmarnock Poems. John Wilson of Kilmarnock printed eight dozen of these leaflets, of which only a solitary example is now believed to exist. J.B. Greenshields of Lesmahagow acquired this rarity from the Glasgow curio-dealer Bell in March 1871 and lent it to the Centenary Exhibition (311). It is of particular interest for the signatures of sixteen of the subscribers. Opposite the name of William Lorimer the annotation 'sent per Charles Crichton' has been heavily scored through by Burns who then added 'The Blockhead refused it'. It is very tempting to suppose that the 'Blockhead' was the father of Jean Lorimer, Burns's 'Chloris', but Jean's father, the farmer of Kemys Hall whom Burns got to know well during his Ellisland period, is unlikely to have subscribed to the Kilmarnock Poems of several years earlier, and Lorimer is not an uncommon surname.

Apart from the Kilmarnock Poems themselves, the next printed relic of Burns must be the *Edinburgh Magazine* of October 1786 which contained the first review of the Poems, unsigned but thought to have been contributed by Dr Robert Anderson. Hard on its heels comes the article by Henry Mackenzie in the short-lived *Lounger* dated 9th December 1786 commending the Kilmarnock Poems and, incidentally, coining that well-worn cliché 'this Heaven-taught ploughman'. Other early reviews appeared in *Critical Review* (volume 63, 1787), *English Review* (February 1787) and *Monthly Review* (volume 75, 1786).

Then there are those poems and letters composed by Burns which first saw the light of day through the medium of the newspapers and periodicals of his lifetime. Peter Stuart, editor of *The Star* (which underwent various changes of name), actually made Burns an offer of a guinea a week (equal to his Excise salary) in exchange for a weekly poem. Burns declined this lucrative offer in 1789 and refused it again, when Stuart repeated it in 1795 in connexion with *The Oracle* which he was then producing. Nevertheless, Burns did contribute several pieces to Stuart's publications. He asked Stuart never to add his name to anything 'except where I myself set it down at the head or foot of the piece'. His 'Ode, Sacred to the Memory of Mrs Oswald of Auchencruive' was signed 'Tim Nettle', the 'Address of the Scottish Distillers', published in February 1789, was signed 'John Barleycorn', and the 'Ode to the Departed Regency Bill, 1789' was signed 'Agricola'. Conversely some scurrilous verses attributed to Burns about the Duchess of Gordon, which first appeared in *The Star* and were reprinted in *The Gazetteer*, were actually composed by Henry Dundas, Treasurer of the Navy. No fewer than 29 poems by Burns were contributed to the press, ranging from 'Address to a Haggis' (in *The Caledonian Mercury* of 19th December 1796) to 'O wat ye wha's in yon town' (in *The Glasgow Magazine* of September 1795. The 'Address to the Toothache' first appeared, posthumously, in *The Scots Magazine* in October 1797, but as late as February 1818 such major works as 'Address of Beelzebub' were making their debut in periodicals — in this instance *The Scots Magazine*, February issue. These first printed appearances of poetic effusions may be found in the *Advertiser*, *Evening Courant* and *Gazetteer* (Edinburgh), the *Courier*, *Glasgow Magazine*, *Mercury* and *Weekly Miscellany* (Glasgow), the *Morning Chronicle*, *St James's Chronicle*, the *Gentleman's Magazine*, the *Morning Star* and *European Magazine* (London). Not all of these were contributed by Burns directly, but were sent in to various papers by friends of the poet, to whom he had sent manuscript copies in the first instance. In addition Burns wrote a number of letters to newspapers, from November 1788 onwards. Cuttings from these periodicals are scarce enough and much sought after, but intact issues of the relevant numbers are of the greatest rarity.

Another source of early printed ephemera consists of proof-sheets of poems. Examples with the poet's own corrections in manuscript are exceedingly rare, but it was also his habit to obtain extra copies of these proofs which he would then distribute to his friends, and there are references to this in several of his letters.

Even in the poet's lifetime his works were pirated

APRIL 14th, 1786.

PROPOSALS,

FOR PUBLISHING BY SUBSCRIPTION,

SCOTCH POEMS,

BY ROBERT BURNS.

The Work to be elegantly Printed in One Volume, Octavo,
Price Stitched *Three Shillings*,

As the Author has not the most distant *Mercenary* view in Publishing,
as soon as so many Subscribers appear as will defray the *necessary* Expence,
the Work will be sent to the Press.

> Set out the brunt side o' your shin,
> For pride in *Poets* is nae sin;
> *Glory's* the Prize for which *they* rin,
>   And *Fame's* their jo;
> And wha blaws best the Horn shall win:
>   And wharefore no?
>
>   RAMSAY,

We, under Subscribers, engage to take the above mentioned Work on
the Conditions Specified.

Proposals for Publishing by Subscription Scotch Poems, 14th April 1786: the only known example, with names of 17 subscribers in manuscript.

— sometimes in entire editions, such as the celebrated Dublin edition of 1787, but more often in the form of chapbooks, sold by pedlars and street-vendors for a penny or twopence each. These pamphlets were generally of very small format and are a prime example of the artless typography so prevalent in the 1790s. Typical of such ephemeral publications were John Lauderdale's pamphlet, c. 1795, containing 'An address to the Deil' with Lauderdale's answer. Stewart and Meikle and Brash and Reid were two Glasgow firms that specialised in producing such chapbooks, and between them they published several editions of 'The Cotter's Saturday Night', 'Tam o Shanter' and 'The Jolly Beggars' as separate works, as well as pamphlets containing small groups of shorter poems, such as 'The Twa Herds' coupled with 'The Antiquarian' (on Captain Grose's peregrinations), or 'The Toothache' coupled with 'Ye banks and braes of bonnie Doon'. Stewart and Meikle were not above printing a genuine work of Burns, such as 'The Inventory' in conjunction with 'The comforts of marriage' and 'The plundered lark' which were not of Burns's composition. A hallmark of these

Dumfries and Burns souvenir booklet, c. 1905.

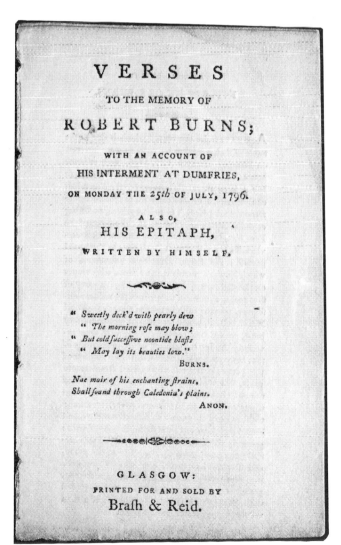

A chapbook published by Brash & Reid of Glasgow, 1796.

Chromolithograph Burns greeting card, Ayr, c. 1900.

chapbooks was the haste with which they were produced, so typographical errors abound. Of particular interest is J. Roach's series entitled *Roach's Beauties of the Poets*, number 21 of which was 'The Cotter' by Robert Burne (*sic*). This curiosity appeared in 1795. Many of these chapbooks were undated, so it is not always certain whether they were contemporary or posthumous. After the poet's death, however, Brash and Reid produced a spate of tiny eight-page pamphlets, of which *Monody on the Death of Robert Burns*, *Elegiac Stanzas applicable to the untimely Death of the celebrated Poet* and *Verses to the Memory of Robert Burns* are fairly typical. Though undated, it is fairly safe to suppose, from internal evidence, that they were published very soon after Burns's death.

Personal documents

Mention has already been made of the obituary notice in the Newcastle newspaper which included a woodcut illustration of Burns. Burns House, Dumfries, has a printer's proof of the article on the death and funeral of Burns which appeared in the *Dumfries Journal* on 26th July 1796. In addition to cuttings from newspapers in July and August 1796 featuring obituary notices of the poet, there are the *Memoir Concerning Burns* by Maria Riddell which appeared in the *Journal* in August 1796, and Robert Heron's *Memoir of the Life of the Late Robert Burns*, which originally appeared in two issues of the *Monthly Magazine* in 1796 and was then reprinted as a pamphlet the following year. No intimation of the poet's death appears to have been printed at the time. This custom was just coming into fashion about that time. Certainly, by the time of Jean Armour's death in 1834, it was well-established, and copies of the death notice and funeral invitation, produced by Robert Junior and printed by J. McDiarmid of Dumfries, are preserved in Burns House and the Birthplace Museum. The latter museum preserves an interesting collection of documents pertaining to the Burnes family. They include a certificate by the kirk session of Dundonald of the good character of William Burnes (1752); no such certificate,

unfortunately, exists in respect of Robert himself. In June 1786 he appeared before Mauchline Kirk Session and subsequently made the necessary three appearances before the congregation. In a letter of 9th July from Mossgiel to John Richmond he writes: 'the Priest, I am inform'd will give me a Certificate as a single man, if I comply with the rules of the Church, which for that very reason I intend to do.' The certificate freed Burns from any obligation towards Jean Armour and effectively wiped the slate clean, but the birth of Jean's twins on 3rd September must have affected its validity. The document itself, unfortunately, has not survived, so we do not know whether it was wholly or partially printed, but probably the latter.

The Births and Deaths Registration Act of 1836, which made registration compulsory and introduced special certificates for these purposes, was originally confined to England and Wales, and was not extended to Scotland until 1855 — far too late to apply to Robert or Jean, or those of their children who died young. I mention this because Burnsians often ask whether death certificates for the Burns family exist. They are on record, in respect of the poet's three surviving sons and, of course, anyone may obtain copies of them for a fee by writing to Register House, Edinburgh in respect of Robert Junior, or to St Catherine's House, London, in respect of William Nicol and James Glencairn. Digressing a moment, there is still much genealogical research needed to be done, especially in respect of the children fathered by Burns on Jenny Clow and May Cameron. Incidentally, the death certificate of Betty Burns (Mrs Thomson) shows her mother's name as 'Ann Hyslop', despite the fact that her mother was Anna Park, the Hyslops' niece.

On 4th June 1787 Burns visited Dumfries and was made an honorary burgess. What subsequently happened to the burgess ticket is a mystery, though it is possible that it was among the papers entrusted to Currie's none too tender care in the period immediately after the poet's death. It came to light at an exhibition of relics staged in Edinburgh's Music Hall in 1859. In 1904 it was auctioned by Sotheby's for £55 and soon afterwards acquired by John Thomson, the proprietor of the Hole i' the Wa' public-house in Dumfries. The ticket was exhibited on the wall of the public bar for many years, but about twenty years ago it was transferred, with other relics, to the burgh museum and is now on display in the Burns Centre. On 29th June 1787 Burns received a similar honour from Dumbarton during his West Highland tour. This document remained in the possession of the poet's descendants until 1923 when it was presented to the burgh of Dumbarton by Mrs Burns Gowring, a great-granddaughter of the poet, and it now hangs in the municipal buildings. The poet's commission as a member of the Company of Archers, the royal bodyguard in Scotland, was likewise retained by Burns's family until the 1850s when it was presented to the national monument on Calton Hill, Edinburgh by Colonel James Glencairn Burns. It was later

The poet's ticket as an honorary Burgess of Dumfries, 1787.

transferred to the municipal authorities when the monument was closed to the public and in recent years has been on display in Lady Stair's House in the Lawnmarket.

Pictorial Stationery and Bill-heads

The letter-sheets used in Burns's day were double sheets of paper of foolscap or quarto size when folded once, to produce four pages. The method of folding them further into three in order to seal them has already been mentioned in the notes on the poet's seals. Most people preferred the quarto sheets and as paper was expensive, sometimes a half-sheet would suffice. As postage was charged on the number of sheets used, space for letter-writing was at a premium, and for this reason alone every inch had to be utilised. If someone had a lot to say, he would fill the pages with writing horizontally, then turn the sheet round and continue at right angles, sometimes using a different colour of ink for clarity. In these circumstances, therefore, there was no incentive to stationers to provide stationery decorated with pictures. As soon as the prohibitive postal charges were drastically reduced in 1840, however, and people could send letters weighing up to half an ounce for a penny, stationers began publishing letter-sheets whose headings were decorated with finely engraved views of scenery and landmarks pertaining to the town or locality in which they were retailed. This custom became especially popular in the seaside towns and holiday resorts, and is regarded as the ancestor of the picture postcard.

From the outset, Scottish stationers were in the forefront of this movement. George Stewart & Co. of Edinburgh was one of the first firms anywhere in the British Isles to publish pictorial stationery, but they were soon followed by Lizars, better known as banknote engravers, Banks & Co. of Edinburgh, and Young & Hamilton of Glasgow. Attractive vignettes were engraved on steel plates and reproduced by the letterpress process. The pictures were quite small to begin with, but by the 1850s it was not uncommon for the picture to occupy up to half a page. With the advent of envelopes the old quarto sheets were superseded by sheets of half that size, and the pictorial element then became even more prominent, in some cases occupying more than half of the front page.

Eventually the principal publishers accommodated collectors by selling pictorial sheets in assorted packets and examples may be found written from addresses irrelevant to the picture actually shown on them. Among the more popular subjects were pictures of Burns's birthplace, the Monument and Auld Brig o Doon at Alloway, and the monument on Calton Hill, Edinburgh. Ellisland, viewed from the opposite bank of the Nith, was another favourite, while Burns House in Dumfries was one of the vignettes featured at the head of quarto sheets which showed other landmarks in the town, with an albino embossed frame. These letter sheets were issued uncoloured, but they may sometimes be found with

Pictorial letter sheets showing Burns Cottage and the Edinburgh momument.

colours applied by hand or lithographed. The Dumfries triptych is known in a colour version. The engravings used for these letter-sheets were originally those which had been produced to illustrate books or were sold as separate prints, but as the size of the letter-sheets was reduced vignettes had to be engraved specially for them. This fashion continued into the 1870s, but then went into decline as the use of pictures in bill-heads and commercial stationery increased; it became 'not quite the done thing' to emulate mere tradespeople. In the past decade, however, the wheel has come full circle, for pictorial notelets have become very fashionable. Examples have been seen showing the Cottage and the Monument, as well as a highly ornate portrait of Burns surrounded by symbols of music and poetry.

Contemporary with the pictorial letter-sheets were pictorial envelopes. Part of the reforms introduced by Rowland Hill in 1840 were prepaid envelopes — in black (one penny) or blue (twopence). These envelopes had an extraordinary motif which covered the front, leaving a small space in the centre for the name and address. Britannia appeared at the top, sending her messengers forth to every corner of the globe, and at the sides were little pictures of people in other lands reading the letters just received from the Old Country. This remarkable composition was designed by William Mulready, R.A. and the envelopes were quickly nicknamed 'Mulreadies'. The pompous design was unpopular, however, and the envelopes were withdrawn from sale in 1841, but not before they had inspired a galaxy of parodies and caricatures by Thackeray, Leech, Spooner and other humorists of the period. Such is the perversity of the public that the caricatures sold like hot cakes whereas the genuine Mulreadies met with little response. The caricatures survived the Mulreadies and, in turn, spawned a new generation of pictorial envelopes which publicised such good causes as temperance, free trade, the abolition of slavery, peace and universal brotherhood. Less serious in their intention were the sets of pictorial envelopes with genre or comic subjects. Fore of London published envelopes with musical, dancing, hunting, racing, shooting, civic, military and Christmas themes, drawn and engraved by the brothers Richard and James Doyle. One of the pioneers of pictorial envelopes was R. Hume of Leith who produced at least a score of different designs. The Hume envelopes had a principal motif on the front, with triangular vignettes on the four flaps that folded over to form the back. Hume's musical envelope number 1 is the most sought after of the entire series, because the front bears the Nasmyth portrait of Burns and the poet's autograph on the left, and a garland of red roses near the space for the stamp. The upper and lower flaps bear the music of 'O for ane and twenty, Tam', while the side flaps have the words of the second and third verses. One of these envelopes fetched £2,100 at a Robson Lowe auction in 1979.

Paradoxically, as pictorial letter sheets went out of fashion this concept was taken over and expanded by tradesmen and all kinds of business concerns. The bill-heads used by shopkeepers and tradesmen in the eighteenth century were very prosaic, and usually representing the artless typography of the local jobbing printer. In August 1795 Burns wrote to James Johnson in Edinburgh. Johnson, as well as compiling the *Scots Musical Museum*, was an engraver and printer and at the end of the long letter, which discussed songs for the *Museum*, Burns added: 'Inclosed is a job which I beg you will finish pretty soon. — It is a Bill, as you will see, for a tavern. — The Tavern-keeper Hyslop is a good honest fellow; as I lie under particular obligations to him, I request that you may do it for him on the most reasonable terms. — If there is any fancy that you would wish to introduce, by way of additional ornament, let me know but I think, the simpler it is, the better. — The **tavern is at the sign of the Globe** — for which reason **it must have a Globe at the top.** — I think the model

Commercial Bill-head, Robinson Bros. of Dumfries.

of the Bill which is inclosed, is a good size but you are a better judge. Let me have a proof sheet, ere you finish it. — I write you in a day or two.—'

Johnson executed the job and sent a proof of the bill-head to Burns who did not reply till about 23rd September, owing to ill health. 'I am highly pleased with Hyslop's bill,' he wrote, 'only you have, in your usual luck, mispelt two words. — The article — *Postages* porter — you have made, *Porterages* porter — pray, alter that. — In the article — Pipes Tobacco — you have spelt Tobacco thus — To*bb*acco — whereas it is spelt with a single b, thus — Tobacco. — When you have amended these two faults, which please do directly, throw off five hundred copies; send them by the very first coach or fly.'

Spelling was not Johnson's strong-point! These letters shed light on the production of the bills used in taverns which, in those days, enumerated all the services provided, from food and drink, right down to hay for the horse. No example of the bill produced by Johnson for the Globe Inn at Burns's request is now known to exist, but ephemera of this sort is just the kind of material which may be lying undetected to this day in the mouldering bundles of vouchers stored in many country solicitor's offices, in the rusting deed-boxes and chests of clients long dead.

Bill-heads of the Globe Inn and Oughton's Cafe.

Letterheads of the Ayr, Calgary and Lochee Burns Clubs.

Presumably the Hyslop bill had some pictorial representation of a globe in the heading. It will be noted that Burns advised Johnson against anything fancy, implying that the fashion for more ornate bill-heads was even then coming in. Thomas Bewick, the illustrator of the rare Alnwick edition of the Poems in 1808, had for almost thirty years prior to that been producing woodcut engravings of great beauty and sensitivity for such mundane articles as tradesmen's advertisements and bill-heads. As early as 1781 he engraved a majestic cock lording it over other farmyard creatures, on the heading used by the Cock Inn at Newcastle, and other early examples of his work include a splendid Chéviot ram against a scenic background, for Thomas Smith of Woodhall (1798) and a suspended sheep, on the bill-head used by a woollen draper. Pictorialism crept into Scottish bill-heads by the end of the eighteenth century, but did not reach its zenith until the second half of the nineteenth century when lithography offered far greater scope than line-engraving.

The tradesmen and shopkeepers of Ayr, Mauchline, Kilmarnock and Dumfries were not slow to incorporate Burns motifs in their bill-heads. Perennial favourites, naturally, were the Cottage, Brig and Monument at Alloway, the Gothic extravaganza in the Kay Park , Burns's statues in Ayr and Dumfries and even the Mausoleum itself. Portraits of Burns himself were also employed, though more sparingly, but they have been recorded in the headings used by purveyors of shortbread, whisky and haggis. The vogue for elaborate pictorial bill-heads declined at the beginning of this century, but as late as the 1930s Oughton's Restaurant in Dumfries was using bill-heads and stationery featuring the statue by Amelia Hill in an Art Deco setting. So far as I am aware, the only commercial establishment in Dumfries which still has a Burnsian letter-head is, appropriately, the Globe Inn which features the Nasmyth portrait with an excerpt from one of the poet's letters '... the Globe Tavern here which for these many years has been my Howff'. The stationery used by Alloway Publishing Limited, which has carved a niche for itself in the field of Burns literature in recent years, has adopted a motif showing a field-mouse on a corn-stalk — an obvious reference to Burns's much-loved poem 'To a Mouse'.

Burns club letter-heads

As lithography gave way to the cheaper half-tone process early this century, there was a brief fashion in commercial stationery for rather fuzzy pictures reproduced from photographs. The generally unsatisfactory nature of these pictures, however, ushered in an era which relied on different styles of lettering for effect. As the pictorial bill-head waned, the use of pictorialism became more popular in the stationery used by Burns clubs and Scottish societies around the world. So far as I can judge, from examples of club stationery which I have seen, the vast majority of the clubs up to and even after the Second World War preferred a simple, non-figural style of letter-head, but a few of the Caledonian and St Andrew's societies overseas adopted a heraldic theme, with thistles, rampant lions and saltire crosses, but never an actual portrait of the bard. In more recent times, however, pictorialism has become the rule. To be sure, there are still a few Burns clubs which prefer a staid approach, with a non-pictorial heading, but most of them now opt for something more eye-catching. Conversely some of the oldest clubs, in Greenock, Paisley, Ayr and Dumfries, were using pictorial stationery by the 1890s, and even the Burns Federation itself had a highly ornate letter-head in the centenary year of the poet's death.

The most popular motif, not surprisingly, is the Nasmyth bust-portrait, often flanked by the poet's dates of birth and death. The stationery used by A' the Airts Burns club also incorporates Burns's autograph. It has to be admitted that the quality of reproduction varies considerably from club to club. Some impressions have obviously come from blocks which ought to have been pensioned off many years ago; others are little more than caricatures of Nasmyth. On the other hand there are a few portraits which have been embellished. Lochee, for example, adds an open book and bouquet of thistles below the bust, while Cumbernauld has an outline of a ploughing scene below the portrait. Airdrie adds an ornate floral frame to the portrait, while the Burns Club of London has the poet's motto — 'Better a wee bush than nae bield' — round the foot of the cartouche. The Ayrshire Association of Burns Clubs used to have a not very good likeness of the bard (closer, in fact, to a certain Irish chat-show host on television) surrounded by a laurel wreath, but in more recent years this has been superseded by a more accurate rendering of Nasmyth framed within the outline of a thistle-head. The Scottish Burns Club of Edinburgh has the Nasmyth bust wreathed with thistles, and 'The Heart ay's the pairt ay' at the foot. Most letter-heads show the portrait in black, but Humberside, Alloway and Burnie (Australia) have opted for Scottish blue, while Canterbury (New Zealand) uses a curious orange-brown shade. Just to be different, the Robert Burns Club of San Diego has the Nasmyth portrait reversed.

By contrast, Archibald Skirving's chalk drawing, though generally highly regarded, has found little favour with the clubs. It is to be found in the heading used by the Burns Anniversary Committee of Rhode Island. The Glasgow District Burns Association has an excellent reproduction of this portrait in the upper right-hand corner while the opposite corner bears a picture of Jean Armour, based on the bust-portrait sculpted by Kellock Brown. For good measure, these letter-sheets have a panoramic view of the Jean Armour Burns houses at Mauchline, for which the Association is responsible, across the foot.

Although eminently suited to letter-heads, the Miers silhouette appears to have been confined to the stationery used by the Calgary Burns club, depicted in deep purple on a rich cream ground with decorative inscription in black and 'A man's a man for a' that' across the foot of the portrait, producing a most eye-catching effect. The Miers silhouette was also used in the stationery connected with the editions of the *Complete Works* and *Complete Letters* published by the Burns Federation in conjunction with Alloway Publishing of Darvel. Kilmarnock Burns club uses the left-facing silhouette by Samuel Houghton, in a laurel wreath with the dates of birth and death at the foot.

A very select group uses the heraldic device as described by Burns to Cunningham and engraved on his last seal, despite the fact that these arms were never matriculated by either the poet or his descendants. This device, in the form of a shield with the woodlark as crest and the two mottoes, appears on the letter-heads used by the Greenock and Paisley clubs whose rival claims to be the oldest Burns clubs dates back to the beginning of the nineteenth century. The armorial badge is also used by the Dumfries Burns club, the Burns Howff club (Dumfries) and the Southern Scottish Counties Burns Association. It is obvious that the Association and the Dumfries Burns club have utilised the same printing block, but the Howff has an altogether more satisfactory version, as befits the club which has raised the money for the poet's arms to be matriculated on behalf of the Burns Federation at long last.

Pictorialism is not entirely dead. The Kilmarnock Bowling club — not a Burns club as such, but a venerable institution dating back almost twenty years before the poet was born — has a picture of the Kay Park monument in its letter-heading. The Sunderland Burns club has a tiny vignette of the Cottage, which is at least recognisable, which is more than can be said for the minuscule engraving in the letter-head used by the Trustees of Burns Monument at Alloway. This engraving, measuring a mere 24 x 10mm, is so microscopic and cluttered with fine horizontal shading in the background, as to be almost illegible. Ayr Burns club, on the other hand, has the most elaborate letter-head of all, with a fine view of 'Auld Ayr wham ne'er a toon surpasses', with the Twa Brigs in the foreground. This vignette is flanked by the club's monogram (left) and the poet's arms (right), the whole ensemble decorated with thistles. One of the most beautiful letter-heads of all time was that used by the National Burns Memorial at Mauchline in the 1890s, with a fine vignette showing the Tower.

Picture Postcards

When Burns wrote, in his verse epistle to Mr McAdam of Craigengillan:

Sir, o'er a gill I gat your card

National Burns Memorial at Mauchline.

J. LEIPER GEMMILL, President.
162 St VINCENT St. GLASGOW.

MARCUS BAIN, Vice President,
WOODSIDE, MAUCHLINE.

THOMAS KILLIN., Treasurer,
168 WEST GEORGE St GLASGOW.

W.S. McMILLAN, Hon Secretary,
102 BATH St GLASGOW.

Letterhead of the National Burns Memorial at Mauchline, 1896.

he was not referring to the postcards we know and use to this day. Postcards were invented in Austria in 1869 and extended to Britain a year later. Oddly enough, as far back as 1777 the French engraver Demaison is said to have invented the first greetings cards, and sent them by post without enclosing them in a cover. His scheme foundered because people were afraid that their private messages might be read by their servants! Be that as it may, it was a well-established custom by the last quarter of the eighteenth century for people to write brief notes on their visiting cards — which were, at that time, about the size of a playing card — and would enclose them either in a letter-sheet or in a small envelope designed for that purpose. Bearing in mind that envelopes doubled the postage, it is unlikely that this custom extended to the General Post, but envelopes could be used at no extra charge in the local Penny Post, operated privately in Edinburgh and environs by Peter Williamson (1773-93), and it is well known that Burns made use of this service. Moreover, cards were often sent under cover privately, by servant or messenger, and such missives would not attract postage at all. There are many references in the poet's correspondence to the sending and receipt of 'cards'.

When reservations, about sending messages through the post that could be read by all and sundry, were overcome, and Austria's experiment was seen to be very successful, the idea was adopted by Britain on 1st October 1870. This expedient answered the criticism that postage had remained at the same level for thirty years and that some cheaper method ought to be introduced for the transmission of circulars and printed matter. The postcard cost only a halfpenny and rapidly caught on as a cheaper alternative to letter-writing, if one only wished to send a brief message. Mr Gladstone was a very enthusiastic user of postcards and by using very tiny writing could cram as much on to a card as most people got in a letter. Appropriately, one of the exhibits at the Centenary Exhibition (1285) was a postcard from Gladstone extolling the merits of Burns and Scott. At the outset, however, the Post Office held a monopoly of postcards. Only the official cards, bearing an impressed stamp, could be sent through the post. Private cards had to be enclosed in an envelope and

transmitted at the full penny rate. This rule was not relaxed until 1894. Other countries had more liberal regulations and permitted the use of privately printed cards, so that a pictorial element gradually crept in from the 1870s onwards.

As soon as the ban on private cards was lifted in 1894, British stationers began producing picture postcards. First in the field was Stewart of Edinburgh, who had led the way with pictorial envelopes half a century earlier. These cards were much smaller than they are today, and conformed to the Post Office 'court' size. Only the name and address of the recipient were permitted on the stamp side. Consequently the picture was confined to a small part of the front, with space for the message underneath. On 1st November 1899, however, the Post Office relinquished the last vestige of its monopoly and stationers were permitted to produce full-size cards like their European counterparts. Britain pioneered the 'divided back' in 1902. A vertical line on the back now separated the message from the address, and this allowed the picture to take up all of the space on the front.

In view of the quarter of a century head start which Continental publishers had over their British rivals, it is hardly surprising that the earliest postcards to portray Robert Burns hailed not from Scotland but from Germany. Burns was one of the literary figures included in a series of German origin in 1889. Two versions exist: one with the Nasmyth bust alone, and the other incorporating scenes associated with the poet. Burns was also featured in the series published by Blum Degen in 1899, along with Shakespeare, Scott, Dickens, Tennyson, Longfellow and Byron. The first British cards portraying Burns appeared at the turn of the century, just before the divided back was introduced. The Edinburgh firm of W. & A.K. Johnston produced several sets of Burns postcards from 1902 onwards, the most sought after being those which reproduced Faed's paintings in chromolithography. Other firms which were early in this field, with some very attractive all-colour cards, included the Art Publishing Company, Stoddart & Company and Raphael Tuck. The last-named firm devoted several of its famous 'Oilette' series to Burns with scenes from his life and works. Thereafter

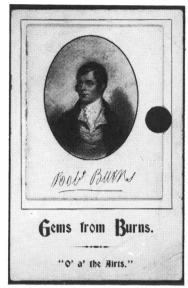

Novelty postcard: the flap lifts to reveal the text of "Of A' the Airts". *Chromolithograph postcard showing Jean Armour and scenes from the life of Burns in Mauchline.*

Chromolithograph postcard issued by the Glasgow and Southwestern Railway, showing Burns Cottage and monument at Alloway.

virtually ever postcard publisher in Britain and many of those in Germany as well, included Burns portraits and scenes in their repertoire. In addition to the artistic chromolithographs of the Edwardian era there were numerous cards which reproduced real photographs in black and white or sepia tones. One of the first in this field was Beecham whose cards included the monument on Calton Hill, the Mausoleum, the Twa Brigs, the Cottage (both exterior and interior views), Lawson's statue in Ayr, the monument at Doonside, Auld Brig-o-doon (sic), Alloway Kirk, the Kay Park monument, Poosie Nansie's in Mauchline, the figures of Tam o Shanter and Souter Johnny at Alloway, the Nasmyth bust-portrait and Burns and Highland Mary by their trysting thorn. Later, such firms as Judges of Hastings and Valentine of Dundee produced much more extensive series of Burns cards. All of the statues, monuments and memorials, in Scotland at any rate, have appeared in postcard form, and to this may be added the statues of Highland Mary and her grave at Greenock, known in both monochrome and coloured versions. One of the rarer cards reproduces a photograph by George Washington Wilson about 1885 of Burns's first house in Dumfries. Cards are also known which show the replicas of the poet's birthplace which were features of the St Louis World's Fair (1904), the Scottish Village at the Imperial International Exhibition in London (1909) and the Aberdeen Exhibition at Olympia (1933). The 1904 replica was subsequently removed to Portland, Oregon but in 1907 it was purchased by the Burns club of Atlanta, Georgia and transferred thither in 1910. Postcards showing the Cottage in Atlanta are known in monochrome as well as colour.

In the 1920s and 1930s, postcards may have lacked the artistic appeal of their Edwardian predecessors, but the range was widened still further. Relatively obscure subjects, associated with the poet because he had visited them, were brought into the Burns orbit, usually with a caption alluding to the connexion, or quoting appropriate lines from his works. Inevitably reproductions of the Nasmyth bust-portraits (but seldom the full-length portrait) and the Skirving drawing proliferated in colour or monochrome, but in recent years a detail from the Hardie painting of Burns in Edinburgh has enjoyed a measure of popularity. The paintings by Hardie and Christie have also been widely reproduced in recent years.

The vast majority of the paintings, prints and engravings illustrative of the poet's works have also, at one time or another, been reproduced in this medium, often being embellished with appropriate quotations. Just when postcards were in danger of becoming too sentimental and sugary, a breath of fresh air was injected by such artists as Dudley Hardy, Phil May, Fred Spurgin, 'Cynicus' (Martin Anderson) and, above all, Donald McGill who would take a line or two from a Burns poem and give it a comic interpretation. Hamish Duncan was a prolific artist whose humorous figures of kilted boy and girl, or old couple, were featured on countless cards illustrating the works of Burns in a pawky, off-beat manner. These cards, signed 'Hamish' were published in Tuck's Oilette series, but this artist also had his work reproduced in the Reliable series, published by Royle. These comic cards had their heyday before the First World War but they then declined in popularity. There are also sepia photographic cards with colour tints showing men and women in sentimental poses to accompany the words and music of some of Burns's great love songs. These song cards were a speciality of Bamforth who published several thousand different varieties, though the number with a Burns theme probably extends to no more than a few dozen. Song cards including works by Burns were also published by Davidson Brothers, Raphael Tuck and Valentine.

Probably the most highly prized of all cards are the beautiful chromolithographs executed by Maclure and Macdonald of Glasgow at the turn of the century on behalf of the Glasgow and Southwestern Railway, whose crest adorns the corner of the picture side. Several of these cards featured scenes in the Burns country, notably the Cottage and the Monument. Because of their railway interest, these rare cards have long been much sought-after by railway enthusiasts, and the Burns angle has greatly enhanced their value.

Several cards of a quasi-political nature were produced in the 1950s, in the period shortly before the poet's bicentenary. Such cards bore rather crude portraits of Burns, with quotations from his letters and poems on the subject of Scottish independence or the rights of man. Relatively few cards, however, celebrated the bicentenary itself — perhaps because the picture postcard, as a commemortive medium, was largely out of fashion at that period. Ironically, the great centenary celebrations of 1896 came just a little too early for postcard commemoration. It is significant that, although the regulations had been relaxed less than two years earlier, no one seems to have considered applying this new medium to the celebrations. Although several photographers produced mounted prints of the celebrations in Dumfries, for example, notably the wreath-laying ceremony performed by Lord Rosebery, not one of them published these pictures in postcard form.

Since the 1970s there has been a renaissance of the commemorative postcard and many fine examples have been produced to mark events of royal and international importance in recent years. It is all the more surprising that so far none of the bicentenaries associated with Burns, from the publication of the Kilmarnock Poems (1986) onwards, have been accorded a postcard tribute, but it is to be hoped that this deficiency will be remedied by the time of the death anniversary in 1996.

From the early years of this century date other kinds of postcard. At one end of the spectrum were the very narrow 'bookmark' cards — just large, enough to bear a stamp and the address, alongside a very brief message. Then there were the novelty cards which had a flap on the picture side. This lifted to reveal a dozen or more tiny photographs folded concertina-fashion. Such cards were not so popular because the Post Office insisted that they be treated as letters and pay the full postage; consequently they are relatively elusive nowadays. Composite cards invariably had a portrait of Burns in the centre, with four or more tiny vignettes in the surrounding space. Illustrated letter cards were developed in the 1920s and consisted of a thin card or glossy paper outer cover, whose flap opened to reveal several postcard-size pictures printed on glossy paper, either concertina-fashion or in the form of a sheet folded in four. The outer cover was often relatively plain, but examples are known with the Nasmyth bust. A typical example is the Mauchline Holy Fair letter-card, published by Dinwiddie of Dumfries, which featured the Nasmyth bust and a tiny vignette of Burns House,

The "Post Book" — a 64-page booklet intended for transmission by post.

Christmas cards depicting Ellisland and Burns House, Dumfries.

Dumfries on the address side. The interior reproduced the famous painting by Alexander Carse, together with a key to the figures depicted. This painting was formerly in the possession of John MacMahon of Castle Tolmie, Inverness and was at one time on loan to Burns House. The letter-card dates from that period, before the painting was transferred to the Birthplace Museum. Perhaps the strangest 'postcard' of all was that produced by Eyre and Spottiswoode. Known as a 'Post Book', it was a 64-page booklet whose paper cover had a gummed flap that could be sealed over the back. The back cover had an all-over thistle and white heather pattern, with a space in the centre for the stamp and address. The front was entitled 'Where we have been and what we have seen' with *The Burns Country* at the top. Three titles were published, the other volumes dealing with Edinburgh and Glasgow (with the Clyde coast), and they were sold for sixpence each. The Burns volume is a remarkable piece of work, with an excellent map, ample text and some very attractive colour illustrations.

Greetings cards

Christmas and New Year cards, dating from the late nineteenth century, are known with verses from Burns's poems. The earliest examples are beautifully chromolithographed with an abundance of cut-paper and embossing. The cards published in the early years of this century, up to the Second World War, were less ornate, although examples are known with pictures of landmarks and scenery associated with Burns and verses to match. A particularly charming series of Christmas cards was produced at one time by Robert Dinwiddie of Dumfries and reproduced vignettes by Alec Graham (who later achieved international renown as a cartoonist). These cards were embellished with raised albino embossing on a coloured ground, a most unusual effect. Many Burns clubs produce their own distinctive cards not only for exchange with kindred societies at Christmas and the New Year but, increasingly in recent years, for St Andrew's Day and Burns Nicht. Several of the older clubs have also produced greetings cards to celebrate their centenaries or sesquicentennials.

Tickets of Admission

Tickets, made of stout carton or pasteboard, intended to denote admission to places of entertainment, are known from the early nineteenth century. Probably the earliest associated with Burns were those produced in 1859 in connexion with the various celebrations marking the centenary of the poet's birth. These tickets are known for admission to the Grand Festival in Belfast, the Glasgow Festival, celebrations in Ayr, Kilmarnock and Dumfries, and the Crystal Palace in London but it is probable that tickets existed for celebrations at a much earlier date, though none has so far been recorded. Apart from the very early, but probably quite informal, dinners held at Alloway, Greenock and Paisley, there was a Burns dinner at Oxford university as early as 1806 and from the formal nature of that banquet it seems likely that proper tickets would have been printed. Similarly, two dinners were held in 1816 which must be regarded as celebrations of Burns on a national scale. These were the Commemoration Dinner in London, held in May to raise money for the Mausoleum fund, and the great Birthday Dinner held in Edinburgh that January, attended by Sir Walter Scott, Alexander Boswell, George Thomson and other leading literary figures of the period. A grand banquet, seating 2,000 no less, was the highlight of the 1844 festival to mark the re-union of the three surviving sons of Burns. As an enormous crowd, variously estimated between 50,000 and 100,000, attended this festival, some form of ticket must have been printed to separate the paying guests from the multitude.

Certainly the 1859 celebrations marked a watershed, and thereafter the ephemera associated with Burnsian events is well documented, due in large measure to James Gould, described in the contemporary press as 'a working-man of Edinburgh'. At a time when artisans laboured sixty hours a week for a pound or less, the working classes had neither leisure nor surplus disposable income with which to indulge in hobbies. Gould must have possessed the characteristics of the true collector — an absolute single-mindedness with the subject he pursued. At the time of the 1859 celebrations he decided to form a collection of menus, programmes, toast-lists, newspaper reports and even advertisements connected with these events. Although tickets are not mentioned specifically in the press report of his collection (1882), these trifles were certainly included, for they are preserved in the volumes which passed eventually into the hands of the Mitchell Library.

The earliest tickets were quite simple in design, with letterpress inscriptions and a minimum of ornament. By the 1880s, however, they were becoming much more ambitious, and frequently incorporated a woodcut portrait of Burns himself, or his heraldic insignia. At the turn of the century these tickets attained their maximum size, some being not much smaller than modern postcards. Artistically, they also peaked about this time, with much use of floral ornament and even embossed and gilded borders. Most clubs suspended their activities, including Burns suppers, during the First World War and from the 1920s onwards tickets have usually been more utilitarian in design. Among the exceptions, however, may be cited some of the invitation cards to civic receptions and banquets in connexion with the annual conferences of the Burns Federation. Other tickets of outstanding design are those which were produced in connexion with certain theatrical shows, pageants and even television shows. Even the rather prosaic tickets issued at the Birthplace museum, the Monument, Burns House and other locations which make an admission charge, should not be overlooked. In this respect Dumfries leads the field in the size and complexity of its 'all-in' tickets, which include circular spaces for the rubber stamps of the local Burns sites. The pictorial rubber stamps are also applied by favour to postcards and other souvenirs on request, and in this guise are discussed in the next chapter.

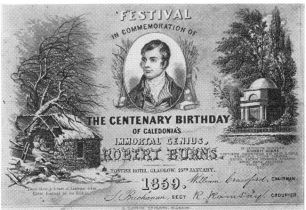

Ticket to the Burns Centenary Festival, Glasgow, 1859 (Allan Stoddart Collection).

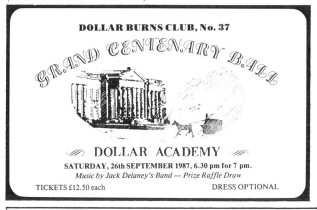

Admission tickets: (a) Burns Exhibition, Glasgow, 1896; (b) Dollar Burns Club Centenary Banquet, 1987.

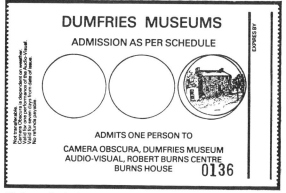

Ticket of admission to Burns House, the Robert Burns Centre and Burgh Museum, Dumfries.

*Cigarette cards depicting Burns and scenes and characters
from his works.*

Cigarette Cards

Older readers may recall the street cry of Scottish urchins half a century ago, as they accosted passers-by, 'Ony fag picturs?' Those little picture cards evolved in 1879 out of the plain card stiffeners inserted in the paper packets of cigarettes, and by 1885 had become a highly developed miniature art form in their own right. The vast majority of the cards now in the hands of collectors date between 1902, when the number of companies was drastically reduced by a series of mergers, and 1940 when paper shortages during the Second World War caused their demise. There were fleeting attempts to revive them in the 1950s and 1960s, but the advent of the cigarette coupons has ousted them completely.

Although the Dublin tobacco company P.J. Carroll had a brand of cigarette named 'Sweet Afton' which one assumes was inspired by Burns, no cigarette cards issued with this brand depicted or pertained to the bard. Other manufacturers paid passing tribute to Burns. Ardath, for example, issued a series of 25 cards in June 1935 entitled 'Famous Scots'. Two years previously Stephen Mitchell of Glasgow had a much more ambitious series of fifty cards in the same theme. One of the earliest sets after the 1902 merger was John Player's 'Authors and Poets'. Burns is featured on one of these very rare cards; fortunately the Ardath and Mitchell cards are fairly common. Burns scenes were included in such sets as 'Scottish Gems', issued in four sets ranging from 50 to 72 in number by J. Duncan of Glasgow; 'Historic Buildings of Scotland', a rare set issued about 1918 by Fairweather of Dundee; 'Beautiful Scotland,' issued by Gallaher about 1920; a set of 48 with the same title by Illingworth of Kendal in 1939; Mitchell's 'Statues and Monuments', a series of 25 released in 1914, and 'Scotland's Story', issued as a set of 50 in 1929; and 'Beautiful Scotland' by J.A. Pattrieouex of Manchester in a series of 48 in 1939.

In 1924, however, the Scottish Co-operative Wholesale Society issued a set of 25 cards entirely devoted to Robert Burns. This series exists in three distinct versions: with a plain back, or with a printed back on either white or cream card, the last-named being the commonest. Cards in a vertical format depicted Robert Burns, Jean Armour, the Mausoleum, the Calton Hill monument and scenes from 'Of a' the airts', 'John Barleycorn', 'Gae bring to me', 'Ye banks and braes', 'Holy Willie's Prayer', 'To Mary in Heaven' and 'Mary Morison'. The horizontal cards depicted Mossgiel, Ellisland, the Twa Brigs of Ayr, the Auld Brig o Doon and Monument at Alloway, Alloway Kirk, the Cottage near Ayr, and Dumfries, as well as scenes from 'Tam o Shanter', 'Flow gently sweet Afton', 'Duncan Gray', 'The Cotter's Saturday Night', 'John Anderson my jo', 'The Twa Dogs' and 'Auld Lang Syne'. A framed set of these cigarette cards may be seen in the Globe Inn, Dumfries.

Trade cards and advertisements

Advertising material is really an extension of the bills and letter-heads discussed previously and in many cases would have been produced by the same jobbing printers, using stock founts of type and occasional woodblock or copperplate engravings by way of illustration. The earliest advertisement connected with Burns — if we except the prospectus for the Poems themselves — is believed to be the small broadsheet which advertised the excursion to Alloway of members of the Burns Club of Greenock and the Greenock Ayrshire Society which took place on 25th January 1803. This interesting advertisement was displayed at the Centenary Exhibition of 1896. Some idea of the advertising material which boldly — nay, quite shamelessly — exploited the 'Immortal Memory' may be gained by perusing the pages at the back of the various catalogues published in 1896 (in Ayr, Kilmarnock, Paisley, Dumfries and elsewhere), as well as in the very early issues of the *Burns Chronicle*. The products which took the poet's name in vain ranged from whisky and haggis to perfume and nerve tonic, and there was even a brand of footwear known as Rabbie Burns Boots! The *Dumfries and Galloway Standard* regularly devotes an issue to the bard at the end of January and the opportunity is taken by local firms to advertise in the Burnsian mode. Seven out of eight of these advertisements will be seen with variants of the Nasmyth bust. Your Burns supper table is incomplete without Dinwiddie's napkins, Burns Cafe offers tasty hot meals served all day, the Globe Inn urges you to visit the poet's favourite howff, and no fewer than four butchers recommend their guid Scots haggis. Of these a special prize for effort must go to Malcolm MacKay of Thornhill for bursting into verse:

> In Thornhill's famous tree-lined streets
> Where Rabbie once passed by
> There is a shop where ye can stop
> And get the real MacKay!

The Burns hairdressing salon may cavil at using the bard's portrait in its advertisement, but we are told 'Rabbie had a distinctive head — you can have your hair expertly styled in the latest fashion… Hair pieces and wigs for Gents a confidential service.'

Two of the above-mentioned businesses also produced trade cards. These were a form of advertisement designed to be handed out and passed around rather like visiting cards. Indeed, the earliest examples of this medium were of the same size and printed on stout pasteboard, with the same tasteful penchant for copperplate engraving. As bill-heads became pictorial, so also did trade cards, but after the First World War they tended to revert to much simpler letterpress motifs. Nowadays there has been a renaissance in pictorialism, as the cards are recognised as a valuable sales aid and have to be as eye-catching as possible. When I settled in Dumfries about sixteen years ago Kevin the hair stylist in Bank Street had the Nasmyth bust on his cards. After all, his premises are where John Syme had his stamp office, and the Burns family lived in the upstairs flat from 1791 to 1793. Mogerley's in nearby Friars Vennel has an interesting trade card which not only features the Nasmyth painting but, on the reverse, gives the most detailed cooking instructions for haggis. Some very attractive cards portraying the bard's widow are used to advertise Jean Armour's Pantry, the restaurant at the Burns Centre, Dumfries.

Playing cards

'The Deil's picture-books', as Burns called them, tongue in cheek, were invented by the Chinese and are believed to have been some kind of written notation for dice. European cards are known, from stray literary references, to have been in use in Venice in the thirteenth century though the oldest pack extant dates from about 1440, the cards being of French manufacture. By the middle of the eighteenth century pictorial playing cards had come into fashion in England, although the antipathy of the Kirk probably militated against them in Scotland to any extent. The cards current in London in the time of Burns were often produced in series with an educational element in their illustrations. There are many novelty packs from this period, with humorous, satirical, erotic or political undertones. The fashion for highly decorative packs declined after 1850, probably in line with the resurgence of puritanism in Victorian Britain. Nevertheless some attractive sets continued to be manufactured. De La Rue had a virtual monopoly of the playing card business in England, but Maclure and Macdonald of Glasgow (who produced some beautiful chromolithographs of Burns) issued a pack of cards which was displayed at

Trade card for Mogerley's, Dumfries.

Trade card for Jean Armour's Pantry, Dumfries.

Trade card for Kevin, Hair Stylist, Dumfries.

Burns Calendar by Holmes MacDougall.

the Centenary Exhibition. The Nasmyth bust was enclosed by a quotation:

> Now, by the powers o verse and prose
> Thou art a dainty chiel.

Less decorative and more commercial packs have been recorded from the early years of this century, again featuring the ubiquitous Nasmyth portrait, while packs showing Tam o Shanter or the Jolly Beggars have been reported, though I have not been able to confirm either of them.

Calendars

Over the years portraits of Burns and pictures of his statues and other landmarks associated with him must have adorned countless calendars. The pictures themselves have often been preserved as attractive examples of chromolithography or photogravure, but it is likely that few of these annual publications have survived intact. Valentine's of Dundee produced a calendar before the Second World War decorated with multicoloured vignettes of characters and scenes around a representation of the Nasmyth portrait. The Mitchell Library possesses a fine example of the very rare Robert Burns Calendar for 1887, which was issued by Duncan Campbell & Son of Glasgow. Now, a century later, the Burns Federation has sponsored a calendar which will undoubtedly rank as a work of art in years to come. I had the privilege of contributing the text to accompany the series of twelve pictures painted by John Mackay.

Menus

How the French word for 'minute' or 'detailed' passed into the English language to denote a list of the courses in a restaurant is curious. The custom of setting out the details of a meal began in France in the early years of the nineteenth century at a time when Napoleon's armies were sweeping victoriously across Europe. Cards setting out the bill of fare were ornamented with patriotic motifs and tiny vignettes of battle scenes. The martial flavour swiftly disappeared after Waterloo but the habit of decorated cards lingered on and soon spread to other parts of Europe. The earliest menus were appearing in England in 1816, and it is tempting to speculate whether either of the two great national Burns dinners held that year

used such cards. The lengthy (and rather verbose) accounts of these events, however, do not mention the actual bill of fare, although we learn that the toast lists were long and varied. Toast lists were similar to menus, and recited the toasts to be drunk, and the names of the gentlemen proposing them and those responding. Eventually it became customary to print the bill of fare on the left and the toast list on the right within an elaborately decorated folder but the earliest menus and toast lists were tall, single sheets printed on one side only.

James Gould, the Edinburgh collector previously mentioned, determined to collect everything connected with the celebrations of 1859. In addition to the tickets and programmes he amassed every menu and toast list he could lay his hands on. As far as possible, he tried also to get the autographs of all those who presided at the various dinners and banquets held throughout the world on that memorable 25th January, and endeavoured to keep up with the Burns Nicht celebrations in the ensuing quarter of a century. Curiously enough only a solitary menu was shown at the Centenary Exhibition, lent by the notable Edinburgh collector H.D. Colvill-Scott, but no details of date or circumstances were given in the catalogue.

In the last quarter of the nineteenth century menus were printed on stout cards, on one side only. The bill of fare occupied a relatively small space in the centre, the rest being lavishly decorated with finely engraved vignettes. The Dumfries Burns Club, for example, had its menu printed on thick pink card, with the Nasmyth bust at the top, flanked by Burns House and the Mausoleum, and showing an elaborate panorama of Tam o Shanter pursued by the witches, with Alloway's auld haunted kirk in the background. Menus continued to be printed on single sheets of very stout card, generally with a decorative back, until the beginning of this century. By the eve of the First World War, however, they had become more elaborate and in some cases resembled large booklets, with up to a dozen pages in stout covers. The bill of fare and toast list occupied the centre spread, but other pages might be devoted to the history of the club, fraternal greetings from other clubs, potted biographies of the club's leading lights, even an illustrated account of the Burns relics held by the club, or details of the poet's associations with the town or district. When the clubs resumed their social activities after the war more modest menus were adopted. Dumfries Burns Club did not meet until January 1920, when it was the club's centenary. The menu was a courageous eight-page effort with the outer cover decorated in gold ink and the civic insignia embossed in gold leaf. Burns himself, after Nasmyth, appeared modestly on page three, while successive pages bore the bill of fare, the list of ten toasts, the roll of presidents and secretaries since 1820, the current office-bearers and greetings to other clubs, from lines which had been sung at the anniversary dinner in 1820. After the dinner the speeches were reprinted in a souvenir book which had a specimen of the menu bound into the centre.

Dumfries Burns Club menu card, 1896.

Burns Anniversary programme, 1897.

Mauchline Jolly Beggars' programme, 1896.

Poosie Nansie's programme, 1899.

Right: Billboard man illustration on programme of 1895.

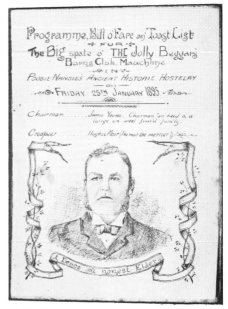

Jolly Beggars' programme, Mauchline, 1895.

Selection of Burns Club and Conference menu cards.

Below: Burns Supper menu from SS Reina del Pacifico, 1937.

Below right: Burns souvenir menu used on British Airways Prestwick-North America routes, 1979.

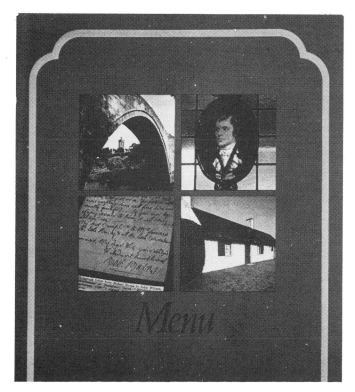

Menus in subsequent years have been more modest, but deserve mention on account of the ornate design of the cover, showing the ghost of Burns hovering over a table on which appears the club's most treasured relics, with Gilfillan's painting of Jean in the background. A view of Ellisland flanks this motif, while a thistle-decked vignette of Burns House appears at the foot.

Looking through my collection of Burns menus at random I note, among the more decorative examples, menus from the Mauchline club's celebrations in Poosie Nansie's printed at 'Ye Burns Press, Mauchline', with a much sharper impression of the Cottage thumbnail sketch than appears on the Alloway Trustees notepaper. Alloway Burns club, before the Second World War, had collotypes of the Nasmyth portrait mounted in a heavily embossed thistle border and a polychrome turned down corner showing yet another thistle. Some of the most elaborate prewar menus were those which showed the sumptuous fare of the Calcutta Burns club, now sadly defunct.

Although many clubs suspended operations during the Second World War, quite a few continued to hold their anniversary dinner. One of the most original menus was that used at the Scottish Burns club's 41st 'yearly foregaither' in 1944. The ghost of Burns is shown over the top table whose principal speakers were depicted in cartoon form by Tom Curr. My menu actually bears the autographs of the speakers above their respective portraits — truly a unique memento.

Among the more interesting or unusual of the postwar menus was that for the dinner at the North British Hotel, Edinburgh, in connexion with the International Burns Festival in 1955; this had a rather Dickensian vignette on the cover, by A. Paterson, showing the toasting of the Immortal Memory. The International Dinner, held at Ayr a week earlier, had as its cover motif the Burns Federation's badge with Centenary bar, while the six inner pages portrayed Burns, gave the bill of fare and reproduced the frontispeice from the Scottish Burns club dinner of 1928 and a facsimile of Burns's manuscript of 'Scots wha hae'. The two centre pages were devoted to 'The Nicht's Ongauns'. What a star-studded occasion that must have been. Four years later the Bicentenary celebrations were conducted on an even more lavish scale, the highlight being the grand dinner held in Kilmarnock by the Burns Federation on 24th January 1959. London's Robert Burns Club claimed a record attendance of 504 at its dinner, but that was as nothing compared with the 700 diners at the bicentenary dinner held by the Burns club of Cuyahago County in the United States, or the vast throng which celebrated the poet's birthday in Moscow's Tschaikovsky Hall.

In the 1960s menus in general became more colourful, due to better facilities for excellent multicolour printing. This ushered in the era in which the Nasmyth bust-portraits and the full-length painting became popular motifs for the covers of club menus, while the paintings by Christie and Hardie have enjoyed widespread popularity in recent years. The oldest clubs have now celebrated their 150th anniversaries and elaborate menus befitting these sesquicentennials were produced in each case.

Among the outstanding menus seen in recent years may be cited those produced by the Burns clubs of Calgary and Canterbury (New Zealand). Calgary's menus have a finely engraved version of the Nasmyth bust on the cover with the poet's autograph below. The inside pages contain a brief biography of Burns, a facsimile of the title page of the Kilmarnock Poems and the text of the 'Address to a Haggis', with an English translation thoughfully provided alongside, or medleys of the bard's shorter poems. The Canterbury menus are a veritable typographical *tour de force*. That produced in 1979 had a very striking cover showing maps of Scotland and New Zealand linked by the poet with stepped pages inside, their contents indicated by apt quotations printed on the leading edges. The 1981 menu, on the other hand, came in the form of a triptych which opened out to reveal the president's message, toast list and programme, and club history on the respective panels, printed in gold ink on a dark brown surface. The 1987 menu of the Burnsians of Rhode Island is the first one I have seen with a reproduction of the Dumfries statue on the cover, but the contents are like a glossy magazine, lavishly illustrated with pictures from the previous year's celebrations. The 200th anniversary of the Kilmarnock Poems at the end of July 1986 has triggered off a spate of bicentennial celebrations which will continue until 1996. Many of these events have been, and doubtless will continue to be, celebrated by banquets and dinners and these, in addition to the usual Burns suppers, are adding many new types of menu to this already immense category of ephemera. The often colourful and elaborate menus produced for Burns suppers aboard ships at sea were a feature of the great cruises of the inter-war period. In more recent times British Airways provided Burns menus on the flights from Glasgow and Prestwick across the Atlantic. These menus, printed by W.R. Royle, had four colour photographs on the cover: the 'Burns Memorial seen through the Brigadoon (*sic*), Alloway', a letter from the poet, the Cottage, and a stained glass window in the Birthplace Museum. Inside, a brief biographical note was illustrated by the Nasmyth portrait, the poet's interleaved copy of the *Scots Musical Museum* and his masonic mark.

Napkins and place-cards

Important adjuncts of menus and toast lists are the paper napkins and place cards. Until the 1930s, however, linen napkins were *de rigueur*, and it was only then that the soft paper variety, designed to be thrown away afterwards, began to come into favour. The earliest examples were comparatively plain, with albino embossed ornament on the borders. Dinwiddie of Dumfries pioneered the pictorial napkin and this continues to form a major part of the company's output to this day. Noel Dinwiddie's reputation as the 'Napkin King' is well-deserved, and Burnsians the world o'er, from Sauchie to Suva, from Mexico to Malaya, dine annually with these indispensable accessories, decorated with portraits of the bard and the words of the Selkirk grace or 'Auld Lang Syne'. Napkins with the Skirving portrait and four quotations are marketed by M. & R. Clark of Glasgow, who also publish a full range of menus and place-cards.

Place cards, or guest cards as they were originally known, were pioneered by Valentine's of Dundee in the early years of this century. Three varieties were available, with cut-out pictures showing the Nasmyth bust (head and shoulders), the head alone on a rectangular base, and the Cottage. Space was provided below the picture for the insertion of the guest's name. In more recent years much larger cards have been published by Whiteholme bearing an oval full-colour portrait of Burns, based on Nasmyth but reversed. Place cards without a publisher's imprint have been seen showing Burns House, Dumfries within a thistle motif, and reproductions of scenes from the 'Cotter', after Faed. Several clubs have place cards decorated with their own name and insignia.

Programmes

Some of the earliest programmes known to exist are also the most elaborate. The Mitchell Library possesses a very fine example of the programme produced at London in 'Commemoration of Burns, the friends and admirers of Robert Burns in London, assembled at Free Masons' Hall on Saturday, 25th May, in aid of the subscription for completing the monument over his grave'. This programme, dated 1816, contains, among other things, three poems, including the 'Ode to the memory of Burns' by Thomas Campbell. Three years later a programme was produced for the festival held at the Freemasons' Tavern in London on 5th May, and this contained a toast list and the words of the songs to be rendered on that occasion. Andrew Park compiled a handsome programme for the 1844 Festival on the banks of Doon, which included some very interesting details concerning the preparation of that event. The Gould collection in the Mitchell Library, of course, is replete with examples of the programmes for concerts and demonstrations connected with the centenary

Burns club syllabuses: Torrance and Burns Howff, Dumfries.

Programme for the Burns Concert to celebrate the Official Switch-on of electricity at Ellisland, 1956.

celebrations in 1859. Among the later programmes which have been preserved in the same library are 'A history of the celebration of Robert Burns' 110th natal day at the Metropolitan Hotel, Jersey City' (1869), the programme of the great Burns concert at the Kibble Palace, Glasgow by H.A. Lambeth's choir (1878), the programme given by the MacLennan Royal Edinburgh Concert Company at Philadelphia (1890), the souvenir of 'A night with Scotland's national poet' in Philadelphia (1894), programmes for James Robertson's first and second Burns anniversary concerts in St Andrew's Hall, Glasgow (1897-8), the book of words and music compiled for the Dumfries Burns Summer Festival (1898) and the programme for Scottish Day at the World's Fair in St Louis, at which a replica of the Cottage was unveiled (1904). Needless to say the celebrations in 1896 yielded a large harvest of programmes for concerts and conversazioni, exhibitions, unveiling ceremonies, processions and pageants.

The earliest playbill known to exist was that produced for the drama 'Robert Burns' staged at the Adelphi Theatre in Edinburgh on 14th August 1844, 'on the occasion of Scotland's Festival in honour of

Paper napkins: (a) "It's coming yet for a' that"; (b) Dumfries Octocentenary banquet.

the Bard'. Subsequent dramatic productions include 'Lights and Shadows' by John Duncan, staged at Dundee in 1879, 'The Angel of Robert Burns' by George Eyre-Todd (Glasgow, 1916), plays by John Drinkwater (1925) and H.F. Lee (1926) both simply entitled 'Robert Burns', Joe Corrie's 'Rake o' Mauchline' (1938), Eric Crozier's 'Rab the Rhymer' (1953) and, probably the best-known of all, Robert Kemp's 'The other Dear Charmer' (1957). 'The True Pathos' by W.B. de Bear Nichol, was staged at Dumfries in 1955. 'A Mauchline Foregathering — a musical and dramatical interlude' by John C. Darlison was popular in the 1960s. The most recent was John Cairney's 'Burns — the Musical' (Glasgow, 1988). Probably the most bizarre of such events, however, was 'A Licht wi' Burns', staged in Dumfries on 24th January 1956 to mark the introduction of the electricity supply to Ellisland Farm. The evening's entertainment was laid on by the South of Scotland Electricity Board and the proceedings were continued the following morning, according to the souvenir programme, with the ceremonial switch-on at Ellisland itself.

The Burns Federation was founded in 1885. In its early years the Federation held an annual general meeting, but it was not until 1893 that these meetings were reported in the *Chronicle*. Five years later the meeting was expanded to include dinner (at which wives of delegates were permitted to be present for the first time), followed by a drive round the Burns country. It is not known whether this annual meeting ran to anything so formal as a printed programme, but in view of the variety of events connected with it, it seems fairly likely. It is singularly unfortunate that the Burns Federation has no archives, so that the survival of programmes from its early meetings has been left entirely to chance. In 1907 the Federation's annual meeting was held outside Scotland for the first time, Sunderland being the venue for a full week-end of meetings, dinners and excursions. By now the number of delegates attending had grown in number, as there were 155 affiliated clubs, and it is thought that some sort of printed programme must have been produced for that occasion. Nevertheless, the earliest programmes for the conferences of the Burns Federation that I have so far recorded date from the London Conference of 1920. Many of these programmes were substantial affairs, amounting in some cases to quite a thick pamphlet, which not only gave the order of events but also biographical notes, words and sometimes music of Burns songs, full details of excursions and outings and, of course, the office-bearers of the Federation and the local organising committee. A collection of the programmes of Burns conferences over the past three quarters of a century would be an invaluable record of the Federation, its deliberations and achievements.

Among the more unusual programmes of recent years was the elaborate folder produced for the Federation's Centenary Conference, held at London in September 1985. This beautiful folder, sponsored by the Clydesdale Bank, was replete with

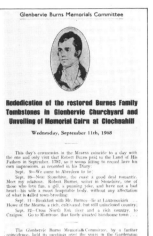

Programmes for the Rededication of the Glenbervie monument (1968), Alloway monument (1973) and the Kilmarnock monument (1978).

reproductions of Burns portraits, engravings from his life and works, his armorial bearings and a scene from the 1859 centenary celebrations in Dumfries, as well as a map of London's West End giving a key to the locations of the various venues and events associated with the conference. A large folder was produced to contain the programme, photographs and press information for the opening ceremony of Land o Burns at Alloway on 21st June 1977. The programme itself was only duplicated, but the lavish cover amply made up for this the Skirving portrait was inset at the top, against an enlargement of the engraving from Hill's painting of the Banks of Doon, which had appeared in *Land of Burns*.

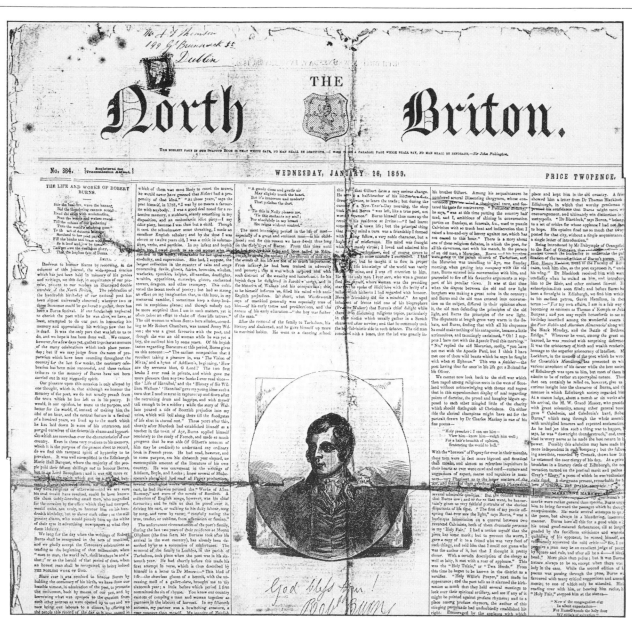

The North Briton, Burns Centenary souvenir edition, January 1859, actually sent through the post.

La Réforme of Brussels, 29th June 1896, with notice of Burns's Death Centenary.

Newspapers and Periodicals

Apart from the newspapers and magazines of the late eighteenth century, previously mentioned, which contained critiques or obituary notices of Burns, the chief interest to the collector of Burnsiana lies in the various souvenir editions or special supplements produced in January each year, around the time of the bard's birthday. Such papers as the *Kilmarnock Standard, Glasgow Herald* and *Dumfries and Galloway Standard* at one time regularly devoted a special supplement to Burns, with lengthy reports of the speeches at the various Burns suppers. Although these supplements have suffered the constraints imposed on modern journalism, they continue in a somewhat attenuated form, although they are generally better illustrated than they were before the Second World War. Several papers also regularly contained supplements devoted to the annual Burns conferences, especially on those occasions when the conference was being hosted by the town in which the newspaper was published. These special supplements usually took the form of four pages with a decorative masthead and articles and reports, supported by advertising matter in which, as already noted, local companies and tradesmen gave their announcements a suitably Burnsian flavour. The former SMT publication *Scotland's Magazine* devoted the entire issue of January 1936 to a 'Burns Hogmanay Number', crammed with excellent articles and having an appropriate Burns motif on the cover.

Souvenir editions of newspapers were produced in 1859, 1896, 1959 and 1966. These differed from the supplements in that Burns was promoted to the front page of the paper itself and a substantial number of other pages were devoted to aspects of the life and works of the bard, together with the contemporary celebrations. The bicentennial celebrations in 1959 even extended to national newspapers and periodicals, including the *Radio Times* which reproduced the Nasmyth bust on the cover.

The dates given above are largely self-explanatory, but 1966 perhaps deserves comment, for it is not a date which is readily apparent as having special significance in the Burns calendar. On 25th January that year, however, the Post Office issued two postage stamps to commemorate Burns and the opportunity was taken by three Scottish newspapers, *The Daily Mail, The Scotsman* and the *Daily Express*, to publish souvenir editions which could be transmitted by post in large envelopes franked by sets of the stamps. The foolscap-sized envelopes were specially printed. The *Daily Mail* cover featured a reversed Nasmyth bust, similar to that which appeared on the 1s3d stamp. The *Scotsman* cover was the most elaborate, with a full-colour reproduction of the Nasmyth bust and a four-line quotation from 'The star o Robbie Burns'. The *Express* cover featured the Irvine statue of the poet, by Pittendreigh MacGillivray. The stamps were cancelled by the pictorial First Day postmark at Alloway. The same concept was used in 1986 when the *Glasgow Herald* sponsored the production of a large-format booklet by John Cairney entitled *A Moment White*, which linked excerpts from the newspaper over the past 200 years to appropriate poems of Burns and comments thereon. This booklet was accompanied by a specially designed envelope which facilitated its transmission by post, but unfortunately no special postmark was sponsored which would have made the package complete.

Many Burns clubs have produced their own newsletters, magazines and bulletins. Some of them, notably the Paisley Burns club, produce a booklet of 36-40 pages in connexion with the birthday celebrations. Others, however, publish magazines monthly or quarterly and these range from the duplicated news-sheets from London (Ontario) to the highly professional *Caledonia* of the Robert Burns Society of Annapolis and *Third Degree Burns* (Calgary). It is probably significant that most of these periodicals are produced furth of Scotland, and play a

A selection of the Burns literature currently on sale at the Robert Burns Centre, Dumfries.

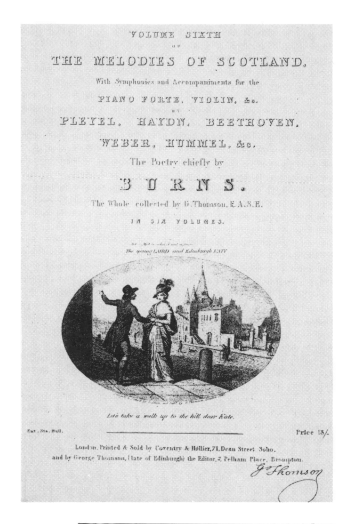

vital role in holding the expatriate Scottish community together. In December 1986 the Burns Federation launched *The Burnsian*, a quarterly tabloid newspaper with the Skirving portrait in the masthead. It is not improbable that the early issues of this paper will become collectors' items in years to come.

Pictorial Music Covers

The application of lithography to the printing of sheet music at the beginning of the nineteenth century raised the music cover to the status of an art form. By 1820 lithography had ousted the traditional and more costly copperplate engraving process, though it should be noted that James Johnson, with whom Burns collaborated on the *Scots Musical Museum*, had perfected a process for using pewter plates. At first lithographed illustrations were confined to the upper part of the cover, the opening bars of music being printed below, but the advent of chromolithography about 1840 led to the illustration filling the entire cover. It has been estimated that between 1820 and 1900 over 100,000 different music covers were produced in Britain alone with a comparable number in the United States in the same period, and numerous examples from Europe. The illustrated sheet music of Victorian times was the equivalent of today's pop record. Songs and ballads were produced on every conceivable occasion, and many of the titles were as ephemeral as the events they celebrated.

Inevitably Burns, who was responsible for so many of the greatest love songs and popular ballads of all time, was well represented in this medium. Countless examples of individual songs by Burns were published as separate works, with suitably decorated covers. In addition, however, Burns was the subject of many ballads, of which 'The Star' is the best-known, and many editions of that song were produced with appropriate motifs on the cover. Among the rarer works which also had pictorial covers pertaining to the bard were Ricardo Linter's 'Reminiscences of Burns, a fantasia for the pianoforte, composed in honour of the Burns Festival on the banks of the Doon' (1844), and 'Tribute to the memory of Scotland's poet, Robert Burns, adapted to an old Scotch air' by T. Oliphant (1859). Apart from songs, dance-music was also published in illustrated covers and many of these titles were fashionable for a season, then vanished for ever. A good example of this, with a Burns theme, was 'The Rantin, Rovin Lancers' whose melody was based on 'There was a lad was born in Kyle'.

Although these beautiful pictorial music covers died out at the end of the nineteenth century there is plenty of sheet music of more recent times with Burnsian themes and these editions of the songs and ballads of Burns are becoming just as collectable, even though the soft pastel shades of the old chromolithographs have long since been superseded by the harsher lines of letterpress and the halftone process. Nor should one overlook the attractive song-sheets and booklets which have been produced over the years by various Scottish newspapers in connexion with the annual Burns celebrations.

Pictorial music covers, mid-19th century, and Burns Federation Song-book.

Posters

Several posters have survived from the 1859 celebrations, and conform to the style of the period. They were printed by means of wooden blocks of various sizes and relied entirely on the ornamental type-faces for decorative effect. Although much more sophisticated processes were available by the time of the 1896 celebrations the posters which have survived from that period show little improvement in style and content. My favourite, however, is that which was produced at the *Standard* office in Dumfries in connexion with the last — and certainly the most bizarre — of all the demonstrations which took place in that momentous year. Wreaths were sent from all over the world, to be laid in and around the Mausoleum on the actual anniversary of the poet's death, but one of the most spectacular of all, sent by Burnsians in New South Wales, did not arrive in time because of problems in connecting with a suitable ship. The problem was caused by the fact that the wreath had been placed inside an enormous block of ice which had to be conveyed in the refrigerated hold

Burns Federation poster, designed by John Mackay, 1986.

of a ship which normally carried frozen mutton. The 'iceberg' as it was nicknamed, arrived by Glasgow and Southwestern Railway goods train on 6th August 1896 and was taken in style to the Mausoleum the next day, immense crowds turning out to view the procession. The poster gave details of the procession of 'The Great Frozen Wreath' and invited local Burns clubs to assemble at the goods yard behind the town band. Incidentally, it is recorded that although the ice had begun to melt *en route*, the 'iceberg' was still too large to squeeze through the gateway at the Mausoleum, which caused a rather embarrassing hold-up.

In fairly recent times, however, there have been several colourful posters which merit attention. British Rail, in the late 1950s with an eye on stimulating passenger traffic during the bicentenary celebrations, produced a poster by William Nicholson which showed a full-length portrait of the bard. Nasmyth's head and shoulders were grafted rather awkwardly on to a standing figure, so that Burns appears to be turning sideways. He was surrounded by landmarks associated with him and scenes from his works. This poster was immensely popular at the time, and was made available by British Rail as a souvenir. One of these posters was acquired by Mogerley's, the haggis specialist of Dumfries, and displayed in their butcher's shop. Eventually Harry Mogerley obtained permission from British Rail to reproduce the poster as a picture postcard, printed by Robert Dinwiddie Ltd. This postcard is still available, as a sort of trade card issued by the shop, and more recently the poster has even been translated into the medium of a printed tea-towel. Dryborough's beer was advertised in an attractive poster depicting Burns characters and scenes around a full-length portrait of the bard, based on the Nasmyth bust. The Scottish Tourist Board produced a multicolour poster in the same genre to publicise the Heritage Trail.

Two posters have been produced as decorative pieces in their own right. The first of these is a remarkable montage entitled 'Robert Burns — Portrait Biography' and was painted about 1985 by Ted Tilby, recognized as one of North America's foremost portrait artists. The central motif is clearly derived from Nasmyth, yet it has a fresh quality about it, especially capturing the 'glowing eye' of which Scott spoke. The portrait is surrounded by eighteen vignettes illustrative of the life and works of Burns. A lithographic edition of this poster was subsequently published in Canada, and it was also used to decorate the dust-jacket of *The Laughter of Love* by Raymond J.S. Grant, published in 1986. Sunprint of Perth, the printers of this book, produced a beautiful poster in 1986, designed by John Mackay, the celebrated illustrator. This work reproduces the Nasmyth portrait by permission of the Scottish National Portrait Gallery, and features sixteen scenes from the poet's life, from childhood to his last days in Dumfries, together with scenes illustrating some of his best-loved poems. Posters of a more commercial nature were also produced about the same time by

Alloway Publishing Ltd to promote the bicentenary edition of the *Complete Works*. Perhaps the most amusing use of Burns in this medium is the large black and white placard produced recently by Digital Equipment Ltd of Ayr, showing Burns seated at a word-processor with the words 'Tam o Shanter' on the visual display unit.

Labels and packaging materials

Doubtless even in Burns's day connoisseurs of a fine malt could tell which distillery a whisky had come from by tasting it, but no attempt was then made to apply brand names to spirits. This practice developed in the course of the nineteenth century, especially after the advent of blended whiskies. By the 1890s, therefore, whisky was usually sold in bottles which bore labels clearly stating the brand. At this period, moreover, many inns and public-houses had their own distinctive label and it is therefore singularly appropriate that Mrs Smith, who kept the Globe Inn, Dumfries until her death at an advanced age in 1928, sold her own brand of whisky. The label was printed in gold ink on white paper and bore a portrait of Burns in recognition of the fact that he had provided the Globe with an endorsement which it proudly uses to this day.

Other brands of whisky current around the turn of the century which exploited Scotland's national bard included 'The Dear Kilbagie', a creamy old Scotch which was marketed by Thomas Stevenson of Johnstone and took its title from a distillery fashionable in Burns's time, 'Tam o Shanter', produced about 1886 by Lang Brothers of Glasgow, 'Auld Killie' by Andrew Thomson of Kilmarnock, whose label showed the monument and statue in the Kay Park, and 'Freedom' old Highland whisky by Macleay, Duff Co. of Glasgow whose label reproduced the Nasmyth bust, flanked by the lines

Freedom and whisky gang thegither
Tak aff yer Dram.

The labels used by R.H. Thomson of Leith were the most elaborate of all, and were a fine example of chromolithography at its best. The Nasmyth bust was prominently displayed, surrounded by little scenes of Burns and Highland Mary, the Cottage and the Monument at Alloway. The brand name 'Robbie Burns' survives to this day, but the rectangular and trefoil-shaped labels feature the Nasmyth portrait alone. This brand was a great favourite in Latin America, where the labels were inscribed 'Robertito' (i.e. little Robert) — 'de los wiskies el mejor' (the best of whiskies). Other distinctive brand labels of more recent times have included 'Poosie Nansie's Mauchline — the Jolly Beggars Brew', 'Glen Catrine' of Ayrshire (with a vignette of the Cottage), 'Begbie's Special' by Slater, Rodgers & Co. Ltd which uses the Peter Taylor portrait of Burns, and 'The Immortal Memory' by Specialised Blenders Ltd. 'Burns Cottage' was the name of a brand of single malt whisky which was packaged in a stoneware bottle (of the type which would have been familiar in Burns's day). The label, of course, depicted the poet's birthplace and a royalty was paid by the promoter to

Whisky and Beer labels, Westwood collection.

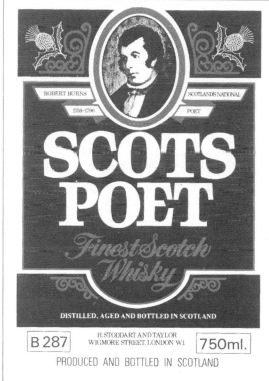

the Trustees of the Cottage. This brand was only available to Burns clubs and, sadly, the experiment in the early 1980s seems to have been short-lived. The Dundonald Burns club arranged for souvenir bottles of Glenmorangie malt whisky to be distributed in 1985 with a special label celebrating the club's anniversary. No doubt other Burns clubs have adopted similar devices at other times. At least one president of the Burns Federation is known to have had his very own whisky labels portraying himself in full regalia.

In view of such poems as 'John Barleycorn' and 'Scotch Drink', it is hardly surprising that the whisky distillers should have derived inspiration from Burns for brand names but it may not be generally known that Burns also inspired a brand of orange squash, marketed in the early 1960s. The Scottish Soft Drinks Company wished to add to their Harmony and Sun-Kool range an orange squash with a distinctly Scottish name. Scores of names were suggested but rejected by the trade mark agents in London as unsuitable for one reason or another. Then, in desperation, the company turned to Gaelic names, but these proved even less practicable. It was at this point that Baron Georges Marchand, a Frenchman and friend of the company's chairman, R.C. Forrest

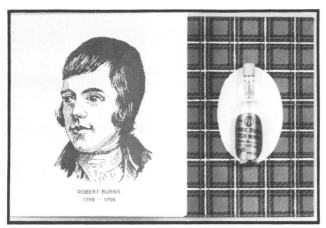

Miniature whisky bottle mounted on a Burns souvenir card.

Dundonald Burns Club miniature bottle of Anniversary Blend whisky.

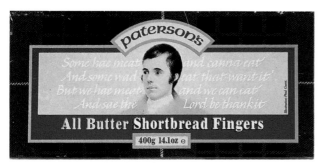

Paterson's Shortbread tin featuring Burns.

Walker's Shortbread tin with the Nasmyth portrait.

Paterson's Shortbread tin with the Selkirk Grace.

"Robert Burns" cigarillos.

French cheroot, with Burns's portrait on the band.

Walker's Shortbread tin showing the full-length Nasmyth portrait.

Home, suggested using the Burns check which he had devised to mark the Bicentenary of Burns in 1959. The Poems of Burns were then consulted and consequently the name Drouthy Bree was concocted. The orange squash went on the market early in 1960 with this name boldly inscribed on a background of the Burns check.

Gilmour and Smith of Kilmarnock, manufacturers of jams, jellies, marmalades and preserves, used labels which took as their trade-mark a picture of the Kay Park monument. Oughton's of Dumfries sold shortbread and biscuits in boxes and tins decorated with labels which showed Church Place, Dumfries, with the poet's statue prominent. In recent years Joseph Walker of Aberlour have produced shortbread in tins decorated with the full-length Nasmyth portrait in various versions, with or without verses of Burns's poems and biographical notes, and petticoat tails in square tins with the bust-portrait and the complete text of 'To a Mountain Daisy' on the back. J. Paterson of Nettlehill, Livingston market shortbread in tins bearing the poet's bust by Paul Guest after Nasmyth, and the Selkirk grace on the lid, and verses from 'Afton Water' and 'Auld Lang Syne' on the sides. David Lauder of Kilmarnock produced souvenir tins in Bicentenary Year with the Nasmyth bust in the centre and the Cottage, Auld Brig and Banks of Doon.

Some tobacco companies have featured Burns or his works. Stephen Mitchell of Glasgow produced a brand of dark flake pipe tobacco known as 'Tam o Shanter' and depicted a sanitised and modernised version of the old toper on the tins and packaging. The General Cigar and Tobacco Company of New York produces to this day a brand of cigar labelled 'Robt. Burns'. A version of this, manufactured in France under licence of the Culbro Corporation of America, is entitled in English 'Fair Play' and bears a curious portrait of Burns superimposed on an antique map of the Indian Ocean. As irrelevant as the background map is the portrait which, although clearly labelled with the poet's name, looks more like the young Goethe! Not surprisingly, this design was not very popular in Scotland itself and has since given way to a tartan motif with a more recognisable imitation of the Nasmyth bust, although the original design is still used on cigar labels, packs, tins and boxes marketed on the Continent. American cigars of a much earlier vintage were the 'Little Bobbie' brand of 5 and 10 cent cigars produced by Straiton & Storm, and later the New Name General Cigar Company. Lest there should be any doubt as to who 'Little Bobbie' was, the cigar-boxes were decorated with a beautiful chromolithograph featuring the Nasmyth bust.

Perhaps the strangest use of Burns in packaging is the barely recognisable and rather crude bust that decorates the paper bags of the well-known Dumfries butcher alongside the slogan 'Mogerley's for Haggis'. It is likely that some of the other brands of haggis, packaged for the extensive export business around the end of January each year, also bore the poet's portrait. Certainly George Waugh, R. T. Gibson and James Wilson, all of Edinburgh, Tulloch of Glasgow and John Gardner of Partick catered specifically to Burns clubs around the world at one time — before the red tape and petty bureaucracy of sundry Customs departments began to look unkindly on imports of Scotland's 'sausage'. R.D. Waddell of Napiershall Street, Glasgow certainly used a portrait of Burns as a trade-mark - a rather gaunt figure which can be regarded as only slightly derivative from Nasmyth.

One of the more unusual mementoes of the Centenary in 1896 was 'Robert Burns Bouquet', a perfume distilled and bottled by William Allan, a Dumfries chemist. Bottles of this perfume were sold for two shillings each or quarter-dozen cases at 5s6d. The label had the Nasmyth bust in the centre at the top, flanked by the obligatory thistles and a commemorative inscription. The brand name was written across the middle, with a row of unidentifiable flowers (daisies?) at the foot, flanking lines from 'The Banks of Nith'.

About 1972, the Westburn Sugar Company of Greenock embarked on a series of sugar bags decorated with portraits and brief biographical notes on Great Scots. Number 8 in this series of 20 was devoted to Burns whose bust, after Nasmyth, appeared in the upper right-hand corner. A. Links & Co. of Glasgow produced the Poetic brand of knitwear whose labels featured the Nasmyth bust, with the Cottage in the background. The Pilgrim Press of Derby print the magenta-coloured labels showing the Skirving portrait, used to wrap the sticks of Robert Burns rock sold in the Alloway souvenir shops. Labels portraying 'Bonie Jean' are used at Jean Armour's Pantry, Dumfries to wrap takeaways.

Luggage labels used to be a familiar feature of hotels around the world, and it was a form of oneupmanship to have one's suitcase liberally plastered with these coloured patches — the more exotic the better. Nowadays people travel as lightly as possible and hotel labels, applied to trunks and cases on departure, are a thing of the past. The Burns Monument Hotel at Alloway had a gorgeous label with a medley of tartans and the poet's heraldic badge in the centre.

The same hotel is the only one, so far as I can ascertain, ever to have produced distinctive match-boxes decorated with a bust of Burns, although it is not impossible that such hostelries as the Globe Inn and the Hole i' the Wa' public-house in Dumfries, and the Tam o Shanter Inn at Ayr may have utilised this advertising medium in years gone by. A black label with the Tower picked out in white and 'Burns Memorial Mauchline' has also been recorded. Match-books with the Nasmyth bust in blue on white were given away as souvenirs of the 1979 Burns Conference in London, Ontario. At the present time match-books with the Nasmyth bust in gold are sold at the Land o Burns Centre, while the souvenir shop at the Birthplace Museum sells two different versions of match-books depicting the Cottage. Jumbo-sized match-books have also been produced as tourist souvenirs, decorated with full-length portraits of Burns vaguely derived from Nasmyth. The well-known match manufacturers, Bryant and May probably included Burns in one of their late-Victorian sets of match-box labels which portrayed historic and contemporary celebrities. In the late 1860s this firm introduced small tin boxes for their new wax vestas and issued them with a large assortment of portraits on the covers. Members of the Royal family were a great favourite, but other portraits included political figures, such as Gladstone, Bright, Disraeli and Lowe, and literary figures such as Burns, Scott and Dickens.

Beer-mats and drip mats

Coasters made of wood or metal will be found in the last chapters of this book, but the thin wood-pulp beer-mat, invented by Robert Smith at Dresden in 1892, revolutionised the bar-equipment industry and provided yet another medium which was ideally suited for advertisements. Wood-pulp beer-mats spread to America about 1910, but it was not until the Twenties that they made their appearance in Britain. Dryborough's — 'brewers in Scotland since Burns was a boy' — were renowned for their Burns Extra

Special beer which had the Nasmyth head on its labels and beer-cans, and the same motif appeared on their beer-mats. As a general rule, beer-mats are either uniface or merely repeat the same motif on the reverse but the Dryborough mats have two stanzas of 'The Deil's awa wi th'Exciseman'. There is a delicious irony in the use of the lines:
We'll mak our maut, and we'll brew our drink,
We'll laugh, sing, and rejoice, man,
And monie braw thanks to the meikle black Deil,
That danc'd awa wi th'Exciseman.

Not to be outdone, drip-mats designed for trays or as place mats have been produced by 'Robbie Burns' whisky, decorated with a view of the Cottage as well as the Nasmyth bust. Under the heading 'Scotland's National Bard' appears a brief biography dwelling on the theme that Burns had three loves: his country, womankind and whisky. Conviviality was, for Burns, one of the most important virtues. 'Auld Lang Syne' and verses from 'A man's a man' are thoughtfully provided for those whose knowledge of these rousing songs is a bit shaky. Drambuie, manufacturers of the whisky liqueur, have produced place mats showing Burns, the Cottage, a ploughing scene and the words of 'To a Mouse'.

Above: Matchbox and match books, luggage label, and knitwear label. Right: Sugar label and beer-mat.

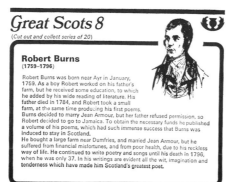

Great Scots 8
(Cut out and collect series of 20)

Robert Burns
(1759–1796)

Robert Burns was born near Ayr in January, 1759. As a boy Robert worked on his father's farm, but he received some education, to which he added by his wide reading of literature. His father died in 1784, and Robert took a small farm, at the same time producing his first poems. Burns decided to marry Jean Armour, but her father refused permission, so Robert decided to go to Jamaica. To obtain the necessary funds he published a volume of his poems, which had such immense success that Burns was induced to stay in Scotland.
He bought a large farm near Dumfries, and married Jean Armour, but he suffered from financial misfortunes, and from poor health, due to his reckless way of life. He continued to write poetry and songs until his death in 1796, when he was only 37. In his writings are evident all the wit, imagination and tenderness which have made him Scotland's greatest poet.

Philately of Burns

Russian stamps of 1956 and 1957.

Although Britain invented the adhesive postage stamp in 1840, this country lagged well behind the rest of the world in using it for commemorative purposes. Britain's first commemorative stamps (publicising the British Empire Exhibition at Wembley) appeared in 1924 — long after the practice was well-established elsewhere — and for many years thereafter stamps were used sparingly to commemorate current events of national, international or royal importance. The very idea of using stamps in tribute to people, past or present, was anathema to the British Post Office.

As the bicentenary year of Robert Burns approached, there were many attempts to raise the matter of special stamps. A major bone of contention at successive conferences of the Burns Federation from 1954 was the progress — or lack of it — in persuading the authorities to issue a Burns stamp. Appeals to successive Postmasters-General fell on deaf ears, and even an appeal to the Prime Minister, Harold MacMillan, himself (the grandson of a Scot whose career, from humble peasant to literary figure, uncannily paralleled that of Burns) failed to budge the Post Office from its entrenched policy of only honouring *current* events. The Post Office regarded the Federation as just one more nuisance among many that plague its corporate life each year with petitions in favour of stamps for all manner of persons, events and worthy causes. Scots, as a whole, felt that this official indifference was tantamount to a national insult and eventually the matter entered the political arena.

On 26th October 1955 Hector Hughes, MP for North Aberdeen, asked the Postmaster General, Dr Charles Hill, if he would consider the issue of a special stamp to commemorate the bicentenary. Dr Hill (best remembered as the Radio Doctor from the wartime period) gave a one-word written answer — 'No!' This terse reply was re-iterated on 9th November when Sir Thomas Moore, MP for North Ayrshire, raised the matter again. Moore said that this would disappoint 'many millions of Burns lovers throughout the country'. Hill refused on the grounds that 'were the Post Office to contemplate issuing stamps to commemorate illustrious persons, the task of choosing among such persons would be more than could be properly accepted.' Mr Alport suggested that a more proper way of commemorating this auspicious occasion would be a reduction in the Excise duty on whisky.

There the matter rested for two and a half years. Outside the House of Commons, however, Burns was not being forgotten. In August 1956 the Soviet Union issued a stamp to mark the 160th anniversary of the poet's death. That the stamp was released a month after the actual anniversary seems to indicate that it was a last-minute decision by the Soviet authorities. The 40 kopek stamp was photogravure-printed in yellow-brown and featured the Nasmyth bust reversed, so that the bard faced right instead of left. The stamp was re-issued the following year. This time the process adopted was the more prestigious and aesthetically satisfying one of intaglio engraving, and a pleasing effect was created by printing the bust in sepia, with a Scottish blue frame.

Twa Plack label

At home, the Scottish Secretariat (publishers of nationalist pamphlets and periodicals) decided to set

'Twa Plack' label produced by the Scottish Secretariat, 1957.

the Post Office an example, and produced a large square label, lithographed in blue by the Scottish Co-operative Wholesale Society in sheets of twenty sold for a shilling. A young apprentice in the printing-works, who had a hand in the production of these historic labels, was George Anderson, later Publicity Officer of the Burns Federation, and its President in 1982. These labels were separated by a form of perforation known as rouletting, using pierced lines instead of punched holes. The basic design consisted of the Nasmyth portrait framed by a wreath of thistles with the Saltire Cross of St Andrew in the background. The side panels bore the words 'Now's the time and now's the hour', a quotation from the Scottish national anthem which Burns had composed. The value was expressed as 'Twa Plack'. A plack was a small copper coin, the sixtieth part of a pound Scots (i.e. two-thirds of an English penny), and although the coin itself had long since ceased to circulate by the time of Burns, the expression was still current in many popular sayings, and, indeed, it figures in Burns's poems to signify a trifling sum.

The original printing was done in indigo; no note of the numbers printed exists, but they must have been small, as this colour is something of a rarity. It was subsequently printed in either deep or light blue and altogether some 150,000 labels were produced. One sheet of twenty was found without any perforations and examples of these labels are now highly prized by philatelists. Even the later printings of the Twa Plack label are none too easy to find, especially commercially used on envelopes where they were sometimes illegally placed next to the postage stamp and thus postmarked. The reason for the scarcity of the Twa Plack label is that many of them were not used on postcards and envelopes at all, which would have led to philatelic preservation, but were more often than not stuck on lamp-posts, walls and even the windows of Glasgow tram-cars! The inspiration of this label was distinctly political rather than philatelic.

The best laid schemes

Easier to find is the second Burns label, in a large oblong format, which the Scottish Secretariat produced in August 1958. This was designed by James

'The best laid schemes' label of 1958.

Leslie and lithographed by the SCWS in sheets of twenty, pin-perforated. The dominant feature was the Scottish flag, with Burns's portrait, his autograph and thistle on the right. Tiny lions rampant embellished the corners and round the frame were inscribed the lines from 'Ode to a Mouse':

> The best laid schemes o mice and men,
> Gang aft a-gley, and leave us nought
> But grief and pain for promised joy.

This label enjoyed a wide popularity and was extensively used on philatelic mail at the time of the bicentenary celebrations the following January.

The campaign hots up

The Burns Federation first made a formal application to the Postmaster General for the issue of a special stamp on 17th May 1957. This application was accompanied by a suggested design in a horizontal format with the Queen's portrait looking left towards a view of the Cottage at Alloway. Between the Queen's head and the Cottage two hands were clasped to signify Brotherhood. The dates 1759-1959, a Union Jack and the lion rampant completed the picture. The Postmaster General's response — if any — is not recorded. On 22nd November 1957, following the debate and resolution at the Burns Conference two months earlier, the Burns Federation published a memorial addressed to all members of Parliament, in the form of a covering letter, with a lengthy memorandum and an off-print of a leading article from the *Kilmarnock Standard* of 21st September posing the question 'Why not a Burns stamp?' In addition, a quarto-sized leaflet was prepared by Kevan McDowall, a Glasgow solicitor who was also 'Stamps Correspondent' of the Federation. This extensive canvassing of MPs was followed up on 28th February 1958 by a four-page letter from the Federation to the Postmaster General himself, under the heading of 'Proposed bicentenary Burns stamps'. Copies of these memoranda and letters were also circulated to influential people in Scotland and England, and constitute interesting collateral material for the Burns philatelist. Unfortunately the correspondence that passed between the Federation and high postal officials has not been preserved by the Federation. The Post Office side of the affair is covered by the thirty-year rule which means that the relevant papers will not become available for study till the end of 1989. Nevertheless, it is clear, from the existing letters and memoranda, that Kenneth Thompson, for the Post Office, dismissed the application on the grounds that a special stamp for a mere poet was out of the question.

On 11th March 1958 the matter was resurrected in the House of Commons. Emrys Hughes, the Welsh-born MP for Ayr, asked the Secretary of State for Scotland what steps were being taken to encourage tourists to come to Scotland in connexion with the celebrations for the bicentenary of Robert Burns. The reply was 'All possible publicity'. Hughes commented that the best possible publicity would be a

A block of labels produced by the Caledonian Society of Southern Africa.

Burns stamp and appealed to the Parliamentary Secretary for Scotland, in whose constituency Burns was buried, 'to impress upon the reactionary Postmaster General the need for doing something in this way.' The following day Emrys Hughes asked the Postmaster General, Ernest Marples, for a specially designed greetings telegram to mark the bicentenary. Marples hedged and said that he would have to defer giving a decision pending the report of the Advisory Committee investigating the telegraph system. Hector Hughes asked for a statement of the Postmaster General's stamp-issuing principles and Marples outlined the, by now, well-known criteria of royal, national or postal events.

During 1958 the campaign spread to other parts of the world and Burnsians were encouraged to write to the British Postmaster General urging him to reconsider the matter. The Caledonian Society of Southern Africa went one better and issued a booklet containing propaganda labels. The booklet was inscribed: 'Get a fellow Scot to join your Caledonian Society' and advertised the *Caledonian*. These booklets contained six panes of ten labels (two rows of five), perforated 10.5 with the outer margins imperforate. The labels, printed by the half-tone process in blue, featured the Nasmyth portrait of Burns. A copy of the booklet was donated to the Tam o Shanter Inn at Ayr and examples of these elusive labels are on display there.

On 10th July 1958 the Burns Federation, which included many MPs, sent a deputation to the Postmaster General. In answer to Emrys Hughes who headed it, the Prime Minister said that the matter had been reconsidered but the Government were unable to alter their decisions. Mr MacMillan published his

letter to Sir Thomas Moore about this decision. Quipped Hughes, 'If Burns had written a letter so long containing so little, any demand for a bicentenary commemoration would not be necessary'. The Prime Minister added, however, that the Postmaster General 'was considering what arrangements might possibly be made for a special franking of letters to commemorate the bicentenary'. Special event handstamps as they are known (discussed later in this chapter) were not uncommon in the Fifties, but the matter was allowed to drag on indecisively and rather shabbily. The Post Office refused to allow a postmark bearing the bard's portrait, on the grounds that it might obliterate the Queen's features on the stamps and this would be tantamount to *lèse majesté* — an ironic statement in view of subsequent events. It was all right for lettering and illustrations in slogan cancellations to blot the Queen's face, but not for a portrait of someone to do likewise!

The bicentenary postmark at Alloway

The Post Office would have been quite happy to provide a special canceller, so long as someone was willing to pay for it but the various interested bodies felt that as a matter of principle such a device should be provided free of charge. In the end nothing extraordinary was provided and all that was done was that Alloway sub-post office was allowed to remain open on the morning of Sunday 25th January 1959 and mail (normally machine-cancelled at Ayr head post office) was exceptionally postmarked with the double circle datestamp of Alloway. More than 27,000 items were hand-stamped at this little post office, the sub-postmistress, Mrs Thomas Mossie, lending her garage to the team of eight men who wielded the datestamp in relays. The bulk of the mail was actually stamped on that day and can be identified by the asterisk slug which is shown in the central position above the date. Some mail, however, could not be postmarked till the following day and although it bears the correct bicentenary date it shows the asterisk moved to the left. A few registered letters were tendered over the counter for postmarking on the Sunday, and the majority of these have the Alloway double-circle datestamp with the asterisk in the central position, indicating that they were really dealt with on the correct date. For some inexplicable reason, however, two or three registered covers were overlooked and were not processed till the following day. The double-circle datestamp was applied on the front, to cancel the postage stamps, and naturally had the asterisk moved to the left. But Post Office regulations demand that the *actual* date of posting must appear on registered covers, so the problem was solved by applying a second datestamp across the flaps, showing the correct date of 26th January. As Alloway post office only had one datestamp, a second had to be made up at short notice from loose type. Such stamps, known as 'skeletons' are normally provided in emergencies such as fire, accidental loss or damage, or burglary at a post office, when a replacement datestamp is required at very short

The very rare 'skeleton' postmark, confined to a few registered covers, Alloway, 1959.

notice, pending the manufacture of another permanent datestamp. Such skeleton postmarks can readily be identified by their large diameter single-circle and the unevenness of the lettering. Understandably these late-cancelled registered covers of Alloway are extremely scarce.

Various souvenir envelopes were produced for the occasion. They ranged from a modest cover bearing line blocks of the Nasmyth portrait and the poet's birthplace, to the colourful cover produced by the Scottish Postmark Group in Edinburgh. Among the more politically inspired envelopes was one emblazoned with the Saltire flag right across it, with a

Bicentenary Souvenir cover decorated with the Saltire Flag.

Below: One of the many different Bicentenary covers posted at Alloway on 25th January, 1959.

Stamps issued in 1959 by Russia and Romania.

portrait of Burns framed inside a thistle in the upper left-hand corner. More daring was the cover, produced by a Nationalist group, which had an imitation 'stamp' impressed in the top right-hand corner, with a crude portrait of Burns and a scroll inscribed '... Man to man the Warld o'er, shall brothers be...' These were treated by the Post Office as 'embarrassing packets' and were not postmarked, though a few of them are known to have slipped unnoticed through the cancelling machines of Edinburgh and Glasgow. Yet another cover, produced by the Scottish Secretariat, bore a facsimile of the Twa Plack label on the left-hand side.

Bicentenary postage stamps and labels

Robert Burns was not without some proper philatelic recognition in his bicentenary year. Unfortunately, it was again left to the Soviet Union to rectify the omission of the poet's homeland. The 40 kopek blue and sepia stamp of 1957 was re-issued, overprinted in red with the dates '1759-1959'. Romania included in her Cultural Anniversaries series of 1959 a 55 lei stamp in slate-blue showing a rather poor and reversed reproduction of the Skirving portrait.

Typeset labels in sheets of ten (two rows of five) were produced in purple on white paper at Ye Burns Press, Mauchline to advertise the exhibition held in the Old Church Halls, Mauchline from 12th to 19th September 1959 to celebrate the bicentenary of the poet's birth. The labels were utilitarian in design and did not portray Burns, but a commemorative inscription and the dates 1759-1959 appeared round the sides of the labels. These labels were issued imperforate but each was surrounded by printer's ornament as a guide for scissors cuts. There is an endearingly old-world ring to the inscription printed at the top of these sheets: 'The Exhibition Committee would esteem it a favour if you would affix these Advertising Stamps to your correspondence — on back (not front) of envelopes, and on parcels.'

A change of policy

By 1961 British postal policy was beginning to relax and the number of special stamps was being stepped up. On 7th November of that year Emrys Hughes asked the Assistant Postmaster General 'if in view of the variety of types of new stamps the Post Office would consider issuing a special Burns stamp'. Miss Mervyn Pike replied in the negative. Hughes said that this would disappoint the Leader of the Conservative Party (Harold MacMillan) who had quoted Burns at the annual Party Conference. Miss Pike said 'I share with the Leader of the House and the Hon. Member a love for Robert Burns and I can best answer him, I think, in the words which Burns wrote in Verses addressed to John Rankine

The breaking of ae point, tho sma', breaks a' thegither.'

Obviously no dangerous precedents were going to be established at this stage.

The burning issue of a Burns stamp next got an airing on 26th February 1964 when Mr Gourlay asked the Assistant Postmaster General, Ray Mawby, if he was 'aware that while we do not begrudge the philatelic recognition of William Shakespeare, it makes the refusal of my Right Hon. Friend the Postmaster General to issue a commemorative stamp for Robert Burns an added insult to Scotland... Would he reconsider his previous decision and issue a Burns stamp next January?' Mawby said that 'if there were the sort of celebrations for Burns that there were now for Shakespeare he would seriously consider it.'

On the face of it, the Government's decision to issue five stamps in April 1964 for the quatercentenary of Shakespeare seemed like a complete *volte face* — more especially as the bard of Avon was actually portrayed on four of them. The Postmaster General, however, argued that the stamps

A pair of 'Free Scotland' labels, 1964.

had nothing to do with William Shakespeare as such, but were commemorating the Shakespeare Quatercentenary Festival at Stratford upon Avon — a major international event which was within the guidelines laid down for the issue of special stamps. When taxed about the inclusion of Shakespeare's portrait, when no one other than royalty had been portrayed before, Post Office officials countered that the use of the Droeshout portrait from the frontispiece of the First Folio was purely symbolic, and that as the picture was posthumous Shakespeare probably looked nothing like that anyway!

These specious arguments provoked sharp reaction north of the Border. The Scottish Secretariat in Glasgow produced a new Twa Plack label, bearing the additional words 'Free Scotland', and printed in sheets of twenty by the SCWS. The public were urged to affix one of these labels alongside every Shakespeare stamp, in defiance of postal regulations. The Scottish Patriots in Edinburgh also produced a Burns label, lithographed initially in maroon in strips of three by Hyslop and Day and sold for threepence each. Designed by Miss Wendy Wood, this simple label had the merit of bearing the best reproduction of the Nasmyth bust up to that time. It was subsequently

reprinted in green (also in strips of three) and then in pairs *se-tenant* sideways in blue. Finally, on 25th January 1965, it was released in red. Approximately 7,000 of each colour were printed.

Two independent groups struck a more petulant note. From Burns's home county of Ayrshire came a series of type-set labels printed on various coloured papers, inscribed 'Boycott the Shakespeare stamps. No stamps for Burns. Why one for him?' These were produced by the Stevenston branch of the Scottish National Party and sold at 1s6d for 100. The first issue of the branch newsletter (February 1964) urged members to boycott the Shakespeare stamps by demanding ordinary definitive stamps a post offices. From the fount of type used, it is thought that the same group was responsible for buff envelopes with the words 'Whaur's yer Wullie Shakespeare Noo?' in seriffed capitals, echoing the cry of the audience at the first night of John Home's tragedy *Douglas* in 1756. In Edinburgh a Shakespeare First Day cover was produced by James Douglas, portraying Burns and inscribed 'Scotland for Ever. We regret having to commemorate William Shakespeare, an alien poet, having been denied the opportunity of similarly commemorating our Robert Burns.'

Above: Anti-Shakespeare Burns cover by James Douglas.

Right: Scottish Patriots label, and Stevenston SNP Shakespeare Boycott label, 1964.

The stamps designed by Gordon Huntly and issued in January 1966.

One of the striking differences between the policy of the Labour Government and that of its predecessors was a more imaginative approach to stamp issues. On 10th November 1964, after only three weeks in office, Anthony Wedgwood Benn announced that a Burns stamp was one of the issues which he was considering. The following week he said that it was too late to issue a stamp for Burns in January 1965, if in fact it were agreed that one should be issued as a result of the review in stamp policy. On 15th December, in reply to a written question by Mr Pounder, Wedgwood Benn stated that one of the aims of his new policy would be 'to reflect the British contribution to world affairs including the arts and science.' Then, on 1st February 1965, the forthcoming stamp programme was outlined in a written answer to Mr Clive Bossom — 'I have decided to issue in January 1966 a Robert Burns stamp'.

As it turned out, the Post Office, which had rebuffed Scotland and her national bard so often in the past, did the thing handsomely. Six well-known Scottish artists were commissioned to produce essays for the two stamps and the high quality of the resulting designs was matched by imaginative treatment of Burnsian motifs. The Post Office produced a commemorative First Day cover showing the Cottage, and a presentation pack containing a set of the stamps and a descriptive leaflet.

The essays for the projected stamps ranged from an unfortunate pair with the quotation 'O my Luve is like a red, red Rose' between portraits of Burns and the Queen, to Stewart Black's novel use of textiles (the Burns check) as a background to the design, bled off into the perforations. The designs submitted by A. B. Imrie were highly regarded and showed the poet's portrait with the Brig o Doon and Alloway countryside. Ruari McLean featured a wreath of flowers and birds in the Victorian style of decorative art. Ian McLeish presented a sketch of Burns, while Jack Fleming adopted a symbolic motif, showing a hand holding a quill-pen, with the Miers silhouette in the background. Gordon Huntly's winning pair was criticised for returning to the symbolism redolent of the 1950s and for his inaccurate depiction of the Scottish flag, which is barely recognisable as such. The 1s3d stamp showed the Nasmyth bust in reverse against a background of plough, thistle, rose, stook of barley, quill-pen and scroll. Tucked away in the corner was the gable-end of the farmhouse at Mossgiel. The 4d stamp reproduced the Skirving portrait — right way round — on blue ground, with ultra-thin diagonal lines supposed to represent the saltire flag. Both stamps used the portrait of the Queen by Dorothy Wilding in a vertical panel above the value, on the extreme right. The 4d stamp was captioned in white lowercase lettering, whereas the

Souvenir booklet prepared by the Post Office in connection with the Burns stamps, 1966.

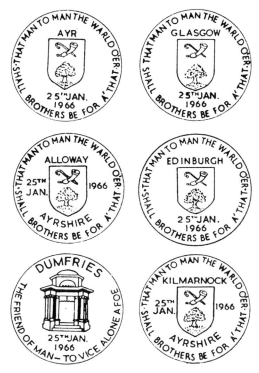

Pictorial First Day handstamps used at Ayr, Glasgow, Alloway, Edinburgh, Dumfries and Kilmarnock, 25th January, 1966.

poet's name appeared on either side of his portrait on the higher denomination. It would have been better had the bard's autograph been used, but instead the words appeared in impeccable copperplate script.

The stamps sold in Southampton and the Glasgow area were issued with phosphor bands printed across their surface to facilitate electronic sorting. Altogether 77,905,176 of the ordinary 4d stamps and 8,738,520 of the phosphor version, and 5,685,096 ordinary and 1,226,160 phosphor 1s3d stamps were sold, in addition to 38,968 presentation packs. The stamps officially went on sale on 25th January but they are known to have been inadvertently sold a day earlier, and envelopes are recorded with that date in the postmark.

At that time the Philatelic Bureau was located in London, but a temporary bureau was established in Edinburgh to cope with orders from collectors all over the world. So successful was this operation, that the Post Office decided to transfer the Bureau to Edinburgh permanently, three years later. The Bureau published an attractive booklet, sold for a shilling, containing articles about Burns (by James Veitch, Editor of the *Burns Chronicle*) and Ayrshire postmarks by James Douglas of the Scottish Postmark Group, and giving details of the artist, the commemorative postmarks and the stamps. Two versions of this booklet exist, a rare variant having no imprint on the back cover.

Apart from the standard First Day postmarks, Shakespeare had been favoured with one special pictorial handstamp. For Burns, however, no fewer than eight special postmarks were provided on the day the stamps were issued. Seven of them, used in Alloway, Ayr, Edinburgh, Glasgow, Greenock, Kilmarnock and Mauchline, featured the poet's armorial badge with the motto 'Better a wee bush than nae bield'. Dumfries, however, had to be different. Its postmark depicted the Mausoleum with the motto 'The Friend of Man, to Vice alone a Foe' — from the epitaph which Burns had written for his father. This distinctive cancellation was designed by Provost Ernest Robertson of Dumfries. In addition to the handstamps used at the eight post offices, a duplicate set of datestamps was held at the Philatelic Bureau and applied to covers sent in by collectors wishing the different marks. The Bureau handstamps differed from those used in the respective offices in size and in minor details of the lettering. Unadopted essays for pictorial handstamps, submitted by George Kay (a naturalised Scot of Polish birth living in Edinburgh), were produced in three designs: a circular type portraying Burns, a vertical rectangle showing a a thistle and the Cottage, and a horizontal rectangle showing a plough and quill pen. The last-named, however, later served as the basis for the handstamps used at the time of the issue of the Burns air letter (discussed later).

Apart from the Post Office official cover, attractive envelopes were sponsored by several organisations. The Southern Scottish Counties Burns Association, for example, published a souvenir envelope whose

vignette showed the kitchen of Burns House in Dumfries. The Burns Federation had its own cover, and there were others which showed the Nasmyth portrait and even Highland Mary's statue in Dunoon. The special covers, produced by the various Scottish newspapers in conjunction with their souvenir editions, have already been described. Greenock Philatelic Society produced a cover featuring the various Greenock postmarks used during Burns's lifetime. Labels, printed in red on orange-yellow paper and properly perforated, were produced. They featured the Nasmyth portrait and had an inscription round the sides signifying that they had been issued to celebrate the commemorative stamps. The origin of these rather superfluous labels is not known.

Philatelic Forerunners

The stamps, labels, postcards and souvenir envelopes of the Fifties which greeted the poet's bicentenary and led to the belated celebration of 1966 were by no means the first appearance of Burns in philately. The late Arthur Blair, a well-known philatelic author and journalist, many years ago turned up the only known example of a small label printed in red, with a crude portrait of Burns in the centre and the words 'Scottish Tour' at top and bottom, and 'Dinna Forget' at the sides. It is obvious that this imperforate label was closely modelled on the Penny Red postage stamps, current from 1841 till 1880. Remarkably, the label must have been used on actual correspondence, for it bears the numeral cancellation 462, used at Tayinloan. Numbered obliterators were introduced in 1844, and for this reason the rumour has gathered momentum that these labels were issued in that year, and some students have even deduced that they were somehow connected with the great Festival on the banks of Doon held that year. If this were true, it would make this Burns label the earliest commemorative sticker in the world, pre-dating the labels issued in Austria in

1845 and the earliest Shakespeare labels, issued in 1864. A closer examination, however, reveals that the '1844-type' cancellation is nothing of the sort. It is a much later type of obliterator not generally introduced till 1864 and, in fact, not allocated to Tayinloan until 1884. As it was superseded by a datestamp in 1887 it may be safe to assume that the label was issued some time between these dates.

A second label of somewhat similar appearance and colour turned up in Vancouver a few years ago and was purchased by a prominent New York collector, Philip H. Reisman, Jr. It appears to be identical but for the inscription round the sides 'Birrell's Scottish Diorama Concert'. Interestingly, it too has a numeral obliterator — 24 — which is known to have been used at Appin from 1879 till the early years of this century. It seems extraordinary that the only examples of either label were both postmarked in Argyll. Further research, however, is required into the 'Dinna Forget' tour and Birrell's Scottish Diorama Concert, to pinpoint the date and purpose of these intriguing labels.

For the Burns Conference at Edinburgh in September 1925 souvenir envelopes with a commemorative inscription were produced, but no labels are known which might have been issued in this connexion. Labels featuring a vignette of the Cottage were produced about 1955 in a series raising funds for the Scottish Council for the Care of Spastics, and a few of these are known to have been applied to souvenir covers and cards posted at Alloway in January 1959.

Subsequent souvenirs

The stamps and postmarks of the 207th anniversary were by no means the last to do honour to Burns. The Fireside Post, a private local post operating in Toledo, Ohio, issued a 5 cent stamp portraying the bard with the inscription 'Fireside Post Celebrates Burns Nicht Jan. 25 1969'. This private post was run by Theodore

A. Jensen who must have some Scottish blood in his veins, as the majority of the personalities commemorated by his stamps have been Scots, ranging from Sir Alexander Fleming to Kirkpatrick MacMillan, inventor of the pedal bicycle. The Burns stamp was reprinted in black and magenta, but there was also a souvenir sheetlet containing a single stamp and this was printed in bright red-orange and released on 25th January 1970.

Peter J. Westwood, now Publicity Officer of the Burns Federation, first became involved with the production of Burns philatelic souvenirs at the time of the stamp issue in 1966. At that time he produced a label showing the Nasmyth bust, with thistles in the corners and a value of 'one groat'. These labels were printed in blue, but an elongated version of this design was printed in green and blue, with the bust in brown and red, red roses alongside. This was not printed as a label, but appeared as the vignette in a souvenir cover, accompanying the words of 'A red, red rose'. The 'one groat' thistle labels were reprinted in bright orange in 1971 and overprinted to mark the National Postal Strike, during which Peter Westwood operated a local post in Paisley. In connexion with that service envelopes with the stamps printed directly on to them were also issued. The groat label was reprinted in black on bright yellow paper later that year to celebrate the centenary of the first England-Scotland Rugby match and in 1985 the design was resurrected for labels printed in brown, with a yellow patch surrounding Burns's head.

In 1969 Peter also produced a set of three labels denominated 4d (blue), 5d (black on green) and 6d (black on yellow), depicting Burns, the Cottage and Burns House in Dumfries, respectively. These labels were issued on 25th January 1969 and coincided with the issue of the QE2 stamps which were cancelled on souvenir covers at Alloway. The 4d stamp was restrospectively overprinted to mark the launch of the ship at Clydebank. These labels were likewise pressed into service during the postal strike of 1971. Unoverprinted, they were used at Paisley, but with an overprint 'GB Delivery' they were employed in the local postal service operated by Messrs Gardiner and Ball at Dumfries. The Paisley labels were re-issued surcharged in the new decimal currency on 15th February 1971.

One of the Westwood labels of 1969.

The Burns Heritage Trail

The year 1974 was a momentous one in the history of the Burns movement, with the inauguration of the Burns Heritage Trail. To publicise this venture the Post Office in Scotland produced a pictorial air letter and provided special pictorial handstamps for use in the same eight offices as before. Two different handstamps were used in each place, on the first day of sale (13th January 1975) and on the poet's birthday. Both postmarks featured a plough, but different inscriptions were used on each date. The air letter was designed by Fraser Haston and had the Nasmyth portrait on the address side, the 'wee, sleekit, cowrin, tim'rous Beastie' on the middle panel and Tam o Shanter hotly pursued by the witches of Alloway, with the quotation 'The carlin claught her by the rump' on the back flap. A few of these air letters are known with the word SPECIMEN overprinted across the stamp; these specimens were distributed to journalists

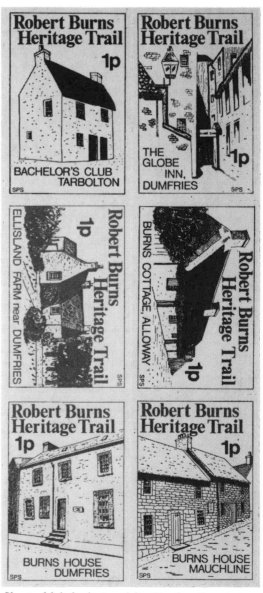

Sheet of labels designed by Gordon Rennie to publisise the Burns Heritage Trail, 1974.

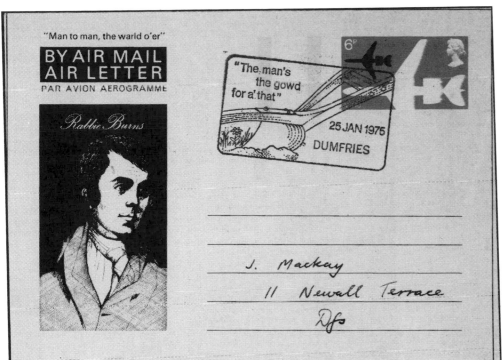

Burns air letter sheet by Fraser Haston, with the pictorial handstamp used at Dumfries, 1975.

Slogan cancellation publicising the Burns Heritage Trail.

Below: Souvenir cover bearing the Westwood labels overprinted during the 1971 postal strike.

and were also affixed to small placards on display at counters in Scottish post offices. The journalists' specimens were overprinted in black by a small steel die, whereas the counter display specimens were overprinted in violet by means of a large rubber stamp.

A novel feature of this air letter was that the various instructions to the user and and inscriptions were matched by appropriate quotations. Thus 'To open slit here' was accompanied by 'An' cut you up wi' ready sleight', while 'By Air Mail / Air Letter' was captioned 'Man to man, the warld o'er'. 'First fold here' and 'Second fold here' were tagged 'Need the world ken' and '... and let naebody see' respectively. 'Sender's name and address' provoked 'O Scotia, my dear, my native soil'. 'Designed by Fraser Haston' was neatly matched by 'My choicest model thou hast ta'en'. Finally the warning 'An Air Letter should not contain any enclosure; if it does it may be surcharged or sent by ordinary mail' inspired the quotation 'The best laid schemes o' mice an' men, Gang aft a-gley'.

Bearing in mind the Post Office aversion to the use of a postmark incorporating a portrait of Burns, an objection raised at the time of the bicentenary, it is interesting to note that the summer of 1975 saw a slogan cancellation in use at Dumfries, Ayr and Kilmarnock, and later extended by popular request to Glasgow and Edinburgh, which featured the Skirving portrait alongside the words 'Burns Heritage Trail'. The slogan was transposed so that the town die normally fell across the postage stamp, but there are many examples in which the poet's features *did* obliterate those of the Queen, but no objection seems to have been raised on this occasion. In addition to the air letter and the slogan postmarks, there was a circular adhesive label showing the Skirving portrait, issued by the Scottish Tourist Board to publicise the Heritage Trail. Labels issued by the Scottish Philatelic Secretariat for this purpose are listed separately later in this chapter.

Souvenir envelopes and special handstamps

Several philatelic events in the past two decades have had souvenir envelopes with a Burns theme. The South-west of Scotland annual philatelic convention, held at the Savoy Park Hotel, Ayr in September 1966, had a cover with a vignette of a reversed Nasmyth bust in black on green, designed by Peter Westwood and used in conjunction with the commemorative stamps, but only an ordinary Ayr handstamp. In 1974 the Solway Philatelic Society hosted the annual Scottish Philatelic Congess at Stirling University and the souvenir cover, designed by J.G. 'Tim' Jeffs of Kirkcudbright, depicted Burns and John Paul Jones, although the matching postmark alluded only to the latter.

On 12th March 1977 a DC 10-30 left the McDonnell Douglas base at Long Beach, California and flew non-stop to Prestwick in 9 hours 6 minutes. The aircraft had been purchased by British Caledonian Airways and was named 'Robert Burns'. Souvenir envelopes were carried on the aircraft, bearing the Long Beach postmark on the American 13c stamp commemorating the 50th anniversary of commercial aviation, with a pictorial cachet printed on the flap and a commemorative inscription on the address side. 247 Burns air letter sheets were overprinted with the airline logo and a picture of the airliner and posted at Ayr for transmission from Prestwick to Gatwick on the last leg of the flight. In addition, souvenir envelopes carried on the Prestwick-Gatwick flight on 13th March bore obsolete Burns 4d stamps cancelled with a private 'postmark' showing a picture of the aircraft. The aircraft was formally named 'Robert Burns, the Scottish Bard' by Colonel B.M. Knox, the Lord Lieutenant of Ayr and Arran, and the aeroplane was subsequently used on the British Caledonian route to Lagos, Nigeria.

There are other postmarks used in Ayr which are of relevance to Robert Burns. On 20th October 1940 a branch post office was established in the square

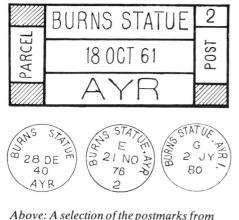

Above: A selection of the postmarks from Burns Statue post office, Ayr.
Right: First Flight Souvenir cover of the airliner 'Robert Burns', Prestwick to Gatwick, 1977.

opposite Lawson's statue of the bard, and this office took the name Burns Statue. This name is to be found in a variety of double- and single-circle steel stamps used at the counter, on registered packets, certificates of posting and pension-books, as well as the rectangular rubber datestamps used to cancel stamps on parcels. Ayr head post office is one of the few in Scotland to have a philatelic counter. On the opening day of this facility, 19th January 1981, a pictorial datestamp, showing the Cottage, was used on souvenir mail. Since then the Ayr philatelic counter has used a handstamp depicting the monument at Doonside. This handstamp is applied to any philatelic mail requested by members of the public, so long as the items posted bear stamps to the value of at least 3p above the minimum postage rate. This attractive handstamp has been applied in recent years to many souvenir covers, when no other special postmark has been made available for the occasion.

The Dumfries Burns club produced two souvenir covers for the poet's anniversary in 1981 and 1982. The first of these had a vignette showing the mausoleum, with Turnerelli's bas-relief, and this was accompanied by a pictorial postmark which showed the Muse of Poetry finding Burns at the plough. Both vignette and postmark showed the Cawthra version of the sculpture, with the poet standing *before* the plough. The following year the cover featured Burns House about 1935 when it was restored to its original appearance. The special handstamp depicted the Spode punch-bowl, purchased by the Burnsians of Dumfries in 1819 and used at the inaugural dinner of the Burns club in January 1820. I designed both of these handstamps and I well recall the reservations expressed by the local postal sales representative on account of the appearance of Burns's portraits in both of them, which were regarded as breaching the Post Office rule against portraits in postmarks. Opposition collapsed, however, when I pointed out that the Trafalgar Square branch office and the London chief office were at that very moment using pictorial handstamps featuring statues of Lord Nelson and Sir Rowland Hill respectively!

Several Conferences of the Burns Federation in recent years have had souvenir covers and pictorial postmarks. A cover showing the bard's portrait in blue was designed by Gilbert May for the Conference at Glasgow in 1978, while the postmark featured the Cottage. This interesting precedent was not followed up until 1982 when the Conference was held in Dumfries. The vignette on the cover reproduced Amelia Hill's statue while the handstamp showed the Mid Steeple, one of the burgh's most prominent landmarks, and alluded to in the patriotic song 'Does Haughty Gaul invasion threat?':

> Who will not sing God Save the King
> Shall hang as high's the steeple.

I had the honour of designing that postmark, too; but all subsequent handstamps and souvenir covers have been designed by the Federation's Publicity Officer, Peter J. Westwood. The poet's armorial insignia, accompanied by bars of music from 'A man's

Handstamp showing the Burns punch-bowl, Dumfries, 1982.

a man' and the poet's signature, formed the elements of the handstamp used at the Centenary Conference in London in September 1985. Kilmarnock was the venue for the 1986 Conference and on this occasion the cover showed John Wilson's printing works where the first edition of the Poems was produced in July 1786, but only the Ayr philatelic counter handstamp was employed. Similarly, although a souvenir cover was provided at the Edinburgh Conference in September 1987 the Edinburgh philatelic counter handstamp, featuring St Giles Cathedral, was used. The cover issued to mark the 1987 Conference portrayed 'Clarinda' (Mrs Nancy McLehose) with whom Burns had a platonic affair 200 years previously.

On the bicentenary of the Kilmarnock Poems in July 1986, however, a souvenir cover was sponsored by the *Kilmarnock Standard* and the pictorial handstamp showed the oak chair in the Birthplace Museum, made from the old Wilson printing press. Both Dumbarton and Dumfries celebrated the bicentenary of the conferment of honorary burgess tickets on Burns in June 1987. Peter Westwood designed the covers sponsored by the Dumbarton Burns club and the Dumfries Howff club respectively. An ordinary Dumbarton rubber datestamp was used to cancel the souvenir covers, and unfortunately all those not intended for purely local addresses were subsequently cancelled a second time at Glasgow, thereby spoiling the effect entirely. The Howff Burns club, however, sponsored a Westwood handstamp featuring the thirteenth century Devorgilla Bridge, with a line from 'The Five Carlins':

Maggie by the banks o Nith, a dame wi pride enough.

In recent years the National Trust for Scotland has sponsored a number of special postmarks to publicise its properties. On 11th June 1985 a pictorial handstamp was used at Ayr to celebrate the 200th anniversary of Souter Johnny's Cottage and this depicted Thom's statue of the Souter. The collecting of Burns souvenir envelopes and postmarks has now become a branch of philately in its own right, and there is even a Burnsiana Collectors Club for philatelists. In recent years Peter Westwood has designed and produced a number of other pictorial covers, from the Federation Centenary Conference of 1985 onwards. Among the souvenir covers may be enumerated those in both ordinary and airmail versions, portraying Burns and 'Bonie Jean' to mark the bicentenary of their first 'unofficial' marriage (1985). Subsequent bicentenaries commemorated in this manner have been Mary Campbell's death at

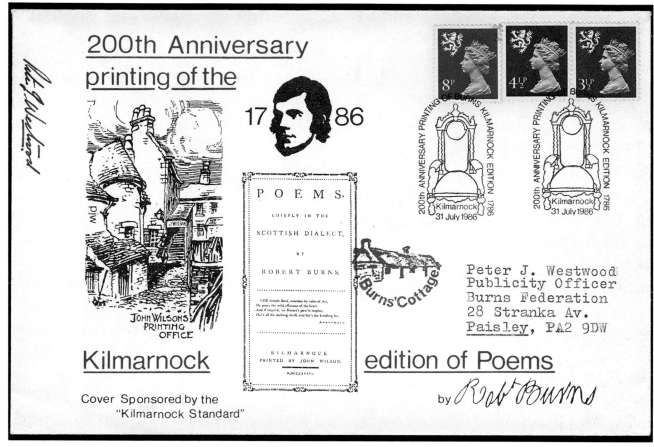

Westwood Souvenir cover celebrating the Bicentenary of the Kilmarnock Edition. The pictorial handstamp shows the Burns Chair in the Birthplace Museum, made from John Wilson's printing-press.

Greenock (20th October 1986) and Burns's first arrival in Edinburgh (29th November 1986). For the 200th anniversary of the proclamation of Burns as Caledonia's bard, by the Grand Lodge of Scotland, there were two covers. One showed the poet being crowned by the Muses, while the other featured the jewel worn by Burns as Depute Master of St James's Lodge, Tarbolton and the masonic inscription which he placed in the Bible given to Mary Campbell when they exchanged vows. The Burnsiana Collectors Club

Cachets used at Burns House (Dumfries), Ellisland and The Cottage, Alloway.

plan to issue souvenir covers at the rate of about six a year over the ensuing period, which will witness the celebration of many bicentenaries associated with the poet, up to July 1996.

Cachets

A cachet is defined as any marking, not being an official postmark, which is applied to a cover or postcard. Sometimes these marks, usually made by rubber stamps, are applied as 'cancellations' to labels and private, local postage stamps. The cachets used by British Caledonian Airways have already been mentioned. Many Burns clubs have used cachets on their mail for almost a century as an identifying mark, thus superseding the wax seals used at an earlier period.

It is surprising that this device was not adopted at the time of the birth bicentenary in 1959 but so far as I am aware nothing of this sort was used. In recent years, however, there have been several pictorial rubber stamps. Peter Westwood has provided a number of such cachets, struck in coloured ink on the souvenir covers for which he has been responsible. A 'double-barrelled' cachet depicting a masonic penny was applied to the covers of January 1987, while a large red cachet featuring the arms of the old royal burgh of Greenock was used on the Highland Mary covers of October 1986.

In 1985 the Scottish National Tourist Board introduced colourful passports listing the places to see along the Burns Heritage Trail, and containing spaces for the application of rubber stamps at each of these

Some of the labels issued by The Scottish Philatelic Secretariat for Clyde Fair International, 1972.

Burns Heritage Trail logbook, for impressions of rubber stamps.

locations. These rubber stamps are also struck on picture postcards and can therefore be classed as cachets in the philatelic sense. Cachets depicting the various landmarks associated with Burns will be found at the Birthplace Museum, the Monument and Land o Burns (Alloway), Culzean Castle (Maybole), Burns House (Mauchline), Dean Castle (Kilmarnock), Burns Museum at 'Wellwood' and the Heckling Shop in Glasgow Vennel (Irvine), Souter Johnny's Cottage (Kirkoswald), the Bachelors' Club (Tarbolton), the Murray Arms Hotel (Gatehouse of Fleet), the Selkirk Arms Hotel (Kirkcudbright), Ellisland Farm, and Burns House, the Burns Centre and the Globe Inn (Dumfries).

Other labels and unofficial stamps

The Scottish Philatelic Secretariat was founded by Dr George Philp of Glasgow in 1968 with the aim of making good the deficiencies in the Post Office policy with regard to the commemoration of events and personalities in Scottish history. The aims of the Secretariat were later expanded to include labels designed to promote Scottish tourism by showing scenes and landmarks of interest. The eighth issue of the Secretariat appeared on 10th June 1972 and showed scenes in the west of Scotland, to publicise Clyde Fair International. One of these labels depicted the Cottage at Alloway. The labels were designed by Gordon Rennie and issued in sheets containing one of each of the six designs, priced at 1p each. A second printing was made and the colours of the Alloway label was altered from grey to blue. The following year sheets of nine labels were issued for a similar event, and on this occasion the Monument at Alloway, and Highland Mary's statue at Dunoon were featured on two of the labels, in myrtle-green and pale blue respectively.

Postmark commemorating Ellisland Farm Bi-centenary.

In 1974 the bicentenary of the death of the poet, Robert Fergusson was marked by two labels tariffed at the then first and second class postal rates. The twopence-halfpenny label featured portraits of Burns and Fergusson his 'elder brother in the muse', while the threepenny label reproduced Fergusson's portrait with the lines written by Burns for Fergusson's tombstone in the Canongate kirkyard. The portraits used on this occasion were the Beugo engraving of Burns (by courtesy of Irvine Burns club) and Alexander Runciman's painting of Fergusson in the Scottish National Portrait Gallery. The labels were designed by Gordon Rennie and printed in sheets of four. Both labels were released on 25th January 1974.

The Secretariat also provided labels for the Tam o Shanter Museum at Ayr, showing the old inn. These labels were originally issued in brown or blue, but later a version was printed in turquoise. These labels were printed in sheets of six, on sale at 1p per label. They were designed by Gordon Rennie who was also responsible for the designs used in a sheet of six labels issued in 1974 to publicise the Burns Heritage Trail. These labels followed the same format as the Clyde Fair labels two years earlier. Four vertical designs featured the Bachelors' Club, Tarbolton (red), the Globe Inn, Dumfries (violet), Burns House, Dumfries (yellow-green) and Burns House, Mauchline (orange), while two horizontal designs showed the Cottage, Alloway (brown) and Ellisland (grey). These labels were likewise priced at a penny each. As with the Clyde Fair labels of 1972, a second printing of the Heritage Trail labels was produced, the layout of the sheet being altered and new colours being adopted. Unadopted essays by Gordon Rennie for this series are known to exist, and include the Mausoleum and Poosie Nansie's at Mauchline.

Robert McCutcheon of Stirling produced a series of labels portraying Burns and issued them on 25th January 1971. These labels, priced at half a crown each, were printed in various combinations of inks and coloured papers, and a special cachet for Burns Nicht was also provided. Large rouletted labels with the poet's head in yellow-brown against the saltire flag were issued in or about 1978. A few of them were subsequently overprinted in three lines at the foot to commemorate the Burns Conference held at Glasgow that year. Undoubtedly the most ambitious Burns labels so far were those issued in a sheet of 24 in 1986

to celebrate the bicentenary of the Kilmarnock Poems. Two rows of six were priced at 5p, two labels were priced at 20p and the rest at 10p. Each label bore a portrait of Burns by Peter Westwood, based loosely on the Nasmyth bust, in the upper right-hand corner. The vignette in each case featured a scene or incident from the poet's life, with a caption in bold capitals and appropriate lines from his poems below. The only exceptions to this were the two 20p labels which respectively depicted the poet's birthplace and the house in which he died. The inscription to the left of the portrait ROBT. BURNS, the date of the scene and the value were inscribed in orange-brown, while the rest was rendered in black ink on yellow paper. The labels depicted the following subjects: the poet's birth in the stormy January of 1759, attending Murdoch's school (1765), tales from Betty Davidson (1766), Murdoch closes the Alloway school (1768), first love and first song (1773), the country dancing school (1779), Rob Mossgiel (1785), first meeting with Jean Armour (1785), Jean Armour's desertion (1786), parting with Highland Mary (1786), publication of the Kilmarnock edition (1786), Jean's return from Paisley (1786), leaving Mossgiel for Edinburgh (1786), patronage of Scottish gentry (1787), marriage to Jean Armour (1788), off to Ellisland (1788), abandons Ellisland farm (1791), residence in Dumfries (1792), faithful Jessie Lewars (1796), last illness and death (1796), and Burns statue, Dumfries (1882). Self-adhesive labels, printed in black on white in a vertical format, were issued by Clackmannan Burns club in 1987 to celebrate the bicentenary of Burns's visit to the area during October 1787. Essays and colour trials for labels were prepared by Peter Westwood for issue in 1987-8. One is based on the original 'one groat' design but is in a smaller format and has the Skirving portrait substituted. Another has an elaborate frame incorporating the bard's two mottoes, while a third reproduces the Miers silhouette of 'Clarinda' and the signature she appended to her letters addressed to Sylvander. Peter has even

Left: Airmail sticker of 1988. Bottom left: McCutcheon postal strike label. Below: Postmark featuring Burns House, Mauchline.

Set of twenty four Kilmarnock Edition Bi-centenary labels.

produced an attractive design for an airmail sticker, incorporating the Skirving head. This was originally prepared in 1971 for John Cockburn who planned to fly round the world in a light aircraft named after the poet. The 'Robert Burns' world flight was to have been funded by the sale of souvenir stationery which had a decorative motif showing the aeroplane and the Nasmyth bust. Unfortunately the scheme foundered for lack of support. The souvenir envelopes are elusive and the airmail stickers were never produced at that time, although they were eventually released in booklets of 54 (six sheets of nine) in 1988 in time for use at the Burns Conference in Hamilton, Ontario.

Bicentenaries celebrated philatelically in 1988 centred on the official marriage of Burns and Jean in March 1788, and the poet's move to Ellisland in June. A souvenir cover was issued at Mauchline for the first of these events. The Scottish Philatelic Congress at Falkirk in April 1988 was hosted by the Ayrshire Philatelic Society whose cover showed the Skirving portrait and the Twa Brigs o Ayr. The Congress handstamp, however, featured Burns House in Mauchline. On 11th June a cover and handstamp were issued at Ellisland, sponsored by 'Cutty Sark' whisky and alluding to the fact that 'Tam o Shanter' was composed there. The postmark showed a view of the farmhouse.

Philatelists the world o'er have always had a soft spot for Rabbie. For many years the cover of *Stamp Magazine*, though published in London, included the second SCWS Burns label on its cover, while the Nasmyth bust appeared on the masthead of volume VI of *Scottish Stamp News*, the organ of the Alba Stamp Group which brings together collectors from all over the world interested in Scottish subjects in philately.

Burns in Numismatics

The poems and songs of Robert Burns contain many references to money in general and certain coins in particular. 'Braid' money was exclusively applied to gold, and 'broad' was the actual name of a gold coin minted by authority of Oliver Cromwell in England. 'Siller' applied strictly to silver coins, but soon came to mean money in general, just as *argent* and *airgiod* are used in French and Gaelic to this day.

Several poems make reference to 'airles' or an 'airle-penny', the coin exchanged to seal a bargain. Specifically it was the penny given by a master signing on domestic servants or farm-hands at the twice-yearly hiring fairs. The opening verse of 'O, can ye labour lea' illustrates this admirably:

> I fee'd a man at Michaelmas
> Wi airle-pennies three.

Pennies were struck in silver in England till the eighteenth century and, of course, survive in this metal to this day in the form of Maundy money. In Scotland, however, base metal was adopted at a much earlier date. The circulation of English pennies was sufficiently prestigious to warrant a separate epithet for such coins. In 'Hughie Graham', Lady Whitefoord offers to ransom the notorious horse-thief:

> Five hundred white pence I'll gie you,
> If ye'll gie Hughie Graham to me.

The last of the Scottish silver pennies were minted in 1496, but such was the inflationary situation at the time that they actually circulated for threepence.

In 'My Collier Laddie' the girl, singing of her lover in the coalmine, says:

> I can win my five pennies in a day
> An' spend it at night fu' brawlie

Fivepene was a farm labourer's daily wage in the 1780s, whereas miners (both men and women) earned fourpence per 30 hundred-weight of coal raised from the coal-face — a good daily average.

Moving up the scale of values, we find several references to the groat, or fourpenny piece. Like the silver penny, however, 'groat' in Scottish parlance was a term that fluctuated widely in actual usage. To be sure, the groat was worth fourpence when David II introduced it in or about 1357. Then it weighed 72 grains, but it was successively reduced to 61, 46 and then 28 grains by 1403. Thereafter its weight remained steady but its nominal value rose to 6d (1406), then increased in weight to 59 grains and it was retariffed at 12d (1451), dropped to 39 grains at the same value, then rose to 1s2d (1484), 1s6d (1526) and ended its days with a small amount of silver alloyed to a large amount of copper in 1586, when it was again worth 12d but had dwindled to a mere 26.25 grains. Thus, when the chorus of 'The Cardin o't, the Spinnin o't' speaks of

> When ilka ell cost me a groat

we would have to know the exact date of the song to determine the actual cost!

The tester crops up in several of the old ballads mended by Burns. This was a Lowland Scots variant of 'testoon' (Gaelic *tasdan*) and meant a shilling. They were struck only briefly in Scotland, in the reign of Mary Queen of Scots, and were obviously modelled on the *teston* then current in France, home-country of the Queen Mother, Mary of Guise. The only reference to shillings themselves, however, occurs in 'Gude Wallace' and that is an anachronism. One line refers to a reward of 'fyfteen shilling' for information leading to the arrest of Sir William Wallace — more than two centuries before the first English testoons were minted.

The sixpence, United Kingdom variety, was a familiar coin in Burns's time and it appears in 'The Henpecked Husband':

> Curs'd be the man, the poorest wretch in life,
> The crouching vassal to the tyrant wife!
> Who has no will but by her high permission
> Who has not sixpence but in her possession.

Numerous poems make reference to three coins which were distinctive to Scotland. Foremost of these was the plack (from French *plaque*, meaning a thin plate). This was a coin of very debased silver — more copper than precious metal, actually — which circulated widely between about 1470 and the end of the sixteenth century. During its currency its value fluctuated between 2d and 4d Scots, but it had disappeared long before Burns's day. It survived in the popular expression 'not worth a plack' and it is in this guise that it appears in several of Burns's poems.

Even more insignificant, however, was the bodle, which Burns occasionally spells as 'boddle' — to rhyme with 'noddle' in 'Tam o Shanter'. It had a somewhat shorter career than the plack, being minted in copper as a twopenny piece from about 1583 till 1697. Originally known as a half-plack, hard-head or turner, it seems to have adopted the name of bodle in the reign of Charles I, although the crowned monogram and thistle motifs remained the same. Charles II placed crossed sceptres below the crown on the obverse, and William III reverted to this style for the bodles minted in his name alone, from 1695 till 1697.

The bawbee was introduced in 1539 as a billon (copper-silver) coin tariffed at 6d Scots, with halves and quarters in similar designs. The derivation of this word is uncertain. The popular belief that it is a corruption of 'baby' because it depicted a baby's head is utter nonsense, although this fallacy probably arose from the fact that the diminutive penny of 1547 depicted the infant Mary Queen of Scots. The bawbee had a crowned thistle obverse and saltire cross reverse and may have taken its name from James Sillibawbee, Master of the Edinburgh Mint in the reign of James V when the coin was introduced. It disappeared from circulation after 1558, but was revived as a copper coin in the reign of Charles II, when 6d Scots was worth an English halfpenny, and was last struck in 1697. It survives in Lowland Scots as a synonym for a halfpenny to this day, and it is in this context that it figures in several poems by Burns.

One of Burns's best-loved songs, and the one which has endeared him most of all to the Socialist world, is 'A man's a man for a' that', his hymn to equality and the universal brotherhood of man. The opening stanza illustrates the point that all men are equal and that titles are but an artificial distinction, in the immortal lines:

> The rank is but the guinea's stamp
> The man's the gowd for a' that.

The 'stamp' or impression of the coin is merely external, and the gold in each person is what really counts.

Guineas appear in several poems and in the poet's lifetime the fourth head and fifth head or so-called 'spade' guineas would have been familiar to him. Originally tariffed at 20s, the guinea had, by the late eighteenth century, become worth 21s or £1. 1s, and its value is alluded to in the poem addressed to his superior in the Excise, John Mitchell, the Collector at Dumfries. This poem, written shortly before he died, shows Burns in dire straits and begging for money:

> I modestly fu' fain wad hint it,
> That One-pound-one, I sairly want it.

A few months earlier he dashed off a quatrain lampooning the decision of the Prime Minister, William Pitt, to put a guinea tax on hair powder, as a means of raising revenue to prosecute the war with France:

> Pray Billy Pitt explain thy rigs
> This new poll-tax of thine!
> I mean to mark the Guinea Pigs
> From other common Swine.

In 'The Twa Dogs', the aristocratic Caesar speaks of the wealthy laird:

> He draws a bonic silken purse
> As lang's my tail, whare, thro' the steeks,
> The yellow letter'd Geordie keeks.

The silk purse referred to here was the type fashionable in the eighteenth century, consisting of a long tube stitched up the side and having draw-strings at the top. The image is conveyed of the guineas with their lettering and profile of George III on the obverse, glinting through the stitches.

In 'The Lass wi' a Tocher' Burns returns to the theme that the girl's dowry is more important than her good looks. The latter, after all, fade away, but the money is another matter:

And e'en when this Beauty your bosom has blest,
The brightest o' Beauty may cloy when possess'd
But the sweet, yellow darlings wi' Geordie impress'd,
The langer ye hae them, the mair they're carest!

Even in the last years of the poet's life, however, the golden guinea was suffering the strain of the protracted wars with France, and paper money was becoming increasingly common, although the Bank of Scotland had, in fact, been issuing notes since 1695. In 1786, when Burns was contemplating emigrating to Jamaica, he wrote twelve lines of poetry on the back of a one-guinea note of the Bank of Scotland (which, in those days, was blank on the reverse). The note,

issued on 1st March 1780, may be seen at the Birthplace Museum:

> Wae worth thy power, thou cursed leaf!
> Fell source o' a' my woe and grief.
> For lack o' thee I've lost my lass,
> For lack o' thee I scrimp my glass...
> For lack o' thee, I leave this much-lov'd shore
> Never, perhaps, to greet old Scotland more.

Burns was associated directly with two men who left their mark in the banking history of Scotland. Patrick Heron (1736-1803) was a partner in the ill-fated bank of Douglas, Heron & Company of Ayr, which failed disastrously in 1773 and ruined many of the prominent families of south-west Scotland. Twenty years later, however, Patrick Heron bounced back as the Whig candidate in the General Election of 1795. Burns contributed four ballads to the election campaign. The third is couched in terms of a mock battle between the opposing factions and in one verse the Tories say:

> The Douglas and the Heron's name
> We set nought to their score:
> The Douglas and the Heron's name
> Had felt our weight before.

This was a side-swipe at the bank failure, hinting that Tory machinations lay behind its collapse. Notes to the value of one pound or one guinea were issued in 1769 and printed in a curious back-hand script, the date of issue, serial numbers and signatures being entered in manuscript.

One of Burns's epigrams, an art-form for which he was justly famous, was addressed to James Gracie, proprietor of the Dumfries Commercial Bank (known locally as Gracie's Bank) which he founded with his son in 1804. In Burns's lifetime, however, Gracie was Dean of Guild and captain of the local volunteers:

> Gracie, thou art a man of worth,
> O, be thou Dean for ever!
> May he be damn'd to Hell henceforth,
> Who fauts thy weight or measure!

One-guinea note of James Gracie's Dumfries Commercial Bank.

Gracie's Bank failed after only four years, with a deficiency of ten shillings in the pound. Its one-guinea notes are still fairly common, but the five-pound notes are rare. Though Burns went through life barely making ends meet, his new-found fame as a poet brought him short-lived fortune. In one of his letters he refers to banknotes being through his hands as commonly as salt-permits, but that was a very brief state of affairs! Although the use of cheques was becoming more fashionable in Burns's lifetime, the usual method of making monetary transactions by post was by banker's order. In a letter of 17th May 1787 from Berrywell near Duns, to Mr Pattison, the Paisley bookseller, Burns mentions a letter from Pattison enclosing an order of the Paisley banking company drawn on the Royal Bank for £22 7s, payment for 90 copies of the Poems. Sometimes Burns would ask Peter Hill to settle bills for him in Edinburgh and debit the sums to his account. From Ellisland in April 1791 Burns wrote to Gracie about a bill of Alexander Crombie which Burns honoured, to his cost. Two months later he wrote to Thomas Boyd, the Dumfries architect who had built Ellisland farmhouse: 'As it is high time that the account between you & me were settled, if you will take a bill of Mr Alexr Crombie's to me for twenty pounds in part, I will settle with you immediately... Mr Crombie cannot take it amiss that I endeavour to get myself clear of his bill in this manner, as you owe him and I owe you.' Thus it can be seen that receipts for the loan of money were often circulated as a form of money in their own right, the 'bill' being endorsed by those through whose hands it passed. Burns mentions this transaction again, in a letter to David Sillar: '...I was considerably richer three days ago, when I was obliged to pay twenty pounds for a man who took me in, to save a rotten credit. — I heedlessly gave him my name on the back of a bill wherein I had no concern & he — gave me the bill to pay.'

Was Burns a numismatist?

Perhaps the most numismatically inspired of all the old ballads mended and reworked by Burns was 'Geordie' which deals with the imprisonment of George Gordon, 6th Earl of Huntly, on treason charges. He was later amnestied during the wedding celebrations of James VI. In one stanza Lady Gordon pleads for the release of her husband and the king demands a ransom of £5,000 which she goes off to raise from her tenantry:

Some gae her marks, some gae her crowns
Some gae her dollars many
And she's tell'd down five thousand pound,
And she's gotten again her Dearie.

This riot of monetary terms vividly illustrates the profusion of denominations current in the reign of James VI. 'Sword dollar' was an alternative name for the ryal, worth 30s, while the 'merk' or mark was tariffed at 13s 4d. The two-merk coin, known as the thistle dollar, was worth 26s 8d. There was no crown as such, but after the king's accession to the English throne in 1603 the sixty-shilling piece was introduced, worth five shillings sterling and therefore intended to be equivalent to the English crown.

Three of Burns's friends were numismatists, a fact which must surely make him unique among his fellow bards. Captain Robert Riddell of Glenriddell, who owned the estate of Friars' Carse near Burns's farm at Ellisland, was a man of great cultural refinement who, with the poet, founded the first public library in the area. Riddell was an amateur antiquary and numismatist of some note, and it is this attribute which Burns highlights in the 13th stanza of the Election Ballad of 1790:

Glenriddell, skill'd in rusty coins,
Blew up each Tory's dark designs.

There is a well-known picture which shows a portrait miniature of Riddell suspended above a table on which are laid out prehistoric flints, fragments of Roman pottery and an array of ancient coins.

The poem 'On Captain Grose' ends with a couplet about Adam de Cardonnel Lawson, Francis Grose's assistant and the author of *Numismata Scotiae*, the first monograph ever published on Scottish coinage:

So may ye get in glad possession
The coins o' Satan's coronation!

— a sly dig at Lawson's preoccupation with coins of immense antiquity.

James, Earl of Glencairn, friend and patron of Burns, was apparently a bit of a numismatist himself, for he acquired on one occasion a coin of immense rarity. This was a silver crown, struck at Oxford in 1644 during the Civil War when the Royalists commandeered the silver plate of the university colleges and melted it down. The silver was then re-issued in the form of coinage whose dies were engraved by Thomas Rawlins. The obverse of this handsome coin shows King Charles I mounted on a charger with a panoramic view of the city of dreaming spires in the background. How Lord Glencairn came by this coin is not known, but it is one of the greatest rarities in English coinage, fewer than a dozen examples being known. The last time that a specimen came up at auction, in June 1974, it fetched £20,000.

It is alleged that Lord Glencairn had this exceedingly rare coin mounted in the lid of a silver snuff box which he presented to Burns at a dinner of the Caledonian Hunt, on 25th January 1787. As I have already mentioned, I confess a certain scepticism about the Earl making such a valuable birthday present to someone whom he had only known for a few weeks at most. But that Burns was deeply indebted to Lord Glencairn he ever afterwards freely admitted and named one of his sons in memory of his late patron. Nevertheless, it is unfortunate that this gift is nowhere mentioned in any of the poet's letters. The box has an eight-line inscription engraved on the base: 'Presented by my highly Esteemed Patron and Benefactor, the Earl of Glencairn 25th January AD 1787 Remuneratio ejus cum Altissimo'. It has been said that this inscription 'unmistakably, as regards the signature at any rate, is in the hand-writing of Burns'. Quite palpably it is nothing of the kind, and was undoubtedly engraved professionally, although

Glencairn snuffbox with the rare Charles I crown inserted in the lid, Burns House, Dumfries.

whether on the orders of Burns or at some later date cannot be determined. The fact that the signature bears some passing resemblance to the poet's autograph, in fact, rouses my suspicions — an attempt, indeed, to pass the engraving off as the bard's very own handiwork. If Burns had actually commissioned an engraver to place such an inscription on the box he would not have insisted on a facsimile of his signature, but copperplate script uniform with the rest of the engraving.

It has to be said that there is no actual record of this snuff box having been in Burns's possession at any time. Nothing was known of it, in fact, until 1877, when it was mentioned by Scott Douglas's edition of the works of Robert Burns, under the date 25th January 1787: 'On this the Poet's birthday the Earl of Glencairn presented to him a silver snuff box... On an inner and carved bottom of the box Burns has, with his own hand, recorded the fact and the date of presentation.'

The snuff box came up at a Christie's auction on 12th July 1894. Sir James Dewar attended the pre-sale viewing and noticed the box among sundry silver articles and coins. On picking it up to examine it, he found that it had a double bottom, and on removing the outer casing he read the aforementioned inscription. Sir James had not seen the catalogue, in which the box was described as having belonged to Burns, so he went back to the sale the following day thinking that perhaps its special significance was not known, but determined anyhow to acquire it. The box was put up at a small figure, but was rapidly run up, and ultimately Sir James found that he had one competitor left, a man on the opposite side of the room, who went on persistently bidding against him. But Sir James was more persistent still and finally the box was knocked down to him at a very large price. When the sale was over Sir James went to the man who had been bidding against him and said 'I suppose you are a Burns worshipper like me and are sorry to have missed the box?' 'Burns!' retorted the man, 'I didn't know the box had anything to do with Burns. I have been bidding on behalf of a Scottish nobleman who very much wants the rare coin let into the lid of the box, to add to his collection!'

The silver snuff box was presented to the Dumfries Burns club at their centenary dinner in January 1920 by Sir James Crichton-Browne, on behalf of Sir James Dewar who could not be present. The snuff box is now on display in Burns House and is undoubtedly the most valuable item on show — whatever its provenance may or may not be.

Medals honouring Burns

Over the past two centuries Burns has been the subject of a number of medals. The earliest of these was a cameo portrait done in glass paste by James Tassie in 1801. It is rumoured that Sir Henry Raeburn had a hand in the modelling of this bas-relief and examples are known which bear his name, but, like the Thomson-Nasmyth painting, it seems probable that Raeburn's name was added after the event to enhance the value. Tassie was born in Pollokshaws, Glasgow in 1735 and studied sculpture in the Fowlis Academy before moving to Dublin in 1763. There he worked for Professor Henry Quin with whom he perfected a white enamel composition which he subsequently used to take casts from wax profiles modelled from the life. The formula of this vitreous paste was carefully guarded by Tassie and his nephew William who succeeded him in the business, and the secret seems to have vanished with the death of the younger Tassie, as no other modeller appears to have used it in more recent times. Tassie moved to London in 1766 and established a business as a jeweller and gem-engraver, specialising in reproductions of classical cameos. He also supplied moulds from which Wedgwood took casts for his celebrated jasperware. His main business, however, came from the wax portraits, usually modelled from the life, which were then duplicated in plaster and then formed the basis for the glass-paste cameo medals. The vitreous enamels created the appearance and texture of time-mellowed ivory, or marble with the faint wandering lines of delicate blue under the surface. James Tassie was largely patronised by his fellow-countrymen and about 500 different medallions were produced. The glass-paste medals were sold at various prices, from half a guinea to two guineas each. The Burns medal was one of the few executed indirectly, but it is a remarkably accurate likeness for all that. A fine example of the Tassie medal is preserved in the collection bequeathed to the Scottish National Portrait Gallery by William Tassie Junior in 1892. The Tassie medal of Burns is not uncommon, indicating its popularity as a souvenir in the early 1800s, and an example was included in a mixed lot of Burnsiana sold at auction in 1986 for £50.

The sculptor and medallist John Henning, like James Tassie, worked originally as a modeller of wax portraits. He was inspired by an exhibition of wax-works in his native Paisley in 1799 to try his hand in this exciting medium. The following year he moved to Glasgow where he was fortunate to secure the patronage of the Duke of Hamilton. Later he moved to Edinburgh where he modelled the profiles of the celebrities of the early nineteenth century. He settled in London where, for twelve years, he was engaged in making plaster replicas of the Elgin Marbles, the work for which he is best remembered, though he also executed the classical friezes for the Athenaeum (1830) and the Royal College of Surgeons (1838). He continued to produce wax profiles which were subsequently cast in plaster and then replicated in bronze, enamels and ceramics. The Birthplace Museum has a very fine wax portrait of Burns by an unknown hand. It is possible that Henning produced it, although it is unsigned. These wax portraits were sometimes lightly tinted to suggest flesh colouring, but the example here noted is in pure white wax. These profiles were commonly mounted on a dark velvet base and then framed and glazed for display on walls and mantelpieces. Henning certainly produced a small medal of Burns in wax, and a plaster cast of this, about two inches in diameter, is in the National Portrait Gallery. Examples of the Henning medal, which shows the poet in profile, were subsequently cast in bronze or silver, and an example, dated 1807, is in the Birthplace Museum. This may also have formed the basis of the undated and unsigned silver medal which was lent to the Centenary Exhibition by R.W. Cochran-Patrick, the foremost Scottish numismatist of his day. The National Portrait Gallery also possesses a plaster replica 4.1cm in diameter, after an unknown artist, donated by the Trustees of the British Museum in 1885. Other anonymous medals of Burns, at the Centenary Exhibition, include an electrotype (lent by Paisley Burns club), a circular portrait of Burns 'embossed in white metal' but not otherwise identified, and a bronze medallion based on the Flaxman statue formerly in the Calton Hill monument.

Several medals were produced in 1844, in connexion with the Grand Festival in honour of the poet at Doonside, held on 6th August that year. A medal in white metal by S. Woolfield of Glasgow has on the obverse a bust after Nasmyth, while the reverse features the Auld Brig o Doon and the Monument, with the legend 'Now do thy utmost Meg, Ere win the Key-stane of the Brig'. Another white metal medal of the same period commemorated the Burns banquet in Glasgow, held in the Kelvingrove Museum. The obverse shows the Muse crowning the seated poet with the legend 'And wear thou this, she solemn said'. The reverse showed the Monument, with the caption 'In commemoration of the banquet August 6, 1844' in the exergue. A small silver medal featured the Nasmyth bust on the obverse with the inscription 'Robert Burns Chief of Scottish Poets — born 25 January 1759, died 21 July 1796'. The reverse had a lengthy inscription contained in a wreath: 'Struck in commemoration of the Great Burns Festival on the Banks of Doon, 6th August 1844'.

The centenary of Burns's birth in 1859 was marked on a comparatively modest scale. Medals, struck by J.

Moore in bronze or white metal, had a portrait of Burns based rather loosely on Nasmyth, with the poet's name at the sides, and the heraldic device on the reverse captioned 'In commemoration of the First Centenary of the Birth of Robert Burns 1759-1859'. The Centenary Committee at Kilmarnock offered a gold medal as a prize in a competition for a poem about Burns. The medal, struck in 18 carat gold, cost the Committee five pounds but it is not known what form it took, who designed or struck it, or whether it portrayed the bard, although it may safely be assumed that it did. The United Burns club of Dunfermline awarded a silver medal in a similar competition to John Houston but, again, no mention of the details on the medal itself appear to have been published. J. Flounders of Argyle Street, Glasgow, produced a Centenary badge which was novel in having the Nasmyth bust reproduced as a photograph mounted on the front.

Several medals were struck to celebrate the unveiling of statues of Burns and the proceeds from sales of these medals helped to defray the costs of the statuary. A large bronze medal, struck by Gillespie Brothers in 1877, celebrated the inauguration of the Glasgow statue, which was featured on the obverse, with a commemorative inscription on the reverse. A bronze medalet was struck to commemorate the inauguration of the Dundee statue. The obverse showed a bust of the poet with the legend 'Born near Ayr 25th Jan. 1759 — died at Ellisland (sic) 21st July 1796. The reverse was inscribed 'In commemoration of the Unveiling of the Robert Burns Statue in Dundee 16th Oct. 1880'. This is a rare medal, doubtless on account of the howler perpetrated on the obverse inscription. Medals in bronze or white metal were produced two years later in connexion with the ceremony at Dumfries. The obverse featured a view of Mrs Hill's statue, captioned 'Dumfries to Burns her gifted son — a loving tribute Robin won', while the reverse was inscribed 'Burns Statue Dumfries by Mrs D.O. Hill. Unveiled by Lord Rosebery 6th April 1882'.

The centenary of the publication of the Kilmarnock Poems was marked by bronze and silver medals sold in connexion with the celebration in the Kay Park. The obverse bore the Nasmyth bust without any inscription, while the reverse depicted the civic arms of Kilmarnock and the legend 'Centenary Demonstration Commemorative of Burns' First Edition 1886'. Six years later Greenock Burns club held a competition for the best bouquet of grasses, and awarded the prize to Joanna Mary Morison. The prize took the form of a medal portraying Burns, but I have not been able to find further details.

The centenary of the poet's death yielded three separate issues of commemorative medals. The unveiling of the statue at Irvine on 18th July was the subject of a bronze medal whose obverse showed the statue by Pittendreigh Macgillivray flanked by the dates 1759 and 1796. The poet's name appeared round the top while the sculptor's name was inscribed towards the right, at the foot. The reverse featured a

Observe and reverse of the Centenary medal by J. Moore, 1859.

Observe and reverse of the 'Daisy' centenary medal, 1896.

bust of John Spiers, whose munificence had procured the statue. The bust was placed in a thistle wreath, and the clasped hands of universal brotherhood appeared below. The medallist showed exceptional ingenuity in accommodating, in an already crowded reverse, a very lengthy inscription: 'In commemoration of the unveiling of a statue of the poet Burns, presented by John Spiers Esqre to the Burgh of Irvine, inaugurated by Alfred Austin Esqre the Poet Laureate, 18th July 1896'.

The main celebration, of course, was held at Dumfries where Burns had died. Philip Sulley, secretary of the Centenary Committee, negotiated with the London firm of medallists, John Pinches, and the correspondence, preserved in the Ewart Library, sheds an interesting light on the way such matters were dealt with, especially the speed with which complex orders could be executed in those days. Sulley first approached the firm in March 1896 and on 30th April preliminary designs were submitted by Pinches. The white metal version was to have a tin clip at the top for ribbon suspension, though the firm were very doubtful whether a clip could be provided cheaply. Two alternative designs for the obverse were sent on 9th May; unfortunately details of the rejected design are not known, as both sketches had to be returned to the company. An estimate for the work was submitted two days later. The cost of engraving and preparing a pair of steel dies was £35. In addition, medals in white metal could be supplied at the rate of £9 7s 6d per thousand, but if the order exceeded 3,000 the price dropped to £8 7s 6d. Bronze and silver medals could be supplied at £40 and £12 10s per hundred respectively. Sulley eventually ordered a hundred of each in bronze and silver and 3,000 white metal, but later extended the latter to 5,000 in all. A sketch of an amended reverse omitting the foliage was sent to Dumfries on 14th May. A revised estimate on 29th May reduced the bill to £25 for 3,000 white metal medals, and the silver and bronze medals were likewise reduced, to £33 15s and £10 respectively. Sample cases followed the very next day. Plain, velvet lined cases cost a shilling each, but with a spring catch they were threepence extra. On 29th June John Pinches dropped a bombshell. The obverse die had cracked during the hardening process, due to a fault in the steel block. It was therefore necessary to get a new die engraved. Consequently, what had seemed like plenty of time ended up as a rush job. Pinches sent four proofs from the cracked die on 2nd July, adding that it would be unsafe to continue using it as an even more serious flaw had begun to develop. Pinches felt confident, however, that he could despatch the order on the night of 17th July in time for the ceremony on 21st. Sulley replied saying that he had hoped to distribute medals on 13th July. On 11th July Pinches despatched by rail 26 silver and 25 bronze medals, completing the first 50 of each. By this time the idea of the tin clip had been abandoned on grounds of cost. Sulley had asked for the white metal medals to be simply pierced with a hole instead. Pinches now quoted an extra 10s per thousand for this work. On

13th July Pinches wrote again, promising to send off a thousand of the white metal medals by passenger train that night, and that the consignment would reach Dumfries at 5.29 am. This letter also mentioned a single example of the medal struck in 18 carat gold, fitted with a suspension bar, at a total cost of £10. It is not known what happened to this unique gold medal, though it is assumed that it was intended for presentation to the Earl of Rosebery who performed the wreath-laying ceremony.

A further thousand white metal medals were despatched on the afternoon of 14th July and a third batch was sent the following day. Pinches pointed out that it was impossible to strike the remaining bronze and silver medals while the white metal medals were going through the press. He offered to do either the bronze and silver medals and then proceed with the final 2,000 white metal medals, or vice versa. A fourth thousand of the latter were sent off on 16th July with a note saying that there was a slight hold-up while a stock of white metal blanks were being procured, and in the meantime the firm would press on with the rest of the bronze medals. Sulley had a leaflet advertising the medals prepared and from this we learn that the silver medal, complete with case, was sold for 11s post free, while the bronze medal was sold for 6s. The white metal version was available at sixpence each, or 45s per 100, carriage paid. The obverse bore an excellent likeness of Burns, based on the Nasmyth portrait with the poet's name and dates round the circumference. The reverse depicted the Mausoleum with the words 'Dumfries Centenary Celebrations' and the date 'July 21st 1896' in the exergue.

A medalet in white metal of unknown manufacture had a left-facing profile flanked by daisies and the inscription 'Dumfries Centenary Celebration — 21st July 1896'. The reverse had a lyre at the top and a lengthy inscription in a wreath of thistles: 'Robert Burns, born January 25, 1759, died July 21, 1796. Interred in St Michael's Churchyard, Dumfries July 25, 1796. 1796 — 1896'.

The commemorative medal reached its zenith at the close of the nineteenth century, but declined rapidly in popularity as other commemorative media were developed. A medal honoured the Sydney statue in 1905 but significantly no medals were struck in 1909 for the 150th anniversary of the poet's birth. No further medals appeared until 1966 when Sandhill Bullion Imports of Leeds, cashing in on the craze for commemorative medals which began with Churchill's 90th birthday and the Apollo space programme, offered 750 fine gold and 1,000 pure silver medals portraying Burns on the obverse, with the Cottage and '207th Anniversary' on the reverse. The very odd anniversary is explained, of course, by the fact that it coincided with the British stamp issue. In more recent years aluminium-bronze medals, (with a brass appearance) were struck in 1981 to celebrate the centenary of the Cottage Trust and these depicted the poet's birthplace. Bronze medals with a proof finish are currently available from the Birthplace Museum and these portray Burns on the obverse and show the

Top row: Dumfries Mausoleum medals by Pinches, 1896. Bottom: Dumfries statue medal, 1882.

Uniface bronze medallion, modern.

Burns and Birthplace medal, 1982.

Obverse and reverse of the Dumfries medal, with bust based on the Reid miniature, 1987.

Cottage on the reverse. In 1986 the Tower Mint of London was commissioned by the Dumfries burgh museum to produce medals whose obverse showed a profile bust of Burns, derived from the Reid miniature. The reverse of these medals bore a laurel wreath containing lines from 'A man's a man' (aluminium-bronze), or had the space within the wreath left blank (silver). This made the silver medal an ideal presentation piece which could be engraved for specific occasions. In 1987 some twenty of the silver medals were re-issued with the date 4th June 1987 engraved on the reverse to signify the bicentenary of the conferment of the honorary burgess ticket on Burns. At the same time, the aluminium-bronze version was supplied in a plush-lined presentation case with a gilt inscription marking the bicentenary. An edition of the aluminium-bronze medal in a much smaller diameter is also currently available, mounted on souvenir teaspoons. The Birthplace Museum also sells uniface bronze medallions 75mm in diameter, showing the Nasmyth bust and designed for hanging on a wall. The Tower Mint also struck a medal in 1988 for the bicentenary of Ellisland.

In recent years the sculptor Ron Dutton has experimented with limited editions of medals cast in bronze, with abstract and symbolic motifs illustrating some of the best loved poems and songs of Burns.

Recto and verso of the Clydesdale Bank £5 note, 1983 version.
(Photographs by courtesy of the Clydesdale Bank Plc.)

£1 promissory note of the Tam o Shanter Burns Club, Coventry, 1987.

Masonic medals: (left) Mauchline St David Lodge bicentenary, (right) Glasgow Masonic Burns club.

Paper money

The Clydesdale Bank was established in Glasgow in 1838, from an amalgamation of the Greenock Union Bank, the Edinburgh and Glasgow Bank and the Eastern Bank of Scotland. Branches were established in the south and west of Scotland, but in the 1870s the Bank opened three branches in Cumberland, much to the consternation of the English banks, who referred the matter to Parliament. The Select Committee appointed to investigate the affair did not make any recommendations, but the Scottish banks took the hint and there were no further incursions into England, other than the opening of branches in London. The Clydesdale Bank was taken over by the Midland in 1919. Four years later the Midland also acquired the North of Scotland Bank, but it was not until 1950 that the two Scottish banks were merged, and for a time the banknotes showed the joint name. The Clydesdale Bank reverted to the shorter title in 1963.

Eight years later an entirely new series of notes was introduced, and had the theme of Scotland's Men of Life and Letters. It was decided that Robert Burns should be the subject of the £5 note and the Bank's design consultant, Lewis Woodhuysen was commissioned to produce a suitable design. To this end he secured the services of Owen Wood, a well-known artist, to provide the original artwork which was then translated into the engraving technique employed in the printing of the notes by Thomas De La Rue.

A very great deal of care went into the production of the artwork. It was decided to use the Nasmyth bust-portrait, but this had to be reversed so that Burns was facing into the note, and thus uniform with the other notes in the series. There have been some comments made concerning which side the poet parted his hair, and the reversal of the picture added to the confusion. The reverse of the note was based on images evoked by Burns's poems — a field-mouse, oats, red roses and the rolling countryside of Kyle where Burns was born. The drawing of the field-mouse came primarily from a photograph in a natural history magazine and Schubert's *Natural History*, *Country Life* and the *Cyclopaedia of Arts, Sciences and Literature*. The first drawing of the oats was not correct as the strain found in Burns's time was a very poor comparison in relation to the modern variety. Similarly, the artist admitted to further botanical ignorance by illustrating the form of hybrid rose more appropriate for twentieth century gardens. The red, red rose to which Burns alluded was the only cultivated variety in existence in his lifetime, and was similar to the native wild rose. This also applied to the sheaf of wheat in the background of the portrait on the obverse. A small number of notes with a 'Specimen' overprint was prepared for circulation in the banking world. The original issue was inscribed 'Clydesdale Bank Limited' on the front, but the most recent notes have had this emended to 'Clydesdale Bank Plc'. The very first note to be issued, with the serial number D/A 000001, was presented by the Bank to the Birthplace Museum, where it is on display.

The Tam o Shanter Burns club of Coventry issues its own scrip, in the form of notes printed in black on pink paper. These notes are uniface and show the Nasmyth portrait in the centre, with 'One Pound' wreathed in thistles and a promise to pay the bearer on demand 'goods or services required equal to the sum written hereon'. These notes are purchased at face value by club members and are subsequently exchanged for food and drinks from the bar, or go towards the cost of admission to the anniversary dinner and other club functions. This is a novel method of maintaining cash flow and it is to be hoped that other clubs emulate this practice.

Miscellaneous badges, medals and tokens

Probably the earliest examples of badges and insignia which portrayed Robert Burns were those adopted by masonic lodges which had a personal association with the bard. Examples of masonic jewels, badges and even copper token pennies with the Nasmyth bust are believed to date from the early years of the nineteenth century, and some fine examples may be seen in the Burns House museum in Mauchline.

Bronze masonic tokens, St David Mauchline 133 Lodge.

Many Burns clubs over the years have provided their members with distinctive badges, usually incorporating an effigy of Burns. The Tam o Shanter Inn has an interesting badge simply inscribed AYR CLUB with a bust of Burns in the centre. This unusual badge, in brass and blue enamelling, is believed to have been current at the turn of the century.

Apart from the magnificent Presidential chain in solid gold with the poet's effigy in bas-relief on the central medal, introduced in 1916, the Burns Federation itself has had a number of badges and medals in the course of the past century. Medals fitted with a ring for suspension from a ribbon have been presented to Presidents on demitting office, and similar medals, with the Federation's insignia, have been awarded to those individuals on whom the honour of Honorary President has been conferred. The idea of introducing medals for award to schoolchildren in the annual competitions held under Federation auspices was first suggested in 1926 by J. M. Menzies of Dumbarton who recommended that a bronze medal be struck. The matter was raised at the Derby Conference in 1927 and expanded to include both gold and silver medals as well. The medals were oval in shape, and had the heraldic device from the poet's last seal on the obverse. The border consisted of thistles, with the Federation name at the foot. The reverse had a similar thistle wreath and the words PRESENTED BY THE in raised lettering, with space below for the school or Burns club making the award to be inserted by engraving. The medal was designed by the architect Ninian Macwhannell and the cost of manufacturing the dies was generously borne by Sir Robert Bruce, a Past-President of the Burns Federation. The bronze medals were sold for 3s 9d, the silver for 7s and the gold for 31s each, although within a year or two it became necessary to sell the gold medals at the prevailing bullion price, as the value of gold began to rise sharply. It is doubtful whether many gold medals were ever distributed, and even the bronze and silver medals are elusive. These much-coveted prizes were discontinued some time before the Second World War and have never been revived.

Originally associate members of the Burns Federation and members of affiliated clubs could purchase a pocket diploma which allowed them, on presentation, to attend meetings of kindred clubs and societies. Something less cumbersome, however, seemed desirable and the idea of a Federation badge or brooch was mooted just after the Second World War. Attractive badges, with the Burns insignia in coloured enamels on a gilt background, were ordered from Thomas Fattorini of Birmingham and made available to Burnsians in time for the annual celebrations in January 1949. Enamelled clasps in matching colours were produced in 1955 and 1959 to commemorate the International Burns Festival and the birth bicentenary respectively. Subsequently the badges and medals of the Burns Federation were produced for some years by Robert Horn of Glasgow. More recently, however, insignia has been produced by James Davie, an Honorary President of the Federation, and Eric Rawlins of Huddersfield, notably the enamelled medallion with the Nasmyth bust, which was issued in 1985 to celebrate the Federation's centenary. This attractive device was produced as a brooch or pendant. Mr Davie has also been responsible for the presidential chains of office and other badges and regalia used by Burns clubs, Caledonian and St Andrew's societies and masonic lodges in many parts of the world.

Selection of Burns Club and Federation medals.

Burns in Ceramics

Spode punch-bowl and whisky jugs, 1819. Dumfries Burns Club.

Visitors to the Cottage at Alloway will no doubt be familiar with the kitchen interior, one of whose features is a dresser with an impressive rack of blue and white platters. In the bad old days, before sophisticated electronic surveillance systems were available, the Cottage used to suffer an appalling turnover in crockery. It seems that pilgrims to the birthplace could not resist the temptation to lean over the barrier and remove a plate or two and make off with the booty concealed about their persons. Tom McMynn, the Curator at that period, was fairly philosophical about it. Each week-end he would go into Ayr and pick up another batch of plates from the nearest hardware shop!

Pottery and porcelain afford the most popular and enduring medium for memorabilia, and examples associated with Burns date back to the early years of the nineteenth century. The first ceramic items commemorating the poet were the three-gallon punch-bowl and set of four whisky jugs which were manufactured by the Staffordshire company of Spode. At the Burns supper held in the Globe Inn, Dumfries on 25th January 1819 it was decided by the friends and admirers of the late bard to open a subscription for the purchase of a porcelain punch-bowl, to be used on all similar occasions. The bowl was duly delivered and was greatly admired at a meeting of the subscribers on 18th January 1820, and it was on that occasion that it was decided to constitute the Dumfries Burns Club. John Commelin was elected president, John Syme was vice-president and William Grierson was secretary. On 25th January 1820 the newly formed club dined in the King's Arms, when some forty gentlemen made excellent use of the new punch-bowl. At that inaugural dinner James Hogg, the 'Ettrick Shepherd', was elected an honorary member.

Interior of the Spode punch-bowl showing the Mausoleum.

Tam o Shanter lidded jug by Ridgway of Hanley.

Staffordshire flatback figures of Tam o Shanter and Souter Johnny, Globe Inn, Dumfries.

The punch-bowl measures 18 inches in diameter and stands on a deep pedestal which was inscribed with the names of the original subscribers and preserved for all time under the glaze. The bowl itself is elegantly decorated with floral motifs — thistles on the outside and vines on the inside. The Nasmyth bust was reproduced in a circular cartouche on the front, in a laureated frame, while Turnerelli's bas-relief from the Mausoleum appeared on the back. The Mausoleum itself was depicted inside the bowl. This commission was a rather unusual one for Spode, and it is significant that the bowl should be illustrated in the definitive history of the firm — although it is unfortunate that the Dumfries Burns club is described therein as 'the first of many throughout the world'.

A feature of the early dinners of the Dumfries club was the extraordinary number of toasts. In 1826, for example, there were no fewer than 34 toasts, including Milton, Homer and Greek Independence! Unfortunately, the punch-bowl was subjected to a great deal of robust — not to say irreverent — treatment at times. Grierson's son, a month old at the time of its purchase, was 'hanselled' in it by the Committee in his father's house at 102 Irish Street. In time, the bowl suffered grievously from careless handling at the convivial table. It was retired from active service and reposed in a damaged condition in Burns House. In November 1977, however, it was decided to have it restored and the Dumfries and Galloway Regional Council voted £800 for its repair. This was sucessfully completed in May 1978 by the Monogram Studio of Congleton, Cheshire — not so far from the original Spode pottery where the bowl was made. It can be seen in its pristine condition to this day in the Burns Centre, Dumfries, along with the handsome silver toddy ladle and the four jugs. The latter were decorated in uniform motifs, showing the Nasmyth bust on one side and a scene from 'Willie brew'd a peck o maut' on the other. The front of each jug is inscribed 'We'll tak a cup of kindness yet, for Auld Lang Syne' around the clasped hands of friendship.

Staffordshire wares

Among the earliest pottery with a Burns theme were the whisky jugs produced by the Staffordshire companies in salt-glazed stoneware with bas-reliefs on the sides. Fortunately it was the custom of the Staffordshire potters to incise their names and the date on the base of their wares. Appropriately, these jugs featured Tam and the Souter with the landlord and landlady. William Ridgway of Hanley produced punch jugs in grey stoneware with the date 1833 on the base. The convivial scenes from 'Tam o Shanter' were rounded off by silver thistle and haggis emblems decorating the mouth of the jug. On 1st October 1835 Ridgway issued a matched set of four jugs in a less ornate style, but still having the scenes from 'Tam o Shanter' on the sides. These jugs of 1835 may be found in various sizes and colours, with or without hinged pewter lids. Somewhat similar jugs were produced on 20th June 1834 by Machin Potts of Burslem , with scenes from 'Tam o Shanter' and 'The

Jolly Beggars' on the sides, a bust of Burns on the front, and a spout in the shape of a woman's head. Scenes from 'Willie brew'd a peck o maut' decorated jugs which may be found in white or grey wares, with or without a covered top. There are also vases in Staffordshire ware with the principal characters from 'Tam o Shanter' in low relief on the sides.

Salt-glazed stoneware of the Staffordshire type was also produced by several of the Scottish potteries in the mid-nineteenth century. The Royal Scottish Museum, Edinburgh has a saut-bucket from the Portobello Pottery, with bas-reliefs of characters from 'Tam o Shanter' on the sides. Whisky jugs from this pottery are also known, as well as from the Caledonian Pottery and the Kirkcaldy Pottery.

Flat-back figures

Apart from the useful wares, the Staffordshire potteries were renowned for their naive ornaments, designed for mantelpiece and ingle-nook. These were hollow moulded earthenware pieces, with a simple oval base and distinctive flattened backs (so that they could stand comfortably on a narrow mantel-shelf), and they suddenly became very popular in the 1840s, having evolved out of flower-vases and spill-holders. What started out as a cottage industry soon developed into a major part of the Staffordshire output and kilted Highlanders, wide-eyed milkmaids and naive spaniels accounted for the bulk of the product. The marriage of Queen Victoria and Prince Albert in 1840 inspired the production of pottery portrait figures and this made the flat-backs more popular than ever. Although most of the figure groups from the 1840s to the turn of the century were of real people, usually contemporary celebrities, it is significant that Tam o Shanter and Souter Johnny were also firm favourites. A fine example in this genre may be seen at the Globe Inn. These figures were often issued unmarked, and it is known that some of the Scottish potteries emulated their Staffordshire counterparts, notably the Rathbone Pottery of Midlothian which was active in the 1860s.

Mugs, jugs and tankards

Earthenware mugs, jugs and tankards, sometimes in matching sets, were produced by several mid-nineteenth century potteries. Much of this ware was workaday pottery distinguished only by a decorative motif, but seldom marked with the maker's name or initials. Tall whisky jugs with smooth white glazes and bas-relief profiles of Burns are thought to date from about 1850. The Caledonian Pottery, operated by Murray and Fullerton in Glasgow in the 1850s, produced large buttermilk jugs which were used by the farmers who rode round the city dispensing this commodity from churns on the back of their carts. This pottery specialised in a form of salt-glazed stoneware known colloquially as 'Bristol ware', and Tam and the Souter were perennial favourites. Similar jugs were a common sight on the counters of taverns at the same period.

Pint-sized mugs in white earthenware, with

Tam o Shanter and Souter Johnny sugar bowl.

Burns Death Centenary mug, Dumfries.

Brownware hot-water jug, Globe Inn, Dumfries.

polychrome underglaze decoration, were fairly plentiful in the second half of the nineteenth century, but were seldom marked. A fine example in the writer's collection has a barely recognisable portrait of Burns on one side and a picture of the Mausoleum on the other, produced at the time of the Centenary celebrations in 1896. The Centenary Exhibition displayed a couple of mugs of this type, one with scenes from 'Tam o Shanter' on the outside, and the other showing scenes from 'Willie brew'd a peck o maut'. The latter mug had a pottery frog crouching inside, the idea being that as you drained the mug the sudden appearance of the frog would frighten you into signing the pledge!

The Globe Inn has an interesting, and possibly unique, hot-water jug. This unmarked piece has a treacly brown glaze with cream panels and *sgraffito* decoration on the sides, with the inscription 'Mrs Smith, Burns Huffy (*sic*), Dumfries 1894'. The Tam o Shanter Inn at Ayr has a brown stoneware jug with the Nasmyth bust of Burns in bas relief. Several interesting vessels were displayed at the two exhibitions held at Lady Stair's House, Edinburgh in 1953 and 1959. Tam o Shanter was portrayed on several jugs, in Fife ware, Clyde pottery and an unidentified pottery (with green and white decoration). Souter Johnny was portrayed on a Fife ware jug, while 'Willie brew'd a peck o maut' was the theme of two different jugs of unknown origins, in stoneware and earthenware with raised relief. Mrs Janet Paterson, from whose collection many of these pieces came, also lent a fine punch-bowl decorated with Burns commemorative motifs.

Whisky jugs were a popular medium for Centenary commemoration. There is a fine example in the Tam o Shanter Inn, showing a portrait of Burns with the Auld Brig of Ayr in the background, transfer-printed in underglaze blue and white. A commemorative inscription appears on the front, below the lip. The brothers John and Matthew Preston Bell operated the Glasgow Pottery in the second half of the nineteenth century, and undoubtedly their best piece of work was the whisky jug with Etruscan polychrome decoration, showing the Cotter's homecoming on one side and the Auld Brig o Doon on the other. A little vignette of Alloway Kirk appears at the front. The Clyde Pottery at Greenock, which flourished between 1857 and 1903, produced jugs and bowls in more sombre hues, a favourite motif being the betrothal of Burns and Mary Campbell — singularly appropriate in view of the fact that it was in Greenock that Highland Mary ended her short life.

Mugs have remained a popular subject for pottery down to the present time. McEwen and Hendry manufactured mugs showing the Nasmyth bust or the Cottage at Alloway to celebrate the bicentenary of the poet's birth in 1959. Lancaster & Sandland of the Dresden Works at Hanley produced an attractive tapered whiteware mug about the same period, with a portrait of Burns and his dates of birth and death. Cartwright & Edwards of Longton, who flourished between 1916 and 1955, issued a mug which had a

Bone china coffee cup and saucer, with polychrome portrait of Burns.

Pair of polychrome jugs by Beswick Pottery, c. 1930, Globe Inn, Dumfries.

Incised stoneware beer mugs by McEwan & Hendry, 1959.

Burns commemorative mug, modern.

Tapered mug by Lancaster & Sandland, 1959.

view of the Cottage repeated on both sides. Denby, best known for their oven-proof stoneware, produced a tankard showing the Miers silhouette and the bicentennial dates, and a matching ashtray. Some time before the Second World War the Beswick Pottery produced whisky jugs with a rather naive portrait of Burns, after Nasmyth, in a floral wreath, on one side. A plough and verses by Burns appeared on the other. A pair of these artless but charming jugs may be seen in the Globe Inn. Among the more recent hollow wares are the tankard by the Border Pottery of Peebles, with a raised bust of Burns in gold on a white ground, An unmarked mug of English origin has a flower-wreathed portrait of the bard on one side and the first verse of 'A red, red rose' on the other, with 'Robert Burns Poet', his autograph and dates on the front. Britannia Designs Ltd issued a mug with a more accurate rendition of the Nasmyth portrait on one side only. The Highland China Company does a white mug with a polychrome view of the Cottage on one side and the national emblems of lion and thistles on the other. J. & A. Kay of Darwen, Lancashire produce brown-glazed earthenware tankards with bas-relief portraits of

Burns on the sides, as well as matching table-lighters and ashtrays. Mugs modelled in the shape of Burns's head are known in unmarked earthenware of the glossy black variety called Jackfield ware.

Aesthetically more attractive are the fine eggshell or bone china coffee cups, with matching saucers, which were produced as souvenirs of the Glasgow Exhibition of 1901. The Nasmyth portrait was reproduced in delicate colouring, while lavish gilding was applied to the rim and handle. Somewhat similar cups and saucers were produced with a nacreous glaze and polychrome vignettes of the Burns statue in Dumfries, so they probably date between 1882 and the turn of the century. Miniature tankards in bone china are known with a view of the Cottage on one side and the inscription 'One for the Road' on the other. The Birthplace Museum has a moustache cup in a yellow brown glaze with Burns scenes transfer-printed in black. This was produced by Ridgway around the turn of the century. Presumably cups and saucers in the same pattern were also produced, as I have seen a sugar bowl and cream jug by the same pottery, with tiny motifs of the Cottage, the Monument and Nasmyth bust.

Jackfield ware portrait mug.

Porcelain coffee cup depicting the Burns statue, Dumfries.

Bicentenary mug by Britannia Designs, 1959.

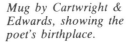

Polychrome whisky jug with transfer-printed scene from "The Cotter's Saturday Night".

Mug by Cartwright & Edwards, showing the poet's birthplace.

Denby stoneware beer mug, with Miers silhouette, 1959.

China mug with bas-relief applique bust of Burns.

Front and back of the "red, red rose" Burns mug.

Ridgway transfer-printed rack plates with portrait of Burns and view of his birthplace.

Rack plates, plaques and roundels

Of all the categories of ceramics, rack plates have the greatest visual impact. They take their name from the old custom of displaying them in racks mounted at the back of the sideboard or dresser, but nowadays they are best displayed on walls. The Ridgway series noted above also included several plates portraying Burns or showing the Auld Brig o Doon, the Cottage, or Midwood's poignant painting of Burns and Highland Mary. Plates of these designs appear to have been in production until the First World War, if not later, to judge by the mark impressed on the back. Of comparable age is the somewhat larger plate by Royal Doulton featuring the Raeburn-Nasmyth portrait of Burns in the centre, surrounded by characters from his life and works decorating the rim. These plates were produced in a very distinctive deep blue glaze, the inclusion of the word 'Royal' in the mark alluding to the title bestowed on the company by King Edward VII in 1902. In recent years Wedgwood have produced a polychrome rack plate in their famous Queen's ware, with the Skirving portrait in the centre. The portrait is flanked by vignettes of the Cottage and Brig o Doon, with Alloway Kirk at the foot. The intervening spaces round the circumference are occupied by a riotous jumble of musical instruments, sheets of music, Highland weapons, fieldmice, saltire flag and a stag's head for good measure. The words of 'A red, red rose' are inscribed on the back. Spode have issued a porcelain plate in a pale blue glaze, reproducing the Nasmyth bust, with large vignettes from the poems in the surrounding area. Rack plates were produced by the Clyde Pottery showing a spirited scene from 'Tam o Shanter', while Wallis Gimson & Company manufactured a polychrome plate with Burns's portrait as the main theme.

Roundels are large circular plates, usually with an absolutely flat back and a front in raised relief. Plaster was the preferred medium for roundels, cast in moulds, but sometimes they were modelled directly in clay and then fired in a kiln. The Globe Inn has a small roundel of Tam and the Souter with tankards raised. Terracotta roundels are known, with the *bisque* rim and bas-relief profile of Burns contrasting with the glazed white field. The Tam o Shanter Inn has a bas-relief profile of the poet in gilded stucco. Joseph Shearer has produced a stoneware roundel with Burns's profile in white on a blue ground, not unlike the blue and white jasperware for which Wedgwood are famous.

Rectangular plaques in high relief were a popular form of three-dimensional picture in the mid-nineteenth century. The Burns Centre, Dumfries has an interesting genre scene from 'The Jolly Beggars' in yellow-brown pottery but such plaques were more usually executed in white stoneware with delicate underglaze colouring. Plaques of this type are known with scenes from 'The Cotter' as well as the interior of the poet's birthplace, inscribed T.A.D. and dated 1908. Whyte's of Edinburgh produced plaques of Burns scenes about 1936 in a ceramic substance called Ivorex, which was intended to have the appearance of carved ivory. The Osborne Pottery of Mount Pleasant, Longton (1909-40) produced rectangular wall plaques in stoneware, with very realistic portraits of Burns, after Nasmyth, in high relief.

Allan Stoddart has a pair of unmarked tiles with portraits of Burns and Shakespeare in black on white ovals with blue marbled surrounds. In more recent years a wide range of tiles has been marketed by Richards showing scenes and maps of the Burns Country, multicoloured on a white ground.

Painted plaster wall plaque of Tam and the Souter, Globe Inn, Dumfries.

Rack plate by Spode.

Wedgwood rack plate.

Blue and white plaster plaque by Joseph Shearer.

Upright cartouche plaster roundel, Mauchline Burns Tower.

Polychrome painted stoneware roundel,

Bas-relief pottery plaque illustrating the poet's birth.

Royal Doulton rack plate, c.1902.

Black basaltes bust by Josiah Wedgewood, Globe Inn, Dumfries.

White alabaster figurine of Tam.

Large parian-ware bust by Minton, 1850.

Statuettes and busts

Josiah Wedgwood patented a very hard ceramic substance known as black basaltes, from a fancied resemblance to the basaltic columns of the Giant's Causeway. This material was capable of being cast and was an ideal medium for small statuary and busts. William Wyon, best remembered as a medallist and coin engraver, also sculpted bas reliefs which were published by Wedgwood as jasperware medallions and roundels. It is not known whether Wyon ever sculpted Burns in this form, but he certainly modelled the poet's portrait in the round. Busts of Burns in black basaltes are known in various sizes with the incised Wedgwood mark and 'W. Wyon' on the reverse. The Globe Inn possesses two of these busts, which may be seen in the Burns room downstairs and the Burns bedroom upstairs.

The Burns Centre, Dumfries has a finely modelled alabaster statuette of Tam o Shanter seated, tankard in hand. Lower down the social scale are the seated figurines of Tam and the Souter in painted plaster, after the carved stone figures by James Thom. The Monument has an interesting plaster figure of Tam o Shanter modelled by Antonio Logotti of Glasgow in 1829 — very much contemporaneous with Thom himself. A pottery group of Tam and the Souter was shown at the 1953 and 1959 exhibitions in Edinburgh, but no further details were given in the catalogue. The English firm of Minton patented a fine-grained, hard-paste porcelain with a matt surface known as Parian ware, from its resemblance to the delicate white marble of the Greek island of Paros. This was enthusiastically copied by other potteries, to supply the insatiable Victorian demand for marble statuary, or at least an acceptable substitute. Hawley Brothers of Rotherham produced busts of Burns. Statuettes of Tam and Souter Johnny, either plain white or delicately tinted, were displayed at the Centenary Exhibition and may, in fact, have been from the Minton factory itself. Parian ware ornaments (with no more precise description) of Burns and Highland Mary were also exhibited on that occasion. I have examined one of these exquisite little statuettes but it is unmarked, and may therefore have been made by the Bells' Glasgow Pottery which also specialised in this medium. Another unmarked figurine in Parian ware reproduced Amelia Hill's statue of Burns erected in Dumfries in 1882, and may have been issued about that time. The Old Prestonpans Pottery also turned out busts of Burns and statuettes of characters from 'Tam o Shanter' in the second half of the nineteenth century.

Miniature busts of Burns, ranging from 7 to 20 cm in height, have been produced in white bisque porcelain in more recent times. Horizon Porcelain Ltd are currently producing attractive little busts derived from Nasmyth's paintings. Earthenware busts, produced at the turn of the century, are known in the form of banks, with a slot for the insertion of coins behind the poet's head. Pottery hollow-ware busts have also been a popular medium for miniature bottles of whisky. They include a bust, after Nasmyth, in a yellow-brown glaze (containing Scotch liqueur), and a curious portrait with long hair, resembling Robespierre rather than Burns, in bisque stoneware. The latter was marketed by the Cumbrae Supply Company of Glasgow on behalf of 'Robbie Burns' whisky.

Many of the busts and statues discussed in Chapter 3 were also published as miniature replicas in pottery or porcelain. These replicas, reduced by the same technique that was used for the bronze statuettes, had the added advantage that they could be decorated in underglaze colour before firing in the kiln. The statues by Flaxman, Lawson and the Stevenson brothers are known to have been edited in ceramic versions, either plain white or polychrome, in various sizes from about 25 to 100 cm.

Minton parian-ware statuette of Burns and Highland Mary.

Minton parian-ware miniature of the Dumfries Burns statue.

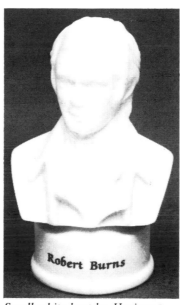

Parian-ware bust of Burns containing "Robbie Burns" whisky.

Small white bust by Horizon Porcelain.

Small brownware bust containing whisky.

Potlids

Decorative earthenware lids of the flat, shallow jars in which cosmetics, and later fish-paste, were sold appeared in the early nineteenth century. They were mainly used on jars containing bear's grease pomade and for this reason the earliest examples showed bears, either in the wild, or in humanoid situations. Bear's grease went out of fashion by 1850, but fortunately the decorated lids had become so popular that they were rapidly extended to other substances, at a time when branded goods were just coming into prominence. Toothpaste, potted shrimps and fish-paste were the commonest products packaged in this attractive manner. The pots and their pictorial lids were produced by four Staffordshire potteries. Felix Pratt of Fenton pioneered the medium in 1847,

Pair of polychrome potlids showing scenes from 'Tam o Shanter', Cauldron Pottery, c. 1860.

but it was soon copied by Mayer Brothers and Elliott, Ridgway of Cauldon and Ridgway of Shelton. Their heyday was the 1860s but they continued till 1879 when the principal designer, Jesse Austin, died. They reproduced the popular paintings of the period, as well as commemorating outstanding historic and contemporary events. Oddly enough, no potlids are known in connexion with the birth centenary of Burns, and by the time of the death centenary in 1896 the potlid was totally eclipsed.

The only potlids with a Burns theme were those produced by the Cauldon Pottery about 1860, when it had passed into the hands of Bates, Brown-Westhead and Moore. The lids were issued in two sizes, medium and large, and there was also a version with a broad plain surround, which was marketed as a teapot-stand. The early versions of these potlids have the creamy fawn colouring distinctive to Cauldon. Lids with the same pictures but a white ground are believed to be late re-issues. Two pictures are known to exist, both derived from paintings by Thomas which were published in the *Art Journal* in 1858. The first shows Tam o Shanter, Souter Johnny, the landlord and landlady

> Fast by an ingle, bleezing finely,
> Wi reaming swats, that drank divinely.

The other lid shows Tam in headlong flight, with Nanie close behind, on the Auld Brig.

Crested china

William H. Goss established the Falcon Pottery at Stoke-on-Trent in 1860 and made his name by pioneering small bone china souvenirs decorated with brightly coloured civic crests. Ironically, these trifles were of secondary importance to his main business, which was porcelain tableware and Parian statuary. Crested china was sold for a few pence as tourist mementoes, mainly of seaside resorts, although they were eventually sold everywhere, even in inland cities and large industrial towns. As the range of civic insignia expanded, Goss diversified into all sorts of novelty shapes, and never overlooked the opportunity to reproduce statues and landmarks in this miniature form. Various statues of Burns are known with civic coats of arms added to the pedestals. Some fine examples of this are to be found in Burns House, Mauchline. Donald Urquhart has a three-handled vase by Goss with the arms of Gourock and Burns, a miniature of the Dumfries statue by Willow Art China with the arms of Dumfries, and an unmarked bust of Burns with the crest of Crianlarich.

Pottery cottages

Apart from the crested novelties, Goss specialised in porcelain replicas in miniature of famous houses, such as Anne Hathaway's cottage and the birthplace of Robert Burns. The latter is a major rarity nowadays, much sought after by Goss collectors. It has to be admitted that these cottages are not particularly accurate, and some artistic licence has been used in embellishing the facade with a two line inscription identifying it. Pottery cottages have come back into fashion lately with collectors, and the

Goss crested china bust of
Burns, Burns House,
Mauchline.

Stoneware model of Burns
House, Dumfries.

Goss crested china statuette of Burns, after
Flaxman, Burns House, Mauchline.

Burns's birthplace, in David Tate's "Lilliput Lane" series.

Small pottery model of Burns Cottage.

Clay pipes with bowls modelled as Burns's head.

Bone china egg-cups depicting the Tam o Shanter Inn and bearing the Selkirk Grace.

German pottery salt and pepper set, c. 1938, shows Tam o Shanter and Souter Johnny. (Allan Stoddart Collection).

Porcelain napkin ring, with Nasmyth portrait, Robert Burns Centre, Dumfries.

Lilliput Lane series, modelled by David Tate of Skirsgill, Penrith, Cumbria, has already established a very high reputation for meticulous accuracy. Burns's Cottage is incredibly detailed, right down to the ladder slung under the eaves and the pitchfork leaning against the wall. Appropriately this model is currently on sale at the Birthplace Museum's souvenir shop, next door to the real thing. There are other models of the Cottage but — you pay your money and you take your choice. Mrs Janet Paterson lent to the 1959 exhibition a pottery bank in the shape of the Cottage.

A very attractive porcelain replica of Burns House, Dumfries can be seen in the Burns Centre. This model has an inscription on the back identifying it, but the mark on the base — 'Willow Art China' — was used by Hewitt & Leadbitter from 1907 till 1926, so that it would appear that this souvenir dates from the First World War period.

Miscellaneous pottery and porcelain

Burns himself was not a smoker — tobacco was taken in powdered form, as snuff, in his day and pipe-smoking did not attain widespread popularity until the Crimean War sixty years after his death. It was a custom of some Burns clubs in the second half of the nineteenth century to provide clay pipes for members at the anniversary suppers, and these pipes had the poet's bust in bas-relief on the sides of the bowls. Burns 'cutties' of this type are believed to have been produced as late as 1922. A more elaborate variant, known in white, yellow or reddish pottery, has the entire bowl modelled in the form of Burns's head. Further up the social scale were the pipes with ivory, ebony or bone stems and porcelain bowls modelled on the poet's features.

Ashtrays with embossed or bas-relief motifs of Burns, Tam o Shanter or Souter Johnny, were at one time a very common souvenir, and may be found with the names of various public houses or hotels inscribed round the rim. In more recent times they have been made available as part of the bar equipment previously mentioned. As smoking has declined in popularity, the vogue for Burns souvenir ashtrays seems to have waned.

Several egg-cups have been noted with Burns motifs. Royal Stafford have produced bone china egg-cups decorated with the words of the Selkirk grace. Tams of England marketed egg-cups with polychrome pictures of the Tam o Shanter Inn, Ayr on the sides. The Burns Centre, Dumfries, has a pair of heavy porcelain napkin rings with the Nasmyth bust-portrait in full colour, but no markings identifying their origin. The Coventry 'Jolly Beggars' Burns club has miniature cradles made of porcelain decorated with Burns motifs. Salt and pepper sets have been noted in the form of tiny coloured figures of Tam o Shanter and Souter Johnny; these little hollow figures were manufactured in Germany some time before the Second World War. Porringers and fruit bowls in reddish earthenware decorated with coloured glazes and *sgraffito* inscriptions of the Selkirk grace were produced about the turn of the century by the Aller Vale Pottery of Devon.

Burns in Woodware

Mauchline ware box with painted portrait of Burns.

The Glencairn snuff-box discussed at great length in Chapter 7 was typical of those used in the eighteenth century: made of silver, with a separate lid which fitted tightly over the box. Cheap boxes were made of wood, but because of the hygroscopic nature of the material, apt to swell or contract according to the climate, it was very difficult to make them with a really tight-fitting lid, and well-nigh impossible to make a wooden box with a lid hinged to the side. Nevertheless, the woodworkers of Finland and Russia who dwelt along the isthmus of Karelia had perfected a tight-fitting hinged lid, by cutting knuckles alternately into the side of the box and the edge of the lid. Snuff boxes with integral wooden hinges spread to Scandinavia and thence to the east coast of Scotland where they were a speciality of the craftsmen of Laurencekirk, notably Charles Stiven. These hinges continued to be fashioned entirely by hand until James Sandy of Alyth perfected a machine for cutting them. James Sandy, bed-ridden from the age of twelve, is one of the unsung geniuses of the Scots, a race noted for its inventiveness. A self-taught artist and inventor in the same mould as Leonardo himself, Sandy made eight-day clocks, fine telescopes and a whole range of useful inventions. The only recognition he had in his own lifetime was the ten guineas awarded to him by the Board of Trustees (of which George Thomson was secretary) for inventing an artificial arm, so ingeniously jointed, that a man who had lost his arm in a threshing accident was able to resume work. This poor helpless cripple deserves to be known as the father of prosthetics, but even the credit for mechanising the snuff box industry has been usurped by Charles Stiven who either purchased Sandy's invention or developed it independently at a later date. The wooden box with its integral hinge, however, remained a monopoly of Kincardineshire till the early years of the nineteenth century.

Hand-decorated boxes

Some time in 1806-7 Sir Alexander Boswell was entertaining friends at Auchinleck House. One of the house-guests, a Frenchman, accidentally broke his Laurencekirk snuff box and it was entrusted to William Crawford, the employee of a local gunsmith, to repair the broken hinge. Having successfully repaired the box Crawford set about imitating the technique for himself. He formed a partnership with his employer, Wyllie to make wooden boxes with integral hinges. About 1819 the partnership split up and Crawford moved to New Cumnock where he established a rival business. By 1825 there were half a dozen craftsmen in Old and New Cumnock making or painting snuff boxes. Crawford became so successful that he was able to commission up and coming young artists of great promise, including Daniel Macnee, Horatio McCulloch and William Leitch to decorate his boxes. The boxes were made of plane (Scottish sycamore) or American maple, but yew and elm were also used occasionally. Plane was the best medium, for its smooth, light surface was ideal for decoration, either drawings executed in pen and ink and then varnished over, or painted direct in oils. There are many examples of small painted wooden boxes dating from the first half of the nineteenth century, with passable attempts at the portraits of Burns. Those by Nasmyth and Skirving were the most favoured, although a fine example of a circular box reproducing the portrait of Burns by Peter Taylor may be seen in the Burns Centre, Dumfries.

From Auchinleck and Cumnock the box industry spread to nearby Catrine, Ochiltree, Stair and Mauchline. Apart from portraits of Burns, the most popular subject for the early painted boxes was 'Tam o Shanter'. The seated figures of Tam and Souter Johnny, after the statues by Thom, were those most commonly depicted, but there were many painted boxes showing dramatic scenes from the great epic, often with such captions as 'Weel done, Cutty Sark!' or 'The carlin claught her by the rump'. Two snuff boxes with a painted scene from 'Willie brew'd a peck o maut' were displayed at the Centenary Exhibition. One of them was additionally inscribed 'Yours ever, Robt. Burns', the implication being that it had been in existence in the poet's own lifetime, although this is highly suspect. The inscription may have been added in or about 1821 when the box was given to the Hon. William Maule, who could claim to have known Burns personally.

By the middle of the nineteenth century there were about sixty box-makers in Scotland, of whom only five were in Laurencekirk and Montrose, one in Lanarkshire, one at Helensburgh and the rest in central Ayrshire. For this reason 'Mauchline ware' came to be applied as a generic term to Scottish woodware, even if it may have come from elsewhere. Snuff-taking began to decline when cigar-smoking first became fashionable in 1815. It lingered on among the poorer classes for another generation, and it was to cater to this end of the market that boxes with mechanical decoration were produced. Hand-painted boxes continued to be produced as cigar-cases, but the small snuff boxes were now decorated by means of engraved transfers. This technique relied on the pantograph, invented by M. Collas of Paris in 1824. In the following year the brothers William and Andrew Smith of Mauchline, then engaged in the production of hones for sharpening razors, established a small factory to make the wooden cases for these stones.

Pair of wooden patch boxes with painted lids: (left) "Weel done, Cutty Sark!" (right) portrait of Burns after Peter Taylor.

Mauchline transfer-printed razor hone case.

Soon afterwards they began diversifying into the manufacture of small boxes and cases of all kinds, imitating the box-makers of the surrounding district. Where the Smith brothers scored over their rivals, however, was in their ability to duplicate the drawings by mechanical means. By 1829 William Smith had opened a warehouse in Birmingham to exploit the rapidly expanding English market, and eventually this developed into a separate box factory. William split with Andrew in 1843, but four years later the separate business was wound up on William's death and thereafter the firm of W. A. Smith operated as a single entity. By now Andrew's son William had come into the business and it was he who really put Mauchline ware on the map.

Tartan ware

The Smith family fortune was largely based on the mania for tartan ware which developed in the 1840s. Not only did they publish what was then regarded as an authoritative handbook on the Scottish tartans (1850) but they churned out vast quantities of small boxes and bibelots decorated with tartan 'painted by machinery'. By the end of that decade the Smiths were employing upwards of eighty people, giving to Mauchline that lucrative light industry which 'Daddy' Auld, writing in the first *Statistical Account* (1792), had hoped would some day be the material salvation of his parish. At the celebrations in Mauchline marking the centenary of Burns's birth, the Smith workmen led the parade and Andrew's youngest daughter, Agnes, crowned the bust of the bard with a laurel wreath. At the celebratory dinner that evening Andrew was croupier, while his son William recited a long poem in praise of Gavin Hamilton.

Transfer ware

This event coincided with a new development which was to revolutionise Scottish woodware in particular, and the British souvenir trade in general. Tartan ware, though still very fashionable in France, was declining in popularity in Britain. Casting around for something to take its place, the Smiths hit upon the idea of decorating boxes with tiny engravings of scenery and landmarks. The introduction of the scenic boxes came at a time when the railway network was virtually completed and the Victorian tourist boom was just beginning. The vast majority of the tartan boxes and cases were entirely decorated in the distinctive patterns, identified by the name of the clan printed in gold at the foot. There were, however, some larger articles that had hand-painted pictures with a tartan surround. At the Centenary Exhibition there was a glove box mechanically painted in tartan, with a vignette of Burns and Highland Mary on the lid.

Pen and ink, hand-drawn or painted boxes continued to be produced, although the relatively high cost of producing them led to their decline, in face of competition from the transfer wares. Scenes and landmarks would be carefully drawn, then engraved on steel and transfers produced from the dies. This technique was already used in the pottery industry, being applied to crockery before glazing and firing. In the case of the woodware, the transfers were applied in black ink to the surface of the sycamore and then varnished over. Eventually the Smiths published woodware decorated with these scenic engravings from all over the British Isles, North America and France, and with great enterprise they produced similar mementoes for the burgeoning Australian tourist industry at the turn of the century. The heyday of Mauchline ware was from 1860 to 1900, but production continued in a more desultory fashion as late as 1933, when the Mauchline boxworks was destroyed by fire. Latterly it had degenerated as an art form, especially after cheap sepia photographs were substituted for the engravings.

Mauchline ware tartan covered case with Nasmyth portrait inset.

Mauchline ware birthday book, formerly the property of the poet's great-granddaughter, Jean Armour Burns Brown.

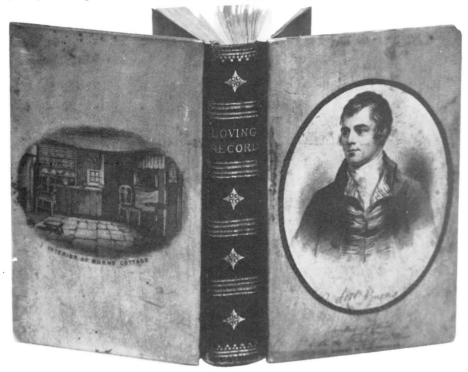

Mauchline ware spill-holder, showing Burns Cottage.

In Chapter 4 I recounted how souvenir hunters and pilgrims to the places associated with Burns began taking away pieces of the bushes and trees at Alloway, Coilsfield and St Michael's churchyard, Dumfries. Many of these fragments survive in the raw state to this day, variously labelled to identify their source, but it was only a short step from preserving such fragments, to converting them into something useful like a snuff box or a paperknife. Snuff boxes, trinket boxes, glove boxes, egg cups, small vases and bowls and needle cases are recorded as having been made from pieces of the trysting thorn at Coilsfield associated with Burns and Highland Mary, from the Crookston yew associated with Mary Queen of Scots and the Elderslie oak associated with Sir William Wallace, from the bed in which Burns died and even the flooring and skirting board of his last bedroom, from the beams and rafters of Nanse Tinnock's at Mauchline and Alloway Kirk, from the old kirk-end tree at Mauchline, blown down in the storm of 27th February 1860, from the platform on which the Auld Brig o Ayr was built, from the rafters of Mossgiel farmhouse, when the roof was renovated in 1859, from the holly-bush at the Mausoleum, the trees which grew around the Monument at Alloway, or on the banks of the Doon, from wood grown in Gavin Hamilton's garden or forming part of the timber of the house in which Robert and Jean were married, the kist prepared for Burns when contemplating emigration to Jamaica and even from wood allegedly taken from the poet's coffin when it was removed to the Mausoleum in 1815. Less directly associated with Burns, and therefore much rarer as a named source, was wood grown on the banks of Ayr. The articles fashioned from this timber not only depicted scenes

Mauchline ware night-light holder showing Burns monument, Alloway.

Trinket box "made of wood which grew near Alloway Kirk".

Mauchline ware napkin ring showing Burns monument, Alloway.

Mauchline transfer-printed ware: circular string box.

Mauchline ware granny fob-watch stand and barrel money box.

Trinket box with Tam o Shanter and Souter Johnny on the lid.

Mauchline ware needlecase showing Auld Brig o Doon.

from the life and works of Burns but bore inscriptions warranting their actual source. Perhaps the most unusual inscription is that which denotes wood 'from the swee of the Tam o Shanter Inn, Ayr'. In the 1860s and 1870s there was a fashion for small diaries, memo books and birthday books containing Burns quotations and having wooden covers decorated with engraved transfers. These wooden book covers often had a lengthy inscription giving their provenance. A good example is 'During the residence of Burns at Mossgiel and for 40 years afterwards the House was sheltered from the East and West Winds by two rows of hawthorn trees from the Wood of which this Memo Book is warranted to have been made.'

Engraved or lithographed portraits of Burns after Nasmyth, with a commemorative inscription surrounding the circular or oval cartouche, are relatively elusive on snuff boxes and card cases, but rare and very much sought after on the tiny volumes of the Poems, or the little book entitled *Scottish Keepsake*, an anthology of Burns songs which the Smiths themselves published. Like the earlier hand-drawn and painted boxes, genre scenes derived from 'Tam o Shanter' were a firm favourite in transfer ware.

This medium, however, appears to have been largely confined to actual scenery and landmarks which may be enumerated, in descending order of popularity: Burns's birthplace, both exterior and interior views, the Monument, Alloway Kirk, Auld Brig o Doon, Scene on the Doon, the Twa Brigs o Ayr, Gavin Hamilton's house in Mauchline, Nanse Tinnock's, Mossgiel, Ballochmyle, Barskimming House, Netherplace and even Ballochmyle Viaduct, though this was not completed until 1845.

Needlecase showing the Dumfries Burns statue.

Twine-holder with photographic view of the Mausoleum.

Work-box decorated with photographic vignettes of Dumfries.

Not all of the Mauchline transfer ware was produced by the Smith boxworks. Rival firms were operated, albeit on a much smaller scale, by Wilson & Amphlet and John Davidson & Sons, as well as by the Caledonian boxworks at Lanark, operated by Archibald Brown (a native of Mauchline) and subsequently by Mackenzie & Meikle. Fierce competition from the tourist mementoes produced in Germany, from china fairings to picture postcards, drove the Smiths to diversify from boxes and small cases into all manner of wooden trifles, such as toothpick and spectacle cases, tea-caddies, wax taper, lip salve, cold cream and tooth powder boxes, ladies' work boxes, thread and twine boxes, barrel-shaped money boxes, spill holders, ferrules, letterknives, watch stands and napkin rings. The finest array of Mauchline ware is to be found in the Pinto Collection, Birmingham, but the Burns House Museum in Mauchline has a representative collection, and many examples are to be found in the other museums devoted to Burns.

Carved wood

The Pinto Collection in the Birmingham Museum also has two deeply carved sycamore table snuff boxes, said to have been carved by a blind man in Glasgow about 1850. These remarkable boxes have high relief carvings on their lids and sides, illustrating characters from 'Tam o Shanter' and 'The Jolly Beggars'. A jewel box carved in a similar fashion, from wood derived from the parlour window-shutter at Nanse Tinnock's, was shown at the Centenary Exhibition of 1896, and parts of John Wilson's printing press were similarly fashioned into carved

Jolly Beggars carved wooden snuff-box, Irvine Burns Club.

Two of a set of carved wooden panels depicting scenes from Tam o Shanter, Irvine Burns Club.

boxes, presumably from the smaller pieces left over from the construction of the elaborate chair in the Birthplace Museum. Examples of bread-boards, cheese-boards and fruit-bowls with Burnsian themes carved round the rims date from the end of the nineteenth century. One of the more spectacular exhibits at the Centenary Exhibition was an oak sideboard, lent by George Bennett, elaborately carved with panels illustrating the works of Burns. The headquarters of the Royal Scottish Zoological Society at Edinburgh Zoo has a large wooden fire surround, beautifully carved with Tam and Meg 'winning the keystane o the brig'. A series of small panels depicting scenes from 'Tam o Shanter' may be seen on the staircase at Wellwood, Irvine, while the Burgh Museum, Dumfries has a long panel decorated with five separate scenes carved in low relief from the

Carved wooden mantelpiece, Belleisle House: (top) Burns, cottage and plough-team, (centre) Tam at the keystane o the brig, (panels) scenes from "Tam o Shanter" and "Death and Dr Hornbook".

Carved wooden panel depicting "Willie Brew'd a Peck o Maut", above the doorway, Belleisle House, Ayr.

Carved wooden panels of "John Anderson, My Jo" and "The Cardin o't the Spinnin o't", Belleisle House, Ayr.

Walking stick with a carved head of Burns and a close-up of the head on the walking stick.

same poem by R. Copeland in 1909. The Birthplace Museum has an intricately carved little panel of 'Death and Dr Hornbrook' (*sic*).

Without doubt, however, the most ambitious and magnificent examples of the wood-carver's art are to be found decorating the main entrance of the Belleisle House Hotel at Ayr. At one time this interesting building was the country seat of the Glentanar family who commissioned European craftsmen to carve the figures, bas-reliefs and friezes that adorn the main hallway. In particular, the fireplace which stands opposite the reception desk shows Tam pursued by Nanie on the Auld Brig o Doon. This scene is shown in white-painted wood against a blue ground, in the manner of Wedgwood jasperware. Above this large panel is a frieze showing Burns at the plough. Smaller painted panels at the sides feature scenes from 'Death and Dr Hornbook', 'Tam o Shanter' and 'The Jolly Beggars', while the Twa Dogs stand guard on the fireside benches. Above the main doorway are further wood panels illustrative of 'John Anderson my jo'.

Both the Irvine Burns club museum at Wellwood and the Tam o Shanter Inn, Ayr have splendid examples of carved walking sticks. The latter pair were presented by Miss M. Gibson of Kilbarchan, her uncle, John Glen, having fashioned them from trees on the Glentyan Estate. The carver has very cleverly exploited the natural grain of the wood in creating lifelike portraits of Burns, the Twa Dogs, Tam o Shanter and Souter Johnny which decorate the handles and stems.

Pyrography — the gentle art of decorating wood with heated needles or fine gas jets — was never possible on a commercial scale because of the time and skill required, but some remarkable examples of this Victorian pastime have been recorded, showing portraits of Burns and scenes from 'Tam o Shanter'. Examples of small wooden coasters are known, however, in which verses from Burns's poems have been burned into the surface by some kind of printing forme applied under heat. Typical of these coasters are those depicting the Cottage with the lines:

> Blythe to meet
> Wae to part
> Blythe to meet aince mair.

A Burns Miscellany

Pair of Stevengraphs (silk woven pictures).

Apart from the major categories of fine, applied and decorative art discussed in the preceding chapters, there is a host of Burnsiana in textiles, metalwork, glass and other materials. Some of this memorabilia comprises the unique productions of amateur artists and craftsmen, but most of it is, or was at one time, produced commercially with an eye on the tourist trade and the Burns cult.

Textiles

It is recorded that at the execution of Burke, the notorious body-snatcher, he was given a handkerchief which he spread between his knees on the scaffold. It carried a portrait of Burns, and some of his many lines on misfortune. Burns himself had died barely three decades earlier, and printed handkerchieves were among the earliest popular mementoes of Scotland's national bard. They came into fashion in the 1820s, and were woven on the Jacquard looms that revolutionised the textile industry after the Napoleonic Wars and threw Scotland's hand-loom weavers out of work. Many of them were crudely designed and, in fact, could trace their origins back to the primitive broadsheets of an earlier generation. Great improvements were made in technique about the middle of the nineteenth century, and the finest examples of silk, linen and cotton handkerchieves and scarves reproducing the Nasmyth portrait date from that period. The fashion waned in the 1870s and had

virtually died out before the great celebrations of 1896. Latterly even cheaper processes supplanted the woven pictures, and for a time there was a vogue for printed handkerchieves, although their overall appearance was generally inferior to the woven versions. This technique was popular as a medium for printing programmes, and Burns House, Dumfries has on display a fine example, printed by Currie of Dumfries, with the details of the unveiling ceremony of the statue erected in 1882.

Thomas Stevens (1828-88) of Coventry devised woven silk pictures in the 1860s as a means of relieving the slump in the ribbon industry. His Stevengraphs, as they were called, achieved immense popularity in the 1880s and were continued after his death, and imitated by rival firms. Genre and historic scenes, reproductions of famous paintings and contemporary subjects and personalities provided the inspiration for these small woven silk pictures. Sportsmen, politicians and military heroes were the favourite subjects, but Robert Burns was also included. Two versions of the Burns Stevengraph are recorded. The earlier of the two has a portrait based on Nasmyth, but in reverse, with four lines of 'Auld Lang Syne' at the top. This appears to have been one of the earlesit Stevengraphs, for it is mentioned in the firm's accounts as far back as 1862, when it was retailed for sixpence. The later version omitted the lines at the top, placed the portrait in a frame with the manufacturer's imprint below, and ROBERT BURNS at the foot. There were also later variants which differed in the title of the song — 'For Auld Lang Syne' or simply 'Auld Lang Syne'. The first version has also been noted in an elongated form, intended as a book-marker. Book-markers, woven in nylon instead of silk, have been revived lately and are available in a number of designs, with the Nasmyth portrait and lines from various poems. These modern counterparts of the Stevengraph are manufactured in the United States. One of Stevens' rivals was William Grant and his company produced woven silks in

Printed tea towels with Burns themes
(Allan Stoddart Collection).

postcard form about 1900. These were headed 'Bonnie Scotland for Auld Lang Syne' and had the words and music of the song in purple, red and blue.

One tends to think of tea towels as being a modern invention but as long ago as 1820 the Kirkcaldy weavers were producing beautiful towels in fine linen with pictorial motifs and a lengthy inscription to commemorate the completion of the Burns Monument at Alloway. Antimacassars and table mats in the same genre were produced for the 1896 Centenary. The linen industry of Northern Ireland has been geared to the tourist trade since the 1950s and numerous tea towels have been produced with printed motifs alluding to Burns and his life and works. The majority reproduce the Nasmyth bust, with the words and music of 'Auld Lang Syne' and other old favourites, or the Selkirk grace. Jean Armour, Highland Mary, Tam o Shanter and other characters from the poems, the Cottage, the Monument, the Auld Brig o Doon and other familiar landmarks of the Burns Country are featured. Perhaps the most interesting of these towels is that produced by Glen Appin, based closely on the British Rail poster designed by William Nicholson in 1959. The more original towels are those featuring the Nasmyth full-length portrait with the Cottage and Monument (currently on sale at the Birthplace Museum) and the towels and aprons portraying Jean Armour and Robert Burns with the words of the Selkirk grace, sold at Jean Armour's Pantry, the restaurant at the Burns Centre, Dumfries. Tom Gourdie, one of Scotland's leading calligraphers, designed 'Sing a Song of Robert Burns', an imaginative presentation of Burns's best-loved songs, which is available from Posthaste Presents as tea-towels, wall-hangings, aprons or place mats.

Several firms, such as Lochcarron Ltd, have produced a wide range of scarves and ties with Burns motifs. It is said that tartan was really a French invention, from the chequered patterns of the Middle Ages known as *tiretaine*. It may therefore have been not inappropriate that the Burns check, which has become immensely popular in recent years, was invented by a Frenchman, Baron Georges Marchand, as a tribute to the bard's bicentenary. Baron Marchand was born in Dunkirk but came to Edinburgh in 1910 where he was employed as French and German correspondent in the woollen firm of George Harrison & Co. Later he represented the company in Holland for a number of years and eventually became senior partner, and Belgian Consul in Edinburgh. He was an ardent admirer of Burns and as himself a poet and composer of some note. The Burns check, derived like the Shepherd tartan from the undyed black and white wool of Lowland sheep, with the admixture of subtle brown and green tints, is a perennial favourite for all sorts of apparel from kilts to scarves, sashes and ties, and may be found on its own or (in the case of men's neckties) with the Nasmyth portrait inset. In 1985 the Dumfries Rotary club acquired its own distinctive tie and this features the Nasmyth bust alternating with the Rotary emblem. Dollar Burns club produced a Centenary tie in 1987, with Burns's portrait surrounded by a commemorative inscription.

In the eighteenth and nineteenth centuries embroidery was a skill practised by women in all classes of society and from the earliest age young girls were taught to work samplers. The Centenary Exhibition had on show samplers which had been worked by Agnes Broun Burnes and Isabella Burns Begg, the mother and sister of the poet. A Mrs M.S. Rollo, however, exhibited a sampler reproducing the Midwood painting of Burns and Highland Mary. The Globe Inn has a fine sampler by an unknown seamstress, reproducing William Allan's seated portrait of the bard. These early samplers relied very heavily on the skill and artistry of the ladies themselves, but in the mid-nineteenth century wool-shops began selling Berlin woolwork kits with a printed canvas showing the outline and colour coding, and this medium has continued to the present time, the Cottage and the Monument being popular subjects, followed by 'Tam o Shanter' and the Nasmyth bust for the more advanced practitioners of the art.

Toddy mats of Paisley work were displayed at the Centenary Exhibition. Oddly enough no examples of the lace produced in the Darvel area of Ayrshire were shown on that occasion. In its heyday the town had over forty lace factories, producing table-cloths, doilies, antimacassars, tray cloths, place mats and centre-pieces. Everything from thistles to profiles of the Queen have been featured in Darvel lace, and Burns's portrait, the Cottage and the Monument were also produced in this medium in mats and tablecloths, as souvenirs of the 1959 bicentenary.

Considering that carpet-making was once a major industry in Kilmarnock it is hardly surprising that Burns should have been immortalised in this medium. Rugs reproducing the Nasmyth portrait were produced at Kilmarnock in the early years of this century. In the 1950s Grays of Ayr produced a very attractive rug for Scott's Crown Carpets Ltd. Using 37

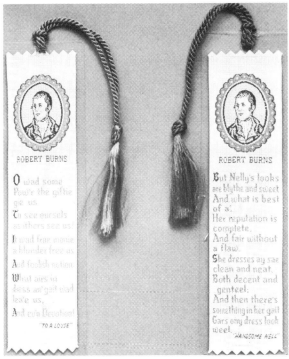

Silk woven bookmarks portraying Burns and quoting lines from "To a Louse" and "Handsome Nell".

different dyes, the artists and weavers combined to produce an unusual tribute to Burns. The Nasmyth bust appeared in the centre, with four vignettes showing the Cottage, Tam o Shanter Inn, Monument and Alloway Kirk. The entire ensemble was surrounded by a border of Wallace tartan, as a reminder of the close association of Sir William Wallace with the royal burgh of Ayr. Many Burnsians mounted this beautiful rug as a wall-hanging. In more recent years there have been rugs with the Nasmyth bust in the centre and oval vignettes showing the Monument through the arch of the Auld Brig o Doon, and the Cottage

To celebrate the octocentenary of the royal burgh of Dumfries in 1986, the Dumfries and Galloway

Rug by Gray of Kilmarnock showing Burns and landmarks associated with him (Allan Stoddart Collection).

Dumfries, Octocentenary collage, Robert Burns Centre. Photo: David Hope.

Guild of Spinners, Weavers and Dyers combined their skills and talents to produce a magnificent tapestry which now graces the foyer of the Burns Centre. The tapestry was designed by Nita Richmond and the work was co-ordinated by Sheila McKay, the Guild's president. Although intended to symbolise eight centuries of Dumfries, it must be admitted that Burns has rather eclipsed everyone else and there is no mention of King Robert the Bruce or John Baliol who also had close connexions with the town. On the extreme left there is a picture of the Globe Inn, the poet's favourite howff, and below that is a fieldmouse and a cluster of daisies, alluding to two of Burns's best-loved poems. Next, there are vignettes of the old Town Mill — now the Burns Centre — and, below, Burns House, the poet's last home. The centre is dominated by Amelia Hill's marble statue. Then there is a view of the burgh museum, originally a windmill and later an observatory and, of course, the repository of relics of the bard. Above this appears the facade of the Theatre Royal with which Burns was so closely associated from the outset. Finally, on the extreme right, there is a splendid view of the Mausoleum, with the steeple of St Michael's in the background. This remarkable *tour de force* has been reproduced as a picture postcard.

For many years the Burns Federation has had its own flag, now unfortunately showing the ravages of time. The question of having a new flag was raised in 1986 by North American Burnsians and, at the time of writing, it is understood that a new flag is being embroidered in Canada depicting the poet's armorial badge. Football clubs and Rotary clubs have long held the tradition of exchanging bannerettes, but this is something new to the Burns movement, pioneered by the Dundonald Burns club in 1981. The club bannerette features the Miers silhouette against a background of local landmarks, together with the club's name, address and Federation number. Past President George Dawes designed this attractive

Stained glass window in "Wellwood", portraying Burns and Jean Armour as well as scenes from their lives (Irvine Burns Club).

bannerette, examples of which may be seen in the local hotels which have given support to the club over the years. It is to be hoped that other Burns clubs will emulate Dundonald's example.

Glass

Several drinking glasses alleged to have belonged to Burns were enumerated among the relics discussed in Chapter 4. One of these is an enormous tumbler which can be seen in Burns House, Dumfries. Its provenance is explained in a ten-line inscription engraved on the side: 'This Glass once the property of ROBERT BURNS was presented by the POET'S WIDOW to James Robinson esq. and given by his WIDOW to her Son-in-law MAJOR JAMES GLENCAIRN BURNS 1840'. The inscription has been quite expertly copper-wheel engraved, a technique that was widely practised in the eighteenth and nineteenth centuries. Some highly decorative goblets, beakers and tumblers were produced in the nineteenth century using the technique of acid etching, but none of these attractive glasses appears to have been considered worthy of a place in the great Centenary Exhibition. In more recent times decorative glassware with a Burns theme has been largely confined to the much cheaper and less aesthetically satisfying medium of painted or enamelled glass, fused to the surface by kiln-firing. Inscribed tumblers and goblets have been produced as souvenirs of Burns Conferences, although the last time this charming memento was presented to delegates was at Stirling in 1984. Several Burns clubs have commissioned their own glassware, usually reproducing the Nasmyth portrait with a commemorative inscription. The Globe Inn has a pair of goblets of French origin with a portrait of Burns and words from 'Auld Lang Syne' or a view of the Cottage. Allan Stoddart has a wine glass with Burns's portrait and the Cottage delicately engraved. Donald Kay, who has established a glasshouse at Mauchline Station, is now engraving crystal goblets with lines of Burns's poetry and appropriate illustrations. Some beautifully engraved crystal bowls and goblets, with portraits of Burns, have been produced by Caithness Glass in very recent years.

Scotland, unlike most other countries of western Europe, had no indigenous tradition of stained glass in the Middle Ages, and what little decorative glass

Dundonald Burns Club pennant.

there was in the great churches and abbeys was invariably destroyed at the Reformation. This was followed by a taboo on ecclesiastical adornment which was only gradually relaxed during the course of the nineteenth century. By that time, however, the traditional forms of stained glass, which relied on building up a picture using pieces of coloured glass like a mosaic bonded by lead strips, were being superseded by the cheaper medium of painted glass, with the traditional coloured glass confined to the leaded borders. Significantly most of the decorative windows in Scottish churches were imported from England. Cottier and Company of London had a thriving business supplying churches, public buildings and mansion-houses with stained and painted glass, and portraits of Burns after Nasmyth were included in their secular repertoire, along with genre scenes from the best-known poems and landmarks associated with the poet. Some excellent examples of nineteenth century stained and painted glass with Burns motifs may be seen in the Birthplace Museum and also in Wellwood at Irvine. The latter also has a street-lamp

Left: Tulip glass engraved with Burns Cottage.

Far left: Glass tumbler engraved to commemorate the Burns Federation Conference at Dumfries.

Centre: Glass tumbler produced by Dumfries Ladies Burns Club No. 1 to mark the centenary of the Burns Federation, 1985.

"AND AYE THE ALE WAS GROWIN' BETTER"

Underglass painted mirror showing a scene from "Tam o Shanter".

mounted above the main entrance showing the Miers silhouette on the panes.

During the Bicentenary year the Burns club of London launched a fund to have a stained glass window dedicated to the poet installed in the Crown Court Church of Scotland. The window was designed by Michael Farrar-Bell and constructed by the firm of Clayton & Bell. Burns is depicted as a ploughman, ruefully contemplating the destruction by his plough of the fieldmouse's nest, and holding in his hand the 'wee, sleekit, cow'rin tim'rous beastie'. The window was dedicated at a special service on Sunday 24th January 1960 and is both a fine tribute from London Burnsians and a splendid example of the art of modern stained glass following traditional forms.

It seems ironic that, although Scotland has in Douglas Hogg of Kelso one of the leading exponents of stained glass in the world today, it was still necessary to go to Iceland for the window dedicated to Burns in St Giles' Cathedral. The campaign to erect a window as a memorial to Burns was launched in 1980 and Leifur Breidfjord of Reykjavik won the design competition. The window itself took more than five years to execute and was eventually produced in England. The result, which is in the modern idiom, has been controversial, the consensus of Burnsian opinion being that something more recognisable as pertaining to the bard would have been preferable. That Breidfjord is probably the most outstanding artist in this exacting medium anywhere in the world today is small consolation to those who would have been content with a more representational memorial.

In the past few years, however, Drew Landsborough (a distant kinsman of the Earl of Glencairn, Burns's patron) has established a glass studio at Dalton near Lockerbie and in partnership with his wife, Mara Eagle, and Ian Morley has been producing excellent stained and painted glass, some of which has had Burns themes. At one end of the spectrum is an elegant nine-piece traditionally fired roundel, with stains and enamels fired on to hand-blown glass. This reproduces the Nasmyth bust in a classical border, with a separate glass panel, suspended by chains, inscribed with lines from 'A man's a man'. Less expensive versions are also available, using colours which do not need to be fired on, thus giving substantial savings in production time, and using only one piece of glass. There are also roundels symbolising 'Auld Acquaintance'. The Decorative Stained Glass Company does not produce one-off pieces, but would be interested in executing orders for Burns clubs prepared to commission a subject or design in an edition of at least 100.

Looking glasses and hall mirrors were fashionable in the second half of the nineteenth century, their upper area decorated with genre scenes in delicate enamels. Examples of these mirrors have been recorded with scenes from 'Tam o Shanter', 'The Jolly Beggars' and 'The Holy Fair'. This fashion declined as it became more commercialised, especially in public houses. The Tam o Shanter Inn has a splendid example of a pub mirror from The Clachan, Ayr, lavishly decorated with scenes from Tam o Shanter.

Mention was made in Chapter 7 of the glass-paste medallions produced by James and William Tassie early in the nineteenth century. James Tassie had an enormous influence on the decorative glassware of Bohemia where glass paperweights were produced with ceramic or glass-paste cameos embedded in them. This technique spread to France and was then considerably improved by Apsley Pellatt of England in 1831. Such paperweights are known as sulphides or incrustations and they are a speciality of the Baccarat glassworks to this day. John Ford, of the Holyrood Glass Works, Edinburgh, produced in 1880 a series of sulphide paperweights portraying Scottish celebrities and Robert Burns was one of those accorded this treatment. The Ford paperweights showed a left-facing bust, after Nasmyth viewed by looking vertically down on the paperweight. A high-domed paperweight, however, is known in which a tiny bust of Burns appears in an upright position, and examples of this sulphide may be seen in the Birthplace Museum and at the Monument.

The majority of the paperweights honouring Burns are of the late-Victorian variety which was extremely popular as a tourist memento and would have been sold for a few pence. The best examples have an engraved and coloured picture on the base, the Monument, the Cottage and the Mausoleum being great favourites. By the end of the century, however, even cheaper weights were being produced with a sepia photograph of scenery and landmarks associated with the poet mounted on the base. Most of these weights are circular with only a slight dome or a flat top, but even larger weights have been seen with a rectangular format, bevelled edges and chamfered corners. These flat picture weights went out of fashion early this century, but with the renewal of collector interest in the 1970s has come a revival. It has to be admitted that the weights now current have little to commend them artistically, with their relatively crude versions of Nasmyth or Skirving portraits or photographs of Burns landmarks. Burns House, Dumfries, has a circular flat weight with a fragment of a letter in the poet's holograph mounted on the base. An inscription indicates that this weight was put together by Thomas H. Ferrier of Hope Street, Edinburgh in July 1883. One cannot help wondering what happened to the old letter of Burns from which the signature was cut out.

In recent years clear acrylic substances have been used as a cheap substitute for glass in paperweights. Alba Crafts currently produce weights of this type, encapsulating some Scotch whisky or a drop of water from the River Doon. These trifles are on sale at the Monument, whose Curator, Glenn Croft-Smith, assures purchasers that he can verify the drop of Doon water — for he witnessed the removal of a bucketful from the stream for this express purpose. At least one prominent collector of Burnsiana in Canada has a proud display of little bottles each neatly labelled to describe the contents personally extracted from the Doon, Ayr, Nith, Afton and other rivers and streams associated with Burns.

I have already discussed the 'iceberg' which was ceremonially installed at the Mausoleum in August 1896. When the ice had melted and the bouquet had wilted someone had the bright idea of preserving sprigs of the exotic flowers in liquid which was sealed in small flasks produced specially for the purpose. These flasks, not unlike the medicine bottles of the period but made of clear, colourless glass, were

Glass paperweight depicting the Mausoleum, Dumfries.

Glass paperweight, c. 1928, depicting Burns Cottage.

Modern paperweight with portrait derived from the Skirving chalk drawing.

Pressed glass bottle depicting the Mausoleum, produced to mark the poet's death centenary, 1896.

Irvine Burns Club silver loving-cup.

produced in at least two sizes. The front of each bottle had press-moulded inscriptions 'Burns Centenary 1896' and 'Mausoleum, Dumfries 1759-1796' with a bas relief view of the Mausoleum in the centre. Most of the surviving examples have long since been emptied of their contents, but a bottle with a piece of New South Wales fern still inside may be seen in the Burns Centre.

Floral tributes

A remarkable memento of the Centenary celebrations at Dumfries in 1896 was a large scrap-book containing the cards from all over the world that accompanied the wreaths and floral tributes laid at the Mausoleum. Sadly, the present whereabouts of this folio volume are not known, although at one time it was preserved in Burns House. The same museum at one time had on display a large framed tribute, consisting of the poet's name and dates of birth and death worked in daisies, mounted on blue velvet. It was probably regarded as an excellent idea at the time, but unfortunately it is the fate of flowers to be 'laid low i' the dust'. Commemoration of Burns in flowers is inevitably one of the most ephemeral tributes, but at least we have photographic records of the flowers arranged in the form of the poet's initials which were worked into the thatch of the Cottage in July 1896, and the flower-beds in front of Greyfriars' Church which reproduced the Miers silhouette to celebrate the Burns Conference at Dumfries in 1973.

Metalware

In Chapter 3 I discussed the reproductions of statues and busts of Burns in silver. This precious metal was a popular medium for presentation pieces in Victorian times, although little use seems to have been made of it for Burnsiana. The Dundee Burns club instituted in 1884 a silver cup for a Football Charity Competition. This handsome cup was designed by Allan Ramsay, a member of the club, and was extravagantly decorated with Burns emblems and mottoes.

The Centenary Exhibition included a set of silver toddy ladles with twisted stems terminating in small busts of Burns. Lower down the social scale are the crested teaspoons and caddy spoons which have long been a popular tourist souvenir. A variant of the normal style, which is decorated with civic crests in enamels, is that which terminates in a portrait of the bard. These spoons have been seen with small bas relief portraits derived from Skirving and Nasmyth, but the more colourful examples have miniatures of the Nasmyth bust in full colour.

An unusual memento of the Burns Conference at Sheffield in 1967 consisted of a cheese knife with a commemorative inscription on the blade. These knives were presented to all delegates at the banquet. Penknives are known with elongated oval cartouches on the handles featuring the Nasmyth bust, the Cottage or Burns House, Dumfries.

The Tam o Shanter Inn has a most unusual replica of the Cottage executed in copper. Closer examination reveals that it is a table lighter, with a slender pipe emitting a gas jet. A slot at the rear was provided for a penny — payment for the light. Doorstops or door-porters were manufactured in the nineteenth century by the Greenlees Foundry of Glasgow in iron, copper or brass, and are known either polished, painted black or decorated in colours. These ornaments show Burns at the plough, with lines from 'To a Mountain Daisy' inscribed on the base. The Nasmyth portrait has been widely reproduced in the form of horse-brasses, usually framed by a horse-shoe or a wreath of thistles. The same motif has been seen mounted on bells, teapot- and iron-stands and other forms of ornamental brassware. Brass door-knockers exist with a small bust of the poet, after Nasmyth of course, as the knocker, against a base which has the Cottage at the top, flanked by seated figures of Tam o Shanter and Souter Johnny. Larger and more elaborate brassware pieces, sometimes intended as mantel ornaments on their own, and sometimes incorporating letter racks, show Burns and Highland Mary.

Andrew & Partners of Harrow, Middlesex produced some attractive figurines and plaques in the 1970s. A bronze figure of a merrymaker seated on a

Three commemorative teaspoons showing portraits of Burns.

Commemorative teaspoons with polychrome Nasmyth portrait (left) and gilt-bronze medallion after Reid (right).

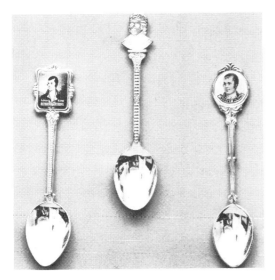

Horse brass with thistles and bust of Burns.

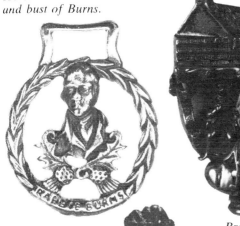

Cast iron doorstop showing Burns at the plough, with quotations from "To a Mountain Daisy" and "To a Mouse".

Brass door-knocker depicting Burns and the Cottage, Alloway.

Brass letter-rack showing Burns and Highland Mary.

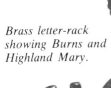

Copper cigarette lighter, modelled in the form of Burns Cottage (Tam o Shanter Inn Museum, Ayr).

Pewter figurine based on the Lawson statue at Ayr.

High relief bronze plaque by Andrew Dishington.

Pewter bas-relief, based on the Nasmyth portrait.

Set of three pewter figurines of Burns, Tam and the Souter.

Napkin ring with niello ornament of the Selkirk Grace.

beer-barrel with foaming tankard raised in salute was entitled simply 'Cheers' and was selected by Ben Truman Breweries for their 1976 Art Collection. It merits a mention here because it was apparently based on a character from 'Tam o Shanter', even though it does not resemble the notion of Tam or the Souter imprinted on our minds by the Thom statuary. A small bust of Burns, based on Nasmyth, stands four inches high, on a two-inch base, and a roundel with a diameter of five inches has the Nasmyth bust executed in high relief. These charming pieces were modelled by Andrew Dishington and produced in cold-cast bronze.

Pewter (an alloy of tin with lead or copper) was the popular medium for hollow wares in Burns's time and we are surely all familiar with the distinctive Scottish measures, from the half-mutchkin to the tappit hen, which are a favourite pub decoration to this day. The idea of applying this humble metal to more decorative objects arose in the early 1970s when the souvenir industry of America was preparing for the celebration of the bicentennial of Independence and explored the various crafts prevalent in colonial times. One of the first companies in Scotland to exploit this medium was Vale of Garnock Crafts which produced pewter figurines of Burns, as ploughman, poet and freemason, as well as a more ambitious group of Tam o Shanter pursued by Nanie. A pewter chess set with pieces inspired by the same poem was also marketed in the early 1980s. Figurines of Tam o Shanter and Souter Johnny have also been issued in recent years. Tankards with a traditional glass base were

Incised silver beer mug by Toye, Kenning and Spencer, reproducing William Allan's seated portrait.

Coaster and plaques in etched copper, designed by T. M. Sandilands of Sanquhar and showing the Mausoleum, Burns House, the Dumfries Statue and the poet's birthplace, Alloway.

manufactured in the mid-1970s by Toye, Kenning and Spencer of Birmingham in sterling silver or hammered pewter, with a bas relief portrait of Burns on the side. Pewter napkin rings have been seen with the Selkirk grace applied in *niello*, a decorative technique perfected in Italy, though more usually associated with Russian wares at the turn of the century. Kathleen Tovey used this process of inlaid black lines on a polished surface for the rectangular plaques showing the front of the Tam o Shanter Inn, Ayr.

Pentland Copper Craft of Penicuik produced coasters as souvenirs of the 1974 Edinburgh Burns Conference, showing the poet's armorial device and a commemorative inscription. These coasters were made of polished copper discs with the detail etched into the surface. The same company offered similar copper coasters in an unlimited edition, portraying Burns and inscribed with his signature.

Scotetch of Sanquhar have produced an impressive range of copper-etched plaques using a similar *niello* treatment on a polished copper surface. These plaques depict Burns House and the Cottage, with portraits after Skirving inset. Similar plaques reproduced antique engravings of Dumfries in the time of Burns, or the engraving based on Lockhart's painting of the bard's funeral. Smaller plaques and coasters are also available showing Burns's portrait above the Cottage or Burns House, and depicting the Dumfries statue or the Mausoleum. These copper plaques were the work of a local artist, Tom Sandilands.

The Centenary Exhibition had a circular snuff box

on show, made of finely carved bone with bronze roundels forming the base and lid. These were decorated by the *repoussé* process, in which thin metal plates were hammered to produce a bas relief effect. In this case, however, the circular plates were probably diestruck by mechanical means. The lid showed a detail from Turnerelli's statuary, with the Muse throwing her inspiring mantle over Burns. The inscription round the circumference alluded to this and was taken from the dedication to the first Edinburgh edition, 1787. The base depicted a plough and lyre, symbolising the ploughman poet. A fine example of this snuff box can be seen in the Burns Centre, Dumfries. In recent years the vogue for reproductions of antique wares has inspired the revival of many old crafts. Toye, Kenning and Spencer, for example, produced a handsome snuff box, hand-painted in vitreous enamels with a portrait based on Skirving, surrounded by a thistle motif filled with translucent blue enamel. This elegant object of *vertuf* was issued in 9 carat gold or sterling silver. More recently Crummles of Poole have produced a series of enamelled patch-boxes in the style fashionable in the eighteenth century. The second in the series was devoted to Burns and featured the Brig o Doon with the Monument in the background on the outer side of the lid. Round the sides are tiny pictures of the Cottage, Edinburgh Old Town, Tam o Shanter

Gilt and enamelled porcelain pill-box by Crummles of Poole, portraying Burns and showing scenes from his life.

"Robbie Burns" whisky enamelled tin tray.

The Burns momument, Alloway, modelled in cork.

Circular snuff box with bronze repoussé lid showing Burns and his Muse, after Turnerelli.

Inn and the Auld Brig o Ayr. Inside the lid is the Nasmyth portrait flanked by the poet's dates, while the bottom of the box is inscribed with lines from 'A red, red rose'. MacRae-Art have revived another traditional art-form lately, in the guise of quaichs in electroplated nickel silver, with the Nasmyth bust, dates and autograph engraved on the inside.

Tiny portrait miniatures of Burns were painted posthumously and were mounted in brooches, rings and pendants in the early nineteenth century. Some examples of these items of memorial jewellery are on display at the Birthplace Museum. In more recent times Toye, Kenning and Spencer have produced pendants and cuff-links which feature a bas relief bust of Burns in various settings.

David Sneddon, one of the founding fathers of the Burns Federation, possessed a magnificent eight-day clock whose brass face was decorated with scenes from 'The Jolly Beggars'. Apart from this, the only example of mechanical Burnsiana that springs to mind is the Musical Portrait produced by Christina Scott of Bishopbriggs. This consists of a reproduction of the Nasmyth portrait, nicely framed and glazed, with a wind-up button on the back. When wound up the picture emits the strains of 'Auld Lang Syne'.

Miscellaneous mementoes

The landmarks associated with Burns have inspired a number of craftsmen to produce models of them. At the Centenary Exhibition models of all the houses in which Burns lived, and the places mentioned in his poems, were represented by scale models constructed by James McDonald, a lamp-trimmer with the Allan steamship line, whose founder, incidentally, was a distant kinsman of the poet. At the top of the grand staircase were exhibited models of scenes in the Burns country which had been fashioned in cork by 'the uneducated deaf mute', Joseph Watson. The models of the Auld Brig o Doon, the Monument, the Cottage, Alloway Kirk and Wallace Tower in Ayr were subsequently deposited by the Ayrshire Deaf and Dumb Mission in the Tower at Mauchline. At the present time, Frank Brown of Dumfries has produced numerous replicas of local landmarks executed in matchsticks, and these have included the sites associated with Burns. One of these detailed matchstick models may be seen in the Globe Inn.

Mention of the Globe reminds me that it is one of the public houses around the world which has a hanging sign featuring the Nasmyth portrait. The Cottage itself was for many years operated as an ale-house, and popularly known as the Burns-heid, from the painted wooden sign which hung outside the door. This ancient sign, weather-beaten and scarred by pilgrims who carved their initials on it, is displayed in the poet's birthplace to this day. Probably the most remote of all such signs are those which decorate the Robbie Burns Bottle Shoppe in Moray Street, Dunedin, with a portrait bordering on caricature. What, one wonders, would the poet's nephew and founder of Dunedin, the Rev. Dr Thomas Burns, have made of that!

Firescreen with silk back and carved, painted panel showing the poet's heraldic device.

Burns Heritage Trail sign indicating Burns House and St Michael's Churchyard, Dumfries. Photo: James Mackay.

Bronze plaque and enamel sign on outside wall of Burns House, Dumfries. Photo: James Mackay.

Painted wooden sign, after Nasmyth, outside the Globe Inn, Dumfries. Photo: James Mackay.

*Skirving portrait in the enamel sign to the Brow Well.
Photo: James Mackay.*

*One of the many decorative cakes produced by
Mrs Molly Rennie.*

Coasters and place-mats with a cork or wooden base and coloured pictures of Burns and the landmarks of the Burns Country have long been a popular souvenir. In recent years there have even been trays and trinket boxes similarly decorated, echoing the Mauchline transfer ware of old. There have even been jigsaw puzzles of the Cottage and Burns House in Dumfries. These mementoes provide further media for the dissemnination of the colour photographs produced originally for picture postcards.

Although books are outside the scope of this survey, there are two categories which merit attention as collectables. The Kilmarnock Poems and many later editions were issued in paper covers and it was then up to the individual to get the books bound to his own taste. In the 1840s, however, trade binding became acceptable and this coincided with the development of machinery capable of blind-tooling. This ushered in an era of beautiful bindings which now attract the serious attention of collectors. A fine example of blind embossing is *The Chronicle of the Hundredth Birthday* (1859) whose binding bore the Reid profile of Burns wreathed in thistles. Colour and gilding became the rage in the 1880s, typified by the pictorial binding designed by John Leighton for Gilfillan's *National Burns*. Pictorial bindings died out in the 1920s when pictorial dust jackets took over.

Miniature books, under three inches in height, are also widely collected. In recent years Ian Macdonald of the Gleniffer private press in Paisley has produced a tiny volume entitled *The Wit of Burns* and a miniature replica of the Kilmarnock Poems.

Mrs Molly Rennie, a past President of the Burns Federation, is noted for her wedding cakes and other confectionery. Included in her repertoire are cakes formed and decorated in the image of the cottage and also embellished with the badge of the Burns Federation in full colour. Mrs Rennie has also produced shortbread using a mould depicting the bust of Burns.

The souvenir shops of Ayr and Alloway, and the sales outlets at the Birthplace Museum and the Monument, have an astonishing array of mementoes to suit all tastes and pockets. At the lower end of the spectrum are the *kitsch*: erasers, plastic pin-backs, key-rings and imitation leather bookmarkers, whose only common denominator is some passable imitation of Burns's portrait. Amid these trifles there is one souvenir destined to vanish in short order — the sticks of Robert Burns rock (made in England). Some years ago I purchased a cake of toilet soap at Burns House in Mauchline which had a multicoloured picture of the Cottage on it. Had I used the soap the picture would have been transferred to the surface and lasted till the end but foolishly I preserved the soap in its plastic wrapper. Now, the delicate transfer is beginning to peel at the edges and I fear that any attempt to lift the lid will destroy the motif utterly. Burns himself would probably have seen the comic side of this, and penned a suitable ode on the transient nature of so much in this world. The poet is alleged to have consoled his wife as he lay dying, with the words: 'Don't be afraid I'll be more respected a hundred years after I am dead than I am at the present day'. He may not have been surprised to learn that his memory is cherished as much now as ever it was but he would doubtlessly be astonished at the range and diversity of the objects — the good, the bad and the ugly — created by each successive generation in his honour.

Bar of soap showing Burns Cottage, Alloway.